Development, Crisis, and Class Struggle

Development, Crisis, and Class Struggle: Learning from Japan and East Asia

Paul Burkett and Martin Hart-Landsberg

St. Martin's Press
New York

DEVELOPMENT, CRISIS, AND CLASS STRUGGLE

Library of Congress Cataloging-in-Publication Data

Burkett, Paul, 1956 May 26-
    Development, crisis and class struggle : learning from Japan and
    East Asia / by Paul Burkett and Martin Hart-Landsberg.
      p. cm.
    Includes bibliographical references and index.
    ISBN 0-312-23250-0
    Economic development—Social aspects—East Asia—Case studies. 2. Economic
development—Social aspects—Japan. 3. Capitalism—East Asia—Case studies.
4. Capitalism—Japan. 5. Democracy—East Asia—Case studies. 6. Human rights—
East Asia—Case studies. 7. Environmental policy—East Asia—Case studies.
8. Marxian economics—East Asia—Case studies. I. Hart-Landsberg, Martin.
II. Title.

HC460.5.B865 2000
306.3—dc21   99-045205

First edition: May, 2000
10   9   8   7   6   5   4   3   2   1

Contents

Preface and Acknowledgments

Our collaborative work began some five years ago, a result of e-mail conversations about events in East Asia. At the time, most economists (including many progressives) were celebrating the East Asian economic "miracle" and, on the strength of the region's performance, capitalism's ability to power third world development; the only debate was over whether free-market capitalism or state-directed capitalism deserved the credit. In contrast, neither of us agreed with the conventional wisdom or accepted the terms of this debate. Both of us were convinced that the East Asian growth process was highly exploitative and unstable. Both of us also believed that only a Marxist approach could illuminate this reality. Motivated by a common desire to expose the bankruptcy in the dominant development discourse and promote an alternative development process that was socially and environmentally responsive to the needs of workers and their communities, we quickly decided to combine our intellectual efforts.

Over the years, we deepened and tested our understanding of the East Asian experience through dialogue and debate with others. The development of our thinking is perhaps best revealed through our published work. In this regard we wish to thank the following publications for allowing us to use portions of this work (although in revised form) in the present book: *Socialist Register* (Burkett and Hart-Landsberg, 1996), *Economic Geography* (Hart-Landsberg and Burkett, 1998), *Against the Current* (Hart-Landsberg, 1998a), *Monthly Review* (Hart-Landsberg and Burkett, 1999), and *Review of Radical Political Economics* (Burkett and Hart-Landsberg, 2000).

The 1997-98 collapse of East Asia's miracle economies has ended the celebration of the East Asian economic "model" and brought great hardship to working people throughout the region. But sadly there has been little if any serious discussion by intellectuals or activists of what the region's experience tells us about capitalism and the prospects for constructing alternative movements for, and visions of, development. Our goal in writing this book was to fill this analytical and political gap.

Development, Crisis, and Class Struggle: Learning from Japan and East Asia shows how a Marxist approach to East Asia can improve our theoretical understanding of, and political responses to, capitalist development and crisis. It also demonstrates how the dominant mainstream perspectives on East Asia lead to truncated visions of development and self-destructive strategies for economic and social transformation. Finally, it shows how advocates of a sustainable and worker-community centered development can and must move beyond the simple dichotomy of free markets versus state activism, by critically engaging with popular struggles in and against particular regimes of capital accumulation. Methodologically, this is an interpretive work that draws broad theoretical, political, and ideological lessons from the East Asian experience, not a high-powered theoretical, statistical, or archival work. Our hope is that this book will be of use to the widest possible audience concerned with issues of development and social change.

This book greatly benefited from the experiences and insights of scholars and activists on both sides of the Pacific. Deserving of special mention are Patrick Bond, Norm Diamond, Seongjin Jeong, Lee Su-Hoon, and Lim Young-Il. We also wish to acknowledge the support and encouragement we each received from our respective families: Suzanne Carter along with Patrick and Molly Burkett, and Sylvia, Leah, and Rose Hart-Landsberg.

Terre Haute, Indiana and Portland, Oregon
August, 1999

Abbreviations

AFTA: ASEAN Free Trade Area
ASEAN: Association of Southeast Asian Nations [Malaysia (joined
              1967), Indonesia (1967), Philippines (1967), Singapore
              (1967), Thailand (1967), Brunei (1984), Vietnam (1995),
              Laos (1997), Burma (1997), and Cambodia (1998)]
CCEJ: Citizen's Coalition for Economic Justice (South Korea)
CDA: Constitutional Drafting Assembly (Thailand)
EGAT: Electricity Generating Authority of Thailand
FDI: foreign direct investment
FEC: Far Eastern Commission
GATT: General Agreement on Tariffs and Trade
GDP: gross domestic product
GNP: gross national product
GTC: general trading company
IMF: International Monetary Fund
JDB: Japan Development Bank
JSP: Japan Socialist Party
KCTU: Korean Confederation of Trade Unions
KMT: Kuomintang Party (Taiwan)
LDP: Liberal Democratic Party (Japan)
LLC: left-liberal consensus
MITI: Ministry of International Trade and Industry
MNC: multinational corporation
NADR: National Alliance for Democracy and National
              Reunification (South Korea)

NAFTA:	North America Free Trade Agreement
NGO:	non-governmental organization
NICs:	newly industrializing countries
NIEs:	newly industrialized economies (South Korea, Taiwan, Hong Kong, and Singapore)
OECD:	Organization for Economic Cooperation and Development
OEM:	original equipment manufacturing
PDR:	People's Democratic Party (Indonesia)
PPBI:	Indonesian Center for Workers' Struggle
PRC:	People's Republic of China
PSPD:	People's Solidarity for Participatory Democracy (South Korea)
SCAP:	Supreme Command for the Allied Powers
SDF:	Self-Defense Forces (Japan)
SEA-3:	Southeast Asian three (Thailand, Malaysia, and Indonesia)
SMID:	Indonesian Students' Solidarity for Democracy
TINA:	"There is no alternative"
TNC:	transnational corporation
UMMDU:	United Minjung Movement for Democracy and Unification (South Korea)
UNCTAD:	United Nations Conference on Trade and Development
WTO:	World Trade Organization

Introduction

This book demonstrates how a careful examination of East Asia can improve our theoretical understanding of, and political responses to, capitalist development and crisis. While the East Asian experience reveals serious shortcomings in the leading mainstream theories of capitalist development, it also contains important insights and lessons for those who seek to build economic institutions and relationships that are democratic, egalitarian, and environmentally responsive. In particular, it shows how a faulty understanding of capitalism can lead to a truncated vision of development as well as self-destructive political strategies for social transformation. On a more positive note, the East Asian experience makes clear that Marxism is still a powerful theoretical framework for analyzing capitalist dynamics; that progressive social change requires the transformation of capitalist structures of accumulation; and that such a transformation requires the building of strong and internationally linked worker-community movements.[1]

East Asia is not the only region from which one can draw these kinds of conclusions. Nonetheless, there are particularly compelling reasons for focusing on this region at this point in history. East Asia was home to capitalism's "miracle economies," economies that are now in crisis. Hence, in studying East Asia one is able to examine capitalism in its full essence, both dynamic and contradictory. In this sense, the present examination should have value for people living outside of, as well as in, East Asia. After all, policymakers and intellectuals from countries throughout the world aspired to the kinds of successes enjoyed by these former economic miracles.

Ideological Struggle Over the East Asian Experience

We are not alone in suggesting that there are important lessons to be learned from East Asia, although few have drawn the conclusions we have. Academics, policymakers, and officials from the World Bank, the International Monetary Fund (IMF), and other international organizations all began singing the praises of East Asia as far back as the 1970s. As the political scientist Robert Wade observed: "Over the past two decades a literature big enough to fill a small airplane hanger has been produced on the causes of East Asian economic success" (1992, p. 270).

The World Bank, for example, published a major study entitled *The East Asian Miracle: Economic Growth and Public Policy* (World Bank, 1993). Said to be the Bank's best-selling monograph ever, this report investigated the policies responsible for East Asia's rapid growth. The Bank explained its decision to focus on East Asia as follows:

> East Asia has a remarkable record of high and sustained growth. From 1965 to 1990 the twenty-three economies of East Asia grew faster than all other regions of the world. Most of this achievement is attributable to seemingly miraculous growth in just eight economies: Japan; the "Four Tigers"—Hong Kong, the Republic of Korea, Singapore, and Taiwan, China; and the three newly industrializing economies of Southeast Asia, Indonesia, Malaysia, and Thailand. (p. 1)

While most commentators have showered praise on all the above-mentioned countries, some have singled out a subset for special attention. Noted economist Alice Amsden singled out Japan and South Korea, arguing that the latter in particular has "succeeded far beyond the non-East Asian late industrializers" and thus "can serve as a useful model from which other aspiring industrializing countries can learn" (1989, pp. v–vi.). Linda Y. C. Lim, on the other hand, focused her praise on Southeast Asia: "After nearly three decades of steady economic growth, the six capitalist countries of Southeast Asia today constitute the world's fastest-growing regional economy" (1995, p. 238).

What made the record of these East Asian countries especially noteworthy was that it stood in sharp contrast to the performance of the rest of the third world. As the IMF explained:

> Korea, for example, experienced almost a ten-fold rise in per capita income between 1965 and 1995, while Thailand saw a five-fold increase, and

Malaysia a four-fold rise. In the developing countries of the Western Hemisphere average per capita incomes doubled between 1965 and 1980 before stagnating over the next 15 years, a period much of which was dominated by the debt crisis and its aftermath. . . . While the [East Asian] success stories illustrate that dramatic improvements in living standards are possible, many countries regrettably are not realizing their potential. In relative terms, most developing countries have failed to raise their per capita incomes toward those of the industrial countries. In fact, Asia is the only major region to have registered significant relative progress, in the sense of having achieved significant convergence towards industrial country living standards. (IMF, 1997a, pp. 76–77)

Many analysts, struck by the geographic concentration of these miracle economies, began to expand their investigations of individual East Asian countries to include the role played by regional economic dynamics. Most concluded that East Asia's success could not be fully ascribed to well-crafted national development policies, and that regional interactions and relationships were also significant.

In short, there was widespread agreement that the eight above-mentioned East Asian countries were success stories worthy of study and emulation. This agreement ran across a wide political spectrum. By the mid- to late 1980s, the model status of the East Asian miracle economies was setting the tone for nearly all development visions and policy debates.

While some theorists did raise questions about the social costs inherent in the East Asian development process—including repression of civil, human, and labor rights, and the destruction of the environment—these costs were considered inconsequential compared to the positive benefits generated by the region's rapid growth and industrial transformation. Moreover, many theorists confidently predicted that these costs would prove to be short-term in nature insofar as they largely reflected the transition *out of* the prior state of underdevelopment. Thus, continued economic growth was seen as the best cure for these social problems.[2]

However, and surprisingly given the almost uniform endorsement of these miracle economies, there was little agreement on the factors that accounted for their rapid growth and the corresponding policy lessons. The most prominent disagreement concerned whether growth and industrial transformation were state-led, or, instead, the natural consequences of market forces. Other debates concerned the precise nature and significance of the regional transmission mechanism. Some argued that regional relationships were insignificant; others that the regional concentration of model countries was the result of a type of learning-by-doing process, where one country, having observed the success of another, introduced similar policies. Yet others credited Japan or China for anchoring a more formally structured regional growth process.

At the risk of oversimplification, East Asia became an intellectual battleground for competing economic development theories and policy strategies. It is important to note, however, that this competition largely excluded Marxism as a theory and socialism as a development strategy. Important Marxist work on Japan and East Asia was either ignored or dismissed by mainstream and even many progressive scholars. One result was that terms such as "imperialism," and "dependency" largely disappeared from the relevant literature during the 1980s and 1990s.[3]

This exclusion was justified (implicitly or explicitly) on the grounds that the East Asian experience had demonstrated the bankruptcy of both Marxism and socialism. South Korea had proved its superiority over North Korea; Taiwan had done the same relative to the People's Republic of China (PRC). The latter was, in fact, eagerly moving to reform its economic structures to become more like South Korea (or according to some, Malaysia). While it claimed to be building "socialism with Chinese characteristics," most analysts saw in this move another convincing sign of the superiority of capitalism over socialism. Finally, the Soviet Union and Eastern Europe, not long after seeking and receiving economic aid from South Korea, formally abandoned their state-planning systems and socialism as even a long-term goal.

While almost all analysts agreed that the experience of the East Asia model economies demonstrated the power of capitalism—more precisely, that there was no alternative to capitalism for development—debate still raged over which model of capitalism was the superior one. In a real sense, then, disagreements in the "learning from East Asia" literature resembled a serious but primarily family feud.

This debate was largely conducted between just two competing approaches, each of which implied a distinct set of political and policy strategies. One side, the less traditional and influential, argued that the East Asian experience demonstrated the importance of the state and state planning (although there was not unanimity concerning the significance and nature of regional dynamics). Those who took this position rejected neoliberalism or what they also called the Anglo-American model of free-market capitalism. Many of these advocates of state intervention had previously supported some kind of socialism. A few even hoped that a more effective and efficient socialism might eventually evolve out of the structures and institutions pioneered by East Asian capitalism. However, the key point is that most of the state interventionists were, at least for the time being, content to promote and perfect a modified capitalist system. Indeed, despite their political differences, the critics of neoliberalism generally agreed that it was possible to use the state to build a more humane and productive capitalism— and they felt that the East Asian experience provided support for their position.

Japan in particular became a model for those seeking to reform the more market-oriented advanced capitalist countries, especially the United States and Great Britain. These scholars and activists generally accepted the same criterion for success as their free-market opponents: competitiveness. But, while arguing that the Japanese system of capitalism was more competitive than the Anglo-American system, they also suggested that one of the main reasons for this superiority was Japan's willingness to embrace state activism and an egalitarian and participatory system of labor-management relations. Thus, they sought to promote social reform by defeating neoclassical orthodoxy on its own terms. By pointing to Japan's large export surplus and high savings and investment rates, they hoped to convince government and corporate leaders that it was in their best interest to adopt Japanese-style systems of economic regulation and organization. In this way, they also hoped to win business and government support for new and more humane labor relations as well as other progressive institutional reforms (e.g., in education, investment planning, and the financial system).[4]

These critics of neoliberalism also believed that Japan could contribute to *third world* development through its productive international investment. Even more importantly, they suggested that the Japanese system could be adapted and adopted by other less developed countries. South Korea, Indonesia, Malaysia, and Thailand were generally seen to be following the Japanese model or at the very least benefiting from Japan's foreign investment and regionalized production strategies. Their rapid growth and industrial transformations appeared to confirm the generalizability of state-led capitalist development. In short, a new conventional wisdom, one that opposed neoliberalism, developed and gathered strength in a close relationship with the rise of the miracle economies of East Asia.

Those on the other side of this debate, the advocates of neoliberalism, tried to rebuff the arguments of the new conventional wisdom by claiming that East Asian growth was the result of market forces, not state activity. For example, a study of Japan and the leading East Asian countries by economist E.K.Y. Chen argued that in all of them, "State intervention is largely absent. What the state has provided is simply a suitable environment for the entrepreneurs to perform their functions" (quoted in White and Wade, 1988, p. 4) Similarly, in seeking to explain why South Korea, Taiwan, Singapore, and Hong Kong had outperformed Mexico, Brazil, Argentina, and India, two eminent neoliberals concluded that:

> the scope of administrative controls was much more limited in the four East Asian NICs [Newly Industrializing Countries] than in Latin America and, even more, India. In the latter case, there were pervasive controls on investment, prices, and imports, and decisions were generally made case by case, thereby creating uncertainty for business and opportunities for corruption, which has remained comparatively limited in East Asia. (Balassa and Williamson, 1987, p. 14)

However, as more studies of the East Asian experience were published, and as the Japanese government itself became more aggressive in promoting its own version of capitalism, neoclassical advocates found themselves increasingly on the defensive.[5] Nonetheless, given the long period in which neoclassical economics had reigned unchallenged—and given the powerful institutional support it received from international development agencies, the U.S. government, and the mainstream media—the advocates of neoliberalism were able to keep the new conventional wisdom from gaining ideological supremacy. As a result, most of the world still credited market forces for East Asia's economic success.

Then came the East Asian crisis of the late 1990s. The crisis surprised everyone involved in the debate; neither side had predicted it. In fact, right up to what was later declared the official start of the crisis (July 1997, in Thailand), both sides continued to celebrate and claim credit for East Asia's record of strong growth. Once the crisis began, moreover, its spread was astonishingly rapid. The IMF's inability to grasp the seriousness of the situation is illustrated by its changing growth forecasts for Thailand: "At the time of the IMF program in August 1997, the projected GDP growth rate for 1998 was 2.5 per cent. By the time of the first IMF review in early December . . . the projection for the GDP growth rate was lowered to 0.6 percent. By the time of the next IMF review in February 1998, GDP growth was projected at a negative 3.5 per cent" (Bello, 1998). The actual outcome was a decline of 7.7 percent.

By early 1998, it was no longer possible to avoid acknowledging the true extent of the economic collapse. As the *Economist* explained:

Plunging currencies and stock markets have put the economic miracle in the deep freeze, and minds are now concentrated simply on survival. At its low point, the Indonesia rupiah was more than 80% down against the dollar, and the currencies of Thailand, South Korea, Malaysia and the Philippines have all dived by 35-50%. . . . The stock markets of all five countries have also seen losses of at least 60% in dollar terms since the start of 1997, and shares in Hong Kong and Singapore too have taken a severe beating. (1998a, p. 3)

Of course, while the mainstream press focused its attention on the declines in currency, stock, and bond markets, the crisis can only be truly understood in human terms. In this regard, the International Labor Organization estimated that "140 million Indonesians, 66 percent of the population, could slip below the poverty line by the end of 1999" (Weinberg, 1998, p. 53). The *Wall Street Journal* reported that Indonesia was running out of medicines; as one pharmaceutical executive put it, "lives are being put at risk because many people cannot afford the 300% to 400% increase in health costs" (Solomon and Linebaugh, 1998, p. A17). In South Korea, surveys by the Korea Chamber of Commerce and Industry found that from December 1997 to May 1998, approximately 80 percent of all households in Seoul had "experienced drops in household income, with the average reduction rate reaching 32 percent" (*Korea Herald*, 1998). Another study reported that "since December 1997, 64 percent of the nation's six million strong middle class has slid down to the low-income bracket" (Ahn, 1999). Similar stories could be told about Thailand and Malaysia (see Chapter 14).

One would think that the crisis might cause some of the participants in the prior debate to seriously question their understanding of the East Asian growth process and development prospects under capitalism, but such was not the case. With only a momentary pause, neoliberal analysts—the very people who had fought a largely defensive battle to uphold market forces as an explanation for East Asia's past economic successes—now offered the following explanation of the crisis: *the East Asian countries had rejected free markets in favor of state direction of economic activity!* East Asia's only hope for recovery was to pursue deregulation, liberalization, and privatization. This was, of course, the same message as before. The difference was that pre-crisis, East Asian countries were held to be models of virtue, shining examples of the benefits of relying on the market. Post-crisis, they were suddenly transformed into models of inefficiency, dark reminders of what can happen when cronyist governments tamper with market forces.

While neoliberals quickly rewrote history, those who had opposed neoliberalism found themselves backed into a corner by the crisis. They had argued that East Asian capitalism was superior to Anglo-American capitalism. Now their model economies were not only in crisis but also yielding (albeit reluctantly) to IMF and U.S. pressure to adopt "free-market" reforms. Some defenders of the new conventional wisdom continued to argue against neoliberalism, claiming that the crisis was caused mainly by premature financial deregulation or by other excesses of economic globalization. But, while their explanations of the crisis contained some elements of truth, their arguments carried little weight. The reason was quite simple: with East Asian economies in crisis, their attempts to argue the superiority of the East Asian system enjoyed little credibility among either the experts or the general public. As a result, their political project of state-centered economic reforms rapidly approached a dead end.

The Need for a Marxist Approach

This book shows that the East Asian experience reveals much about the close relationship between the contradictions of capitalism and the shortcomings of mainstream development thinking. More specifically, its shows that neither variant of mainstream theory sketched above has a sound explanation for the East Asian experience of growth and crisis. Moreover, neither mainstream approach has much to offer in the way of solutions to the region's current economic problems. Neoliberals press policies that will only intensify East Asia's dependence on foreign capital, income inequality, repression and exploitation, and environmental destruction. Not surprisingly, they defend these policies mainly by arguing that there are no viable alternatives; they have largely run out of success stories to promote in defense of their position.

At the same time, the new conventional wisdom has little of value to offer in opposition to neoliberalism. Its understanding of capitalism, its criteria for successful development, and its political strategy for achieving anti-neoliberal reforms are all badly flawed. Tragically, the logic of the new conventional wisdom has left many of its proponents defending increasingly unpopular regimes in East Asia in the hope that neoliberal policies can be resisted and past development strategies renewed.

The East Asian experience demonstrates, in other words, the need for a sounder understanding of how capitalism operates—a theory that, in revealing the deeper forces generating both growth and crisis, can guide political and policy responses in liberating directions for workers and communities. This book demonstrates that Marxism—a Marxism structured by the specifics of East Asian history and class relations—can provide this necessary analytical framework.

Stated differently, this book reasserts the relevance of a long and vibrant tradition of Marxist work on Japan and the rest of East Asia. As noted above, this considerable body of work has generally been ignored even by leftists, especially in the United States. Sadly, many of these leftists have become caught up in development-model fads. As a result, they spend far too much time designing economic strategies for technocrats, often in competition with mainstream economists, at the expense of what is truly needed: the critical development of analyses and alternatives based on real world contradictions, conflicts, and popular challenges to the status quo.

Rejecting the notion that "there is no alternative" (TINA) to capitalism, the present analysis is geared toward supporting the construction of a socialism from below. Socialism is not equivalent to state control or state planning, or even equity in some generic sense. Socialism is the antithesis of capitalism; as such, it means worker-community power and self-development in and through collectively and democratically managed economic and political relations. The task of socialist intellectuals is to help construct popularly based and structurally informed analyses and development visions. The first step in this task is to point out the contradictions of capitalist development regimes from a human, social, and ecological standpoint. These contradictions, like the ideology of TINA itself, must be seen as particular instances of capitalism's class-exploitative and antisocial character.

In sum, while making no claim to original statistical or even historical discovery, this book does offer an empirically based and theoretically coherent Marxist perspective on East Asia—one that bears strongly on debates in the areas of development policy and social transformation. The paths broken and rediscovered here are methodological, political, and ideological.

An Overview of the Book

Part I critically examines the five dominant non-Marxist perspectives on East Asian development: neoliberal and structural-institutionalist (Chapter 1); "flying geese" and Greater China (Chapter 2); and dependency approaches (Chapter 3). This critical survey specifies the key forces that each perspective sees driving growth, as well as the most likely barriers each sees to continued growth in East Asia. While pointing out the main analytical shortcomings of the five non-Marxist perspectives in light of the East Asian crisis, Part I also sets out the elements of a Marxist framework capable of overcoming these difficulties in a politically useful way (see especially Chapter 2). Part I concludes by highlighting the negative political consequences of a false understanding of the East Asian experience, using left-liberal interpretations of Japan as a case study (Chapter 4).

Any meaningful attempt to understand the East Asian experience must be anchored by a critical examination of Japanese capitalism. Unfortunately, all of the perspectives examined in Part I suffer from an inaccurate or partial grasp of Japan's capitalist development, both domestically and in terms of Japan's regional connections and power. Part II accordingly presents a more holistic and historical interpretation of Japanese development and crisis. The political need for such an historical perspective is first demonstrated by examining Japan's current economic crisis and its ideological interpretation by the mainstream western press (Chapter 5). Subsequent chapters step back historically to analyze the development of the pre–World War II Japanese political economy (Chapter 6), the post–World War II working-class struggle to remake this political economy (Chapter 7), and the political and economic dynamics that led to its eventual renewal (Chapter 8). Finally, the nature and contradictions of Japan's postwar growth "miracle" (Chapter 9) and the socio-economic dilemmas underlying the country's current structural crisis (Chapter 10) are interpreted in light of the prior historical analysis.

Part III examines the causes of the broader East Asian economic crisis. Most development economists had argued that the rapid economic growth of countries such as Thailand, Malaysia, and Indonesia (the Southeast Asian three—SEA-3), following the earlier experiences of first Japan and then South Korea, Taiwan, Hong Kong, and Singapore (the East Asian Newly Industrialized Economies—NIEs), demonstrated the benefits of export-led growth. A significant number of economists also credited regional economic dynamics, in particular those shaped by Japanese foreign direct investment, for the regional advance. The present analysis also ascribes considerable importance to the regional investment and production activities of Japanese, and then NIE-based, capital. However, following Steven (1990, 1996), it is shown that the successive waves of Japanese foreign investment represented responses by Japanese capital to the class-based and competitive contradictions of Japan's own accumulation process. The expansion of NIE-based foreign investment in the SEA-3 was also undertaken in response to the contradictions of export-led growth, although in the NIEs' case these contradictions were accentuated by economic dependency on

Japanese capital. The result of all this foreign investment activity was a hierarchical regionalization of investment and production, leading to an intensification of competitiveness pressures on working people throughout the region, economic instability and, eventually, economic crises not only in Japan but also in the NIEs (Chapter 11) and the SEA-3 (Chapter 12).

Part IV considers responses to the crisis. According to mainstream economists, East Asia's economic successes demonstrated that it was in principle possible for all third world countries to develop by means of capitalism. And, as discussed earlier, these successes played a crucial role in the growing dominance of TINA-type thinking even among many leftists. The East Asian crisis has thrown mainstream development theory into crisis precisely because it threatens this ideology. In fact, the "stability" and "discipline" currently demanded by international financial institutions and transnational corporations threatens to echo the TINA notion back onto capitalism as "this is no alternative!" In developing these points, Part IV first demonstrates the failure of mainstream theorists to offer either a plausible and consistent explanation for, or an effective response to, the crisis (Chapter 13). An attempt is then made to move beyond TINA and toward a new development perspective serving socialism from below—a perspective informed not by technocratic policy analysis, but by worker and community struggles against the capitalization of human existence in East Asia and elsewhere (Chapter 14).

PART ONE

Alternative Perspectives on East Asia: Ideology in Development Visions

Chapter 1

A Marxist Perspective on the Neoliberal Versus Structural-Institutionalist Debate

The East Asian crisis has abruptly ended both mainstream and left celebrations of the region's highly dynamic and competitive capitalisms. The long post – World War II sequence of economic "miracles" involving first Japan, then the newly industrialized economies of Asia (NIEs: South Korea, Taiwan, Hong Kong, and Singapore), the rapidly industrializing countries of Southeast Asia (SEA-3: Indonesia, Malaysia, and Thailand), and, lastly, China, attracted the interest of development economists across the entire political spectrum. East Asia was widely admired as the only region where the barriers to "late industrialization" had been overcome, and the miracle economies were widely held up as models for other less developed countries.

The economic crisis has sent the celebrants of East Asian capitalism scrambling in various directions searching for answers as to what went wrong, with the lessons drawn for other countries now being overwhelmingly negative. Adding to the confusion is the fact that prior to the crisis, there had been sharp disagreements among economists and policymakers over the factors promoting East Asian industrialization and growth. It is necessary to sort through this theoretical confusion as a first step toward the development of a coherent and politically useful understanding of the crisis. Accordingly, Part I of this book undertakes a critical examination of the five most popular (non-Marxist) theoretical approaches to East Asian capitalism: neoliberalism, structural-institutionalism, "flying geese," Greater China, and dependency theories. It is shown that none of these approaches is satisfactory, in large measure because none fully captures the contradictions inherent in the region's economic development. By focusing on these contradictions, Marxism can provide a politically useful foundation for understanding the East Asian experience and informing a working-class response to the region's crisis.

Methodology

In examining the five perspectives on East Asian industrialization, Part I draws specific connections between their analytical failures and their idealizations of capitalism. In addition, their basic development visions are shown to either remove popular class-based movements from discussion, or to treat such movements as disruptive forces to be managed in pursuit of predetermined growth strategies. This tendency to marginalize grassroots-democratic development visions from theory and policy agendas afflicts even the more left wing of the dominant perspectives, for example, those that reject free-market explanations of East Asia's development successes.

The following examination also distinguishes among the five approaches according to whether they interpret industrialization dynamics at the level of individual nation-states or in terms of regionwide processes. The two dominant perspectives, neoliberalism and structural-institutionalism, focus on the nation-state. But while neoliberals stress the importance of free-market forces and comparative advantage, structural-institutionalists highlight the key role of strong developmentalist states engaging in market interventions. By contrast, both flying geese and Greater China approaches emphasize regional dynamics. The flying geese perspective argues that Japanese corporations initiated a diffusion of product and process innovations from more- to less-developed East Asian countries, thus supporting a collective regional advance in welfare. Greater China approaches meanwhile credit East Asia's economic vibrancy to China's reemergence as a regional economic power anchoring a complex nexus of regional economic interdependencies drawing entrepreneurial energy from expatriate Chinese business families. The fifth perspective, dependency theory, also highlights regional investment and trade relations; but it does so from the standpoint of subordinate actors in the regional system, especially working people and communities in the countries other than Japan. In this way, dependency analyses challenge the East Asian advocates who claim that the downsides to the East Asian "miracles" are little more than transitional "external costs" of industrialization and growth.

Each of these approaches is evaluated using a three-step procedure. First, the key forces or governing mechanisms that each perspective sees driving and shaping industrialization and growth in East Asia are specified. This specification is conducted on the level of basic development visions, with analyses of particular countries and processes referred to only as necessary to define these visions. Second, the actual or potential barriers that each approach sees to continued growth and development of the miracle economies are outlined—again at the level of basic visions. Finally, the main analytical gaps and internal contradictions of each approach are highlighted. This third step is the one most directly informed by Marxism as well as by the problems the East Asian crisis poses for each dominant perspective. A full analysis of East Asian development and crisis is not attempted at this point (see Parts II and III); but the need for an independent Marxist perspective is motivated by the demonstration of how the dominant approaches idealize East Asian capitalism.

Neoliberalism Versus Structural-Institutionalism

The present survey begins with an examination of the two most influential (and competing) approaches to explaining East Asian development: neoliberalism and structural-institutionalism. Neoliberalism is the dominant approach not only to the East Asian experience but to all international economic developments.[1] Its advocates argue that the economic success of Japan, the NIEs, and the SEA-3 was due to their governments having allowed comparative advantage in international trade to direct the allocation of productive resources. By creating stable, non-inflationary, and open economic environments, governments encouraged domestic firms to take advantage of low unit labor costs and engage in labor-intensive export-oriented production. The focus on exports enabled firms to overcome inadequate domestic demand and reap increasing returns to scale and associated learning-by-doing effects from greater production. With productivity rising faster than real wages, East Asian countries were able to secure rapid increases in output and employment without threatening their low unit labor costs and export competitiveness. This process of export-driven growth was further enhanced by a government commitment to relatively loose restrictions and "realistic" taxation rates on export-oriented foreign capital. Such a commitment was especially important to the SEA-3 countries, enabling them to attract the foreign direct investment (FDI) they required to overcome the "natural" market imperfections (rooted in high transactions and information costs) otherwise hindering their development of technology, finance, and marketing.

Neoliberals generally see two main external threats to East Asia's continued economic success. First, because East Asian exports are largely sold in the developed core countries, core protectionism represents a serious potential barrier. Neoliberals, of course, strongly warn core countries against pursuing this policy. The second external threat, especially for the NIEs and the SEA-3, is growing export competition from lower-wage countries, in particular China. Neoliberals believe there is only one way for these countries to overcome this threat: they must upgrade the technical level of their production by increasing their human capital formation (education and training). At the same time, however, they caution that this must be achieved in ways that do not increase either government deficits or tax rates. Otherwise the stable non-inflationary environment required for competitiveness and inflows of foreign capital will be undermined.

Neoliberals also foresee an internally generated threat to growth. They expect that the interest groups pressuring NIE and SEA-3 governments will become more numerous and powerful as a result of a natural correspondence between modernization and representative-democratic government. While claiming to welcome this correspondence, neoliberals worry that interest group pressures (e.g., for improved job security and workplace safety, economic equality for female workers, social welfare expenditures, and environmental regulations) could undermine economic stability and competitiveness. Their suggestions for countering this danger include an independent central bank, maximum freedom of short- and long-term capital movements, and strengthening the power of the executive.

Structural-institutionalists have criticized the neoliberal approach for its failure to recognize how East Asian states actively shaped investment and trade activity, especially in Japan and the NIEs. The success of such industrial policies contradicts neoliberalism's starting assumption of a *given set* of comparative advantages.[2] Among the state interventions commonly cited are investment and export subsidies; protection of newer industries and enterprises from imports in exchange for their achievement of export targets; government control over the sectoral and inter-enterprise allocation of credit; and strategic planning of the new industrial activities to be developed, which often entailed a leading role for state enterprises. Like neoliberals, structural-institutionalists emphasize the need for technical upgrading to deal with competition from lower-wage countries. But unlike neoliberals, they suggest that planned import-substitution industrialization and export-led growth are not competing but rather complementary means of achieving this goal. Through the right combination of rewards and penalties, governments can engineer a maturation of protected infant industries into dynamic, globally competitive firms and sectors (Jaymin Lee, 1997). However, this strategy requires an unusually autonomous state, both internally and vis-à-vis other states and multilateral organizations.

Structural-institutionalists thus see threats to the developmental state as constituting the main danger to continued East Asian growth. The most serious threat comes from the U.S. government, the IMF, and the World Bank, all of which demand that the East Asian countries liberalize their economies. Many structural-institutionalists also fear that domestic political democratization could undermine state cohesion and independence of action. They also share neoliberal views on the importance of controlling wage costs and maintaining a stable macroeconomic environment (even though structural-institutionalists define stability more as a prerequisite for effective state planning and direction of industrial activity).

Structural-institutionalism clearly offers a more accurate description of the East Asian experience than does neoliberalism. Government policies in the miracle countries (especially Japan, Taiwan, and South Korea) bore little resemblance to the neoliberals' preferred free-market regime. Problems also exist with the neoliberal argument that transnational corporations (TNCs) promote development by helping countries overcome "natural" market imperfections. Insofar as "market power may be achieved via economizing on transaction costs" (Pitelis and Sugden, 1991, p. 11), the neoliberal approach to transnationals "cannot necessarily discriminate between market power and efficiency considerations" (Yamin, 1991, p. 77; cf. Hymer, 1970). Neoliberals assume that market "imperfections" (international inequalities in terms of access to production methods, funding sources, and sales opportunities) are "exogenous to the TNCs" even though these imperfections are often "created, perpetuated and maintained by TNCs in their attempt to increase their monopoly rent" (Cleeve, 1994, p. 1). Transnationals can use their technological, financial, and marketing resources to establish monopolistic power in key sectors of an economy and, in doing so, they may "correct" market failures in ways that do not yield desirable results for the host economy. Structural-institutionalists have shown an acute awareness of these issues. Amsden (1989), for example, shows that a strong government negotiating stance and state acquisition of technical expertise were both integral elements in the effective transfer of productive capabilities from transnationals to South Korean *chaebol* (family-run industrial and financial conglomerate enterprises).

Common Theoretical Shortcomings

The relative historical accuracy of structural-institutionalism has caused many to embrace it as the preferred alternative to neoliberalism.Yet the two approaches share important shortcomings, due to their significant common ground on the level of basic development visions. Most clearly, they both espouse essentially national visions of industrialization and growth. Insofar as they see many success stories in East Asia, they both assume that the miracle countries have individually followed similar strategies albeit with important international elements (e.g., openness to global competitive pressures and export opportunities; state accommodation versus planning of changes in comparative advantage). There are limits to such national-level analysis, however.

To begin with, one may question whether export-led growth is a viable strategy for large numbers of less developed countries given core market limitations and protectionist pressures. The fallacy of composition at work is evident here from the inadequate responses of both neoliberals and structural-institutionalists to the overproduction problems afflicting the East Asian economies. The region's export-led growth strategy has generated large amounts of excess capacity in a number of key industries, including autos, memory chips and other semiconductors, chemicals, and shipbuilding. This overproduction, together with attempts by governments to sustain demand *via* competitive devaluations, is a prime factor underlying the region's economic crisis (Mandel, et al., 1997).[3] Yet structural-institutionalist analyses of this crisis downplayed or even ignored the role of overproduction. Instead, blaming the crisis on financial liberalization and speculative capital flows, advocates of this theory continued to assert the fundamental "soundness" and competitiveness of *individual* miracle economies (especially South Korea), without seriously addressing the prior regional and global buildup of excess capacity (Amsden and Euh, 1997; Chang, 1997;Wade andVeneroso, 1998). Neoliberals such as Sanger (1997), while recognizing the region's overproduction problems, blamed them on misguided and corrupt investment policies followed by East Asian governments. The question as to why all these governments would suddenly follow such faulty policies in unison was swept under the rug.[4]

Given their common focus on national industrialization policies, neoliberalism and structural-institutionalism are also unable to adequately address the regionalization of Japanese and NIE-based capital. As a result, the regional spread of industrialization tends to be explained in terms of demonstration effects of prior country successes on policy thinking in other countries where political and social preconditions of the "general model of late industrialization" happen to be present (Amsden, 1991, pp. 285-286), or in simple terms of "spill-over effects from the fast growth of the more nationally focused, governed-market economies of East Asia" (Wade, 1996, p. 26). Growth in the SEA-3 *was* clearly spurred by a tidal wave of FDI emanating from Japan and the NIEs (UNCTAD, 1996a, Part 2; Athukorala and Menon, 1997, pp. 165 170). Structural-institutionalists have recognized that the wave of FDI inflows into the SEA-3 neither followed nor corresponded with a period of intensive import-substitution industrialization such as occurred in Japan and (less completely, in a more dependent form) in the NIEs (Wade, 1993, pp. 438-439). Yet, they largely sidestep the problems that the regionalization of late industrializing countries' capital creates not only for the extension of their statist strategy to other countries, but also for the successful late industrializers themselves.[5]

The neoliberal and structural-institutionalist strategies both emphasize improvements in international competitiveness; but to remain internationally competitive, NIE-based firms may have to transnationalize, partly by increasing their ties to core-country based transnationals.[6] Such "homegrown" transnationalization poses especially serious problems for structural-institutionalism insofar as it increases the independence of domestic enterprises from government planning mechanisms. In South Korea, trade and foreign investment gains gave the *chaebol* more autonomy from a weakening state, enabling them to use more profits for foreign investment and speculation rather than productive domestic investments (Hart-Landsberg, 1993, Chapter 10). Moreover, the success of late industrializing country firms in penetrating core markets generates strong pressures on these latecomers to open up and deregulate their own economies. Such liberalization strengthens the incentive for domestic firms to internationalize their operations, since these firms will no longer be able to rely on fat profit margins in protected home markets (Schuman, 1996).

This vicious circle highlights the danger of identifying the economic strength of individual *nation-states* with that of domestically based *enterprises*. It also reveals structural-institutionalism's inadequate allowance for endogenous economic liberalization pressures that can disrupt state planning mechanisms. Structural-institutionalists have recognized the promotion of neoliberal policy designs by U.S.-based transnational capital (Wade, 1992, p. 319; Wade and Veneroso, 1998, pp. 18-21); but they have ignored the internationalization of NIE and Japanese business (and of allied government functionaries) as a homegrown force working toward the deregulation of production, investment, labor markets, and external capital flows

(Petras, 1998b, pp. 152-153). Underlying structural-institutionalism's false identification of national *economy* with national *capital* is an idealized unity of "national interest" itself—an abstraction from the class divisions characterizing capitalist nation-states.

This brings up another common ground of neoliberalism and structural-institutionalism: their desocialized, technical conceptions of industrialization and development. The political and social *context* enters into neoliberal and structural-institutional analyses through its influence on state policies. Nonetheless both approaches treat industrialization itself as largely an engineering and management problem (Hart-Landsberg, 1993, pp. 93-98). As a result, both treat popular economic and political struggles as potential disruptions of a preconceived industrialization strategy. The possibility that such struggles reveal shortcomings and tensions in the preferred strategy is ignored; for both approaches, these struggles are a problem to be managed or suppressed.

This technocratic bias creates serious problems for both perspectives. Neoliberalism's insistence on strict control of wage pressures by any means necessary clearly contradicts its advocacy of a free-market, non-interventionist economic environment. Moreover, neoliberal calls for insulation of fiscal and monetary policies from popular participation contradict the neoliberal vision of a natural correlation between democracy and modernization (Cumings, 1997a). Neoliberals deal with the latter contradiction by using highly limited definitions of democracy (e.g., periodic elections), or by supporting representative "participation" in economic policy deliberations only to the extent that it proves useful for legitimizing neoliberal policies.[7] Similarly, structural-institutionalists appear interested in political opening and "labor peace" only insofar as they are consistent with, or help provide the necessary stability and legitimacy for, the predetermined state-interventionist development strategy (Amsden, 1989, pp. 324-329). As the East Asian crisis spread and deepened in 1997-98, structural-institutionalists joined neoliberals in expressing fears that popular unrest might threaten the region's long-term security and prosperity (Kristof, 1997b; Chang, 1997; *Economist,* 1998b). Neither approach considered popular resistance to IMF austerity as pointing a way out of the crisis to a more human, democratic, and sustainable form of development. For both, development choices were best left to the technocrats, while the best that could be hoped for from democratic institutions was the effective *management* of popular unrest.[8] In short, both theories are seriously flawed as frameworks for understanding East Asian economic dynamics and as guides to action.

A Marxist Alternative

One can begin finding a way past this theoretical confusion and political dead end by considering a Marxist approach to East Asian development and crisis. Such an approach recognizes that the region's competitive successes involved not just effective management of production, investment, and macroeconomic policies, but also effective extraction of surplus value from workers by (state and private) capital and its effective conversion into means of expanded exploitation and monetary accumulation. Capitalist accumulation is based on and reproduces class divisions *and* market competition among enterprises and workers. Thus, as individual enterprises, nations, and regions are more or less successful in appropriating social resources and applying them to the exploitation of workers, the resulting capitalist development is necessarily *uneven*.[9] Production as a social and material process requires a relatively stable institutional framework; yet competition and class struggle work against such stability. This creates a need for elite management by state and business organizations on national and international levels. The uneven success of such management is itself a cause and effect of the uneven development of capitalist accumulation.

The Marxist perspective suggests that because state and business organizations are "institutional forms of class domination, which express a particular configuration of class struggle" (Clarke, 1988, p. 85), one should not idealize them as elements of a model whose reproduction is unproblematic if state and business managers fulfill their proper functions. Insofar as these institutions are shaped by "the social and political struggles unleashed by the contradictory tendencies of capital accumulation" (p. 85), they reveal much about the class tensions, and unrealized worker-community needs and capabilities, built into the most successful accumulation regimes. For example, the productivism and competitiveness of Japanese labor-management relations rested on the ability of Japanese capital to appropriate and rechannel the creative impulses demonstrated by Japanese working people in the massive production control and unionization drives immediately after the Second World War (see Chapters 7 and 8).

By highlighting the suppressed worker-community potentials underlying East Asia's competitive successes, such a perspective can help integrate contemporary popular aspirations and struggles into new visions of development. Then, instead of treating resistance to IMF austerity as a threat to East Asian development, or as a popular rejection of one technocratic policy in favor of another (more statist) one, we can find in this resistance prefigurations of a democratic development. As Jeong and Shin (1998, p. 14) point out, workers' "opposition to massive layoffs" and demands for job and wage security, and so on, can "function as a transitional program towards fundamental transformation" during a period of economic crisis when "workers' right to live" is least likely to be assured within capitalism—especially insofar as the resistance is consciously linked to previous struggles which, however briefly, went beyond capitalist relations toward a worker-community controlled economy.

From a Marxist perspective, it also makes no sense to treat the most competitive capitalisms as if their successes can be generalized to other countries. Capitalism always generates losers and winners—"an accumulation of misery, corresponding with accumulation of capital" (Marx, 1967, p. 645). Not everyone—not even a majority—can be a winner. Yet neoliberalism and structural-institutionalism treat East Asian development as in principle replicable in other countries. The competitiveness of Japanese export-led growth, however, was underpinned by work times, labor intensities, labor force flexibilities, and shares of capital in value added all well above socially acceptable levels in other core countries. The repression of militant Japanese labor and democracy movements in the immediate post-World War II period, and the Japanese region's special Cold War position, were essential conditions of capital's relatively great power over labor in Japan. This power explains the Japanese state's greater ability to concentrate on industry and trade strategy vis-à-vis other capitalist states (Halliday, 1978; Moore, 1983; Steven, 1990). Similarly, South Korean accumulation was facilitated by work times and rates of exploitation (and of industrial accidents) well above international standards even for third world countries. This labor control was carried out by a militarized state owing its existence to the Cold War environment of a divided Korea and to the repression of a militant People's Committee movement by U.S. occupation authorities immediately after World War II (Cumings, 1981; Hart-Landsberg, 1998b, pp. 70-77). The Cold War atmosphere was essential to the export-led growth of Japan, South Korea, and Taiwan insofar as the United States "sought to showcase the advantages of capitalism over communism and thus opened its markets to Asian imports" (Petras, 1998a, p. 10). And just as Japan's export-led growth had earlier been jump-started by Korean War procurements (Sweezy, 1980, pp. 7-8), both Japan and the NIEs "benefited from the ten-year U.S.-Indochina war via military contracts and trade concessions" (Petras, 1998a, p. 10).[10]

Finally, Marxism sheds light on the role of overproduction problems in East Asian development and crisis. For Marxists, competition involves efforts by individual firms to gain surplus profits at the expense of other firms; but before these profits can be realized in the market they must be produced through the extraction of surplus labor from workers. The fundamental basis of overproduction is the drive of individual firms to increase surplus value-products without regard for the extent of the market as determined by the class-exploitative distribution of purchasing power (Clarke, 1990-91, p. 454). Overproduction is a form of uneven development insofar as it results from the *uncoordinated* expansion of productive capacity by competing enterprises, as the firms enjoying surplus profits and growing market shares are the ones which most efficiently exploit their workers through the private application of socially developed productive forces (pp. 454-455; Clarke, 1988, p. 81). This helps us understand why the high growth rates of the East Asian miracle economies depended not only on high rates of domestic investment but also on trade surpluses with less competitive nations—once more negating the notion of a more progressive and dynamic form of capitalism in principle achievable by all countries. Fueled by high rates of domestic exploitation, East Asian capitalism featured correspondingly large gaps between domestic production and domestic wage-based demand. During high-growth periods this gap was filled by exports (facilitated by the Cold War) and by the high investment rates such exports helped support. Recent overproduction problems are, in short, inseparable from the historical circumstances and competitive dynamism of East Asian capitalism.

Chapter 2

Flying Geese and Greater China Approaches: The Limits of Regionalized "Modernization"

While neoliberalism and structural-institutionalism remain the dominant mainstream perspectives on development, other theories have been advanced to explain the East Asian experience. Among the most important are the flying geese and Greater China approaches, each of which enjoys significant support in East Asia (and among boosters of Japan and China, respectively). Both approaches were developed in response to specific East Asian dynamics, in particular, the regionally structured process of East Asian industrialization.

The Flying Geese Approach

The flying geese approach was first formulated in the 1930s by the Japanese economist Kaname Akamatsu.[1] Drawing upon Japan's experience as a "follower" country, Akamatsu argued that development was best promoted by a "dynamic infant-industry" strategy in which "a developing country . . . goes through industrial upgrading, step by step, by capitalizing on the learning opportunities made available through its external relations with the more advanced world" (UNCTAD, 1995, pp. 258-259):

> The economic nationalism of the developing countries at first establishes consumer goods production on the basis of national capital, and then it proceeds to the national capitalization of industries so far operated by foreign capital and, further, to the production of capital goods by national capital. This series of developments signifies that the developing countries advance

through the stages of homogenization with the industries of the advanced countries. (Akamatsu, 1962, p. 8)

The resulting "wild geese flying pattern" of industrialization contains three "sub-patterns":

The first basic pattern is the sequence of import—domestic production—export. The second pattern is the sequence from consumer goods to capital goods and from crude and simple articles to complex and refined articles. The third pattern is the alignment from advanced nations to backward nations according to their stages of growth. (Akamatsu, 1961, p. 208)

Akamatsu did not expect a static pattern of flying geese. In his vision, "some of the less-advanced countries always remain in a stagnant state falling more and more behind . . . while others, like Japan, join the ranks of advanced countries" (Akamatsu, 1962, p. 18). He also saw "the economies of advanced countries [as] sometimes stagnant and sometimes making leaping advances," and even allowed for cases where "the 'lead goose' eventually tires and falls back; its position [being] taken over by a more vigorous one which has moved up from behind in the flock" (p. 18; UNCTAD, 1995, p. 258).

Contemporary flying geese perspectives significantly modify this original formulation. Rejecting Akamatsu's focus on the actions of individual follower countries and fluid international industrial rankings, flying geese theorists now argue that it is mainly the leading country, Japan, that motivates regional growth and that Japan can and should be the permanent "lead goose." They stress that only the correct mix of industrial policies in the leading country can ensure the continuous technical upgrading of the leader's productive base and foreign direct investment as required for the region-wide diffusion of industrial growth. Ozawa (1993), for example, emphasizes how the "sequential structural upgrading" of Japan's industry from labor-intensive textiles and simple electronics goods (1950 to mid-1960s), to heavy and chemical industries (late 1950s to early 1970s), to automobiles and more complex electronics goods (late 1960s to present), to computer-aided manufacturing and other information-intensive areas (early 1980s onwards)—involved successive waves of outward direct investment, thereby "recycling" previous leading sectors to the NIEs and (later) the SEA-3.[2]

Modern flying geese approaches also draw a sharp distinction between vertical and horizontal divisions of labor among leaders and followers (see, for example, Doner, 1993, pp. 173–174). The vertical divisions are said to be based on *absolute* cost advantages in different levels of technology. Here, the lead goose (Japan) operates at the highest level (less standardized, more information-intensive products and processes, such as the development of more powerful computer memory chips) while followers focus on lower- and middle-rung areas (e.g., more standardized electronics assembly operations) in which their lower wages give them the upper hand. Horizontal divisions, meanwhile, are shaped by the *comparative* advantages of different following countries at similar levels of the technological hierarchy (e.g., international complementarities in the production and assembly of different car parts). The followers' replication of Japan's integrated industrialization patterns is thus seen as a regional one, whereas Akamatsu's original approach saw this replication as achievable by individual following countries.[3]

One of the main strengths of the flying geese approach is that it does recognize Japanese capital's growing role as shaper of an integrated East Asian political economy. Japanese direct investment in Asia exploded in the second half of the 1980s following the Plaza Accord of 1985, under which the United States, Japan, the United Kingdom, Germany, and France agreed to support a large appreciation of the yen (and of the other main non-dollar currencies) against the U.S. dollar. Between 1985 and 1989, annual Japanese direct investment rose by a factor of four in Taiwan, by a factor of five in Malaysia and South Korea, by a factor of six in Singapore, by a factor of 15 in Hong Kong, and by a factor of 25 in Thailand (Pempel, 1996/97, p. 18). Beginning in 1994, Asia became the second largest continental destination for Japanese FDI. That year, Japanese firms invested $17.8 billion in the United States, $9.7 billion in Asia, and $6.2 billion in Europe. The following year totals were $20.3 billion, $10 billion, and $5.3 billion, respectively. Japanese direct investment in *manufacturing* is now greater in Asia than in the United States. In 1994, Japanese manufacturing FDI was $5.2 billion in Asia compared with $4.8 billion in the United States; in 1995 the totals were $6.5 billion (Asia) and $4.2 billion (United States) (Terry, 1996, pp. 189–190).[4]

In accord with this regional focus, the flying geese approach generates its own concerns about potential barriers to continued industrialization. Akamatsu recognized that industrial diffusion could generate trade conflicts between leaders and followers (1961, p. 204). Modern flying geese analyses have argued that protectionist pressures may, by disrupting the given leadership function of Japanese business, upset the harmonious flight of the different national geese. However, they suggest this problem can be avoided if governments conduct ongoing national consultations with leading corporations and regional consultations with other governments (see, for example, Seki, 1995, p. 14).

Flying Geese Limitations

The flying geese perspective has serious theoretical weaknesses. For example, despite its empirical grounding in the regionalization of Japanese capital, one may question the modern flying geese perspective's insistence on Japan as permanent lead goose. Akamatsu's original formulation, allowing for a reshuffling of leader and follower positions in line with changes in competitive advantage, seems more consistent with the realities of capitalist uneven development. Moreover, the flying geese approach itself suggests that specific national strengths are largely a function of industrial policy decisions and thus cannot be taken as "given." The leadership question is important given the potential inequalities arguably built into the vertical and horizontal divisions of labor among leading and following geese.[5] But even from the standpoint of leading countries in general and Japan in particular, the flying geese approach presents a highly idealized vision of capitalist development. It presumes that regionalized creative destruction fulfills the needs and capabilities of Japanese workers and communities even though it is driven by the profit interests of Japanese capital. Capital's use of industrial restructuring and relocation to undercut workers' power throws this presumption into question.

Contrary to the idealized claims of flying geese proponents, the regionalization of Japanese capital has taken the form of a recurrent crisis-driven pattern of scrap-and-build accumulation, each round of which was carried out largely at the expense of Japanese labor (Steven, 1990).[6] In the 1960s, wage pressures and trade conflicts caused light industries (including textiles and simple consumer electronics), which had been Japan's leading export sector in the 1950s, to be run down and scrapped in favor of the heavy and chemical industries. This process entailed a crowding of predominantly female light-industry labor into low-wage service employment and the household sector. Then, when the 1973 oil crisis and domestic environmental protests raised heavy industry costs, this sector was itself largely scrapped and relocated abroad while the new leading domestic sector became the machine industries, especially cars and electrical machinery. The success of this transition hinged on the conversion of machine industries from production mainly for the domestic market to a strong export orientation, which was achieved by keeping unit labor costs low largely through the expanded use of temporary and subcontracted labor. Eventually, trade tensions with the United States, the 1985 Plaza Accord, and the subsequent "high yen crisis" led Japanese corporations to relocate significant portions of the machinery industries offshore as well. This overall process of scrap-and-build both hinged upon and reinforced the encapsulation of core-industry workers' militant and creative energies in enterprise unions as well as the deep gender- and education-based divisions in the Japanese working class (Steven, 1990).[7]

Apart from its effects on workers, Japanese scrap-and build accumulation ultimately conflicted even with the industrial dynamism and competitiveness championed by flying geese theorists. Although repeated restructuring of the industrial base maintained the dynamism of the Japanese economy until the mid-1980s, its eventual result was a definite hollowing out of domestic industry, that is, the growing substitution of foreign investment and financial speculation for productive domestic investment (UNCTAD, 1996a, pp. 94–101). The transnationalization of Japanese capital has been a constant source of competitive pressures on Japanese working people since the 1960s, constraining the growth of the domestic market and thereby reinforcing the export-dependence and trade conflicts built into Japanese economic growth. But it has also eroded the domestic industrial base required to sustain Japan's past rapid growth (see Chapter 10). With its seemingly permanent growth recession, historically high rates of unemployment, downward pressures on wages and work conditions, and its banking system in shambles, the Japanese economy of the 1990s hardly resembles a dynamic lead goose.

Flying geese advocates also acknowledge the important, although secondary, role played by NIE-based foreign direct investment in SEA-3 industrialization. But as in the case of Japan, they largely assume that the resulting regional industrial restructuring had only positive implications for workers and communities in the NIEs themselves. Unfortunately, this assumption is no more reasonable for the NIEs than for Japan. It was hardly coincidental that the post–1980 growth of outward direct investment from both South Korea and Taiwan corresponded to powerful protests against authoritarian regimes that had supported rapid export-led accumulation by repressing domestic labor, especially women in light-export industries. These democratic struggles led to the end of formal military dictatorship, mushrooming labor organization, and rising wages.[8] Meanwhile, Japanese investment in the SEA-3 was creating new lower-cost export competition for the NIEs, further spurring South Korean and Taiwanese firms to shift their own production to lower-cost locations, including the SEA-3 countries and China.[9] The result of all this foreign investment was, among other things, the regional build up of excess capacity, and intensifying competitive pressures on workers and communities in the NIEs (Steven, 1997).

Other important aspects of this Japanese-led regionalization process, including the extreme import dependency and structural trade deficits built into SEA-3 manufactured export growth, are addressed in Chapter 3. For present purposes, the crucial point is that the flying geese approach does not overcome the idealizations of capitalism that are common to neoliberalism and structural-institutionalism. Although the Japanese origins of the flying geese approach have meant that its proponents tend to favor structural-institutionalism on the national level, the overriding imperative for those that advance this approach remains to keep the East Asian region open to Japanese corporate capital. This imperative, combined with the false identity of interests between Japanese capital and workers throughout the region, has even blinded flying geese theorists to the harsh realities of economic crisis. Hence, with the East Asian crisis in full swing, Edith Terry offered the strange reassurance that although "the Japanese model may be discredited in theory, . . . in practice it is thriving—just as Japanese economists had been predicting for the better part of a century—in the developing, hard-struck economies of Asia" (1998, p. 6).

Indeed, the "shared vision" of flying geese proponents, namely "a rapid move towards greater economic integration regionally and an even more rapid shift towards integration between the Japanese and Asian economies" (Terry, 1996, p. 189), is not fundamentally different from the vision propounded by neoliberal advocates of NAFTA, GATT, and the WTO. The flying geese approach joins with neoliberalism in branding any popular opposition to the regionalization of capital—including the coalition of workers, farmers, women, urban poor, environmentalists, indigenous peoples, and peace activists who gather every three years in Asia under the banner of The People's Plan for the Twenty-first Century (Hart-Landsberg, 1994)—as parochial interests standing in the way of modernization.[10] Like neoliberalism and structural-institutionalism, it sees popular aspirations and struggles as potential disruptions of a predetermined development strategy, not as sources of inspiration for the strategy itself. They are problems to be managed, not human-social phenomena with whom to be critically engaged. Thus, despite its new insights, the flying geese approach remains an unsatisfactory alternative to neoliberalism and structural-institutionalism.

The Greater China Approach

The Greater China approach sees the People's Republic of China (PRC), together with the significant concentrations of expatriate Chinese businesses in other East Asian countries, especially Hong Kong and Taiwan, as the main organizer and anchor of regional progress.[11] According to its proponents, the recent development of East Asian trade and investment networks makes possible the reestablishment of a dynamic China-centered regional economy. Post-1978 reforms in the PRC set the stage for this "relinking" of China proper with expatriate Chinese capital. Hong Kong and Taiwanese foreign direct investment helped launch China's export-led growth. Chinese-led enterprises from Hong Kong, Taiwan, and Singapore also helped, in concert with Chinese entrepreneurs in Thailand, Malaysia, and Indonesia, to promote the industrialization of the SEA-3. The PRC, in turn, provides a critical outlet for NIE and SEA-3 exports.

Within this framework, some Greater China analyses place more emphasis on the development impulses and regional economic autonomy generated by the PRC's state-directed economy, and these analyses draw inspiration from structural-institutionalism (see, for example, Selden, 1997). Others emphasize the energetic entrepreneurship of expatriate Chinese business, with its family-run enterprises and informal relations of economic reciprocity. These latter analyses combine neoliberal and culturalist conceptions of economic relationships. Yeung (1997, pp. 1–2) even scolds "economistic and Western-centric" approaches for taking inadequate account of "the role of *guanxi,* or personal relationships in social and business networks." Despite such anti-economistic pretensions, however, Greater China analyses often contain a large dose of old-fashioned small-business ideology, emphasizing the dynamism of family-based enterprises and business networks relative to the established TNC giants and allied national governments (Lever-Tracy et al., 1996). In fact, elements of both structural-institutionalism and neoliberalism are often found in particular Greater China analyses. Hsing (1996), for example, credits the growth of Taiwan-PRC investment networks to a strong cultural affinity between expatriate Chinese business practices and the flexible-bureaucratic traditions of the Chinese state. In conjunction with recent reforms increasing the autonomy of Chinese local governments, this affinity evidently created fertile ground for reciprocal "gift-exchanges" between Taiwanese investors and Chinese government officials.

Challenging Japan's status as the lead East Asian goose, Greater China theorists have argued that Japan's regional prominence in the post–World

War II period derived from United States imperial power just as much or even more than from Japanese strength. The United States encouraged and supported Japan's regional leadership in order to reduce its own cost of maintaining an open global system of investment and trade. U.S. economic and (especially) political and military influence over Japan, and East Asia more generally, is still substantial enough to preclude any meaningful talk of Japan as a lead goose.[12] As a case in point, not long after the start of the East Asian financial meltdown the Japanese government attempted to create an Asian Monetary Fund to provide emergency loans and support "a gentler form of adjustment in the region, while consolidating Japanese political influence" (Gill, 1999, p. 6). The United States aggressively and successfully vetoed the attempt.

At the same time, the reemergence of the PRC as a major regional force is said by Greater China theorists to reduce East Asia's dependence on the United States (and by extension Japan) both economically and politically. The economic strength and dynamism of the PRC and of Chinese regional investment and trade networks thus improves the terms on which East Asia is integrated into the world economic system, thereby enhancing the region's chances for sustained economic success (Hamashita, 1997).

While recognizing the tensions and instabilities *internal to China proper* as a potential threat to the region's prosperity, Greater China analyses treat the PRC's worsening interregional inequalities, corruption, inflation, unemployment, social polarization, and environmental destruction as manageable side effects of economic dynamism, especially given the "substantial regulatory and organizational powers" retained by the Chinese state (Selden, 1997, p. 337; cf. Shu-Ki, 1996, pp. 36-37). Greater China theorists also worry that East Asia's complex array of competing capitalist and imperial state interests could generate disruptive conflicts. Perhaps the most important tension is that between Japan's "lead goose" project and China's emergent regional economic interests (Yam, 1995, p. 65). Trade and diplomatic conflicts between the United States and the East Asian countries (especially China and Japan) are also a major concern—with the deep-rooted political antagonism between Taiwan and the PRC always lurking in the background as a potential destabilizing force (Sung, 1993, p. 128). A truly dangerous escalation of conflicts is considered unlikely, however, so long as the behavior of the leading East Asian states, particularly China and Japan, is conditioned by their common need for continued economic and military cooperation with the United States (Selden, 1997, p. 338). The United States thus emerges as a key conflict manager in a multipolar regional power structure anchored by Greater China (Zhao, 1997).

Greater China Limitations

The Greater China approach suffers from a number of problems. To begin with, it underestimates the regional presence of Japanese capital compared to Chinese-organized investment and trade flows. It is true that Chinese-led firms from Hong Kong and Taiwan dominated the initial direct foreign investment flows into the PRC, they were also (together with Singapore-based Chinese firms) a major source of direct investment in the SEA-3 countries during the 1980s. But these facts are not inconsistent with a regional hierarchy headed by Japan—a hierarchy based on differential control over technological, marketing, and financial resources.[13] Bowles and MacLean (1996, p. 399) present data indicating that during the 1985-88 period, Japan emerged as the leading direct investment source for all four East Asian NIEs, with FDI-inflow shares ranging from 30.9 percent for Taiwan, to 31.9 percent for Hong Kong, 39.2 percent for Singapore, and 51.8 percent for South Korea. Meanwhile, Japanese direct investment in the countries of the Association of Southeast Asian Nations (ASEAN) eclipsed that of all four NIEs combined for three of the five years from 1986 through 1990 (p. 400; see also UNCTAD, 1995, pp. 49-50).

Subsequent reports revealed that Japanese corporate capital was building a stronger position in China as well, as the PRC tried to upgrade its production into higher value-added areas. Sender (1995, pp. 50-52) observed that China's share of total Japanese outward direct investment had "grown by leaps and bounds and has now reached 6.7% . . . fast coming up on the 7.7% share of ASEAN." The *Economist* (1996, p. 63) noted that "in 1990, direct investment by Japanese firms in China totaled only $349 million. That figure rose by a factor of ten by 1995-96." In fact, "a survey of Japanese companies in January [1996] by Japan's Export-Import Bank found that China was easily the most popular place to invest" (p. 63).

In its structural-institutional variations, the Greater China approach also tends to exaggerate the industrial planning capabilities of the Chinese state and the structural stability of the PRC political economy. Selden (1997, p. 337), for example, mentions the weakening of the Chinese planning apparatus by privatization and liberalization; but he argues that the Chinese state still possesses considerable potential as a developmentalist state based on "its own heavy industrial foundations, a relatively comprehensive if inefficient complement of industries including electronics, and its own (limited) research infrastructure." The reality, however, is that the most dynamic sectors and regions of the Chinese economy are those which lie outside the shrinking realm of government planning and state enterprise (Cheng,

1999, p. 45). One aspect of this uneven development is the focus of inward direct investment from Hong Kong, Macau, Taiwan, and South Korea on China's coastal provinces, especially Guangdong and Fujian in the southeast and (more recently) the Jiangsu-Shanghai region to the north. At the end of 1993, the former two provinces accounted for 46.5 percent of the stock of FDI in the PRC, with the latter region taking up an additional 12.9 percent (Lever-Tracy, et al., 1996, p. 67). According to UNCTAD, this concentration of FDI-based manufacturing activity is itself

> losing momentum as the transfer of labor-intensive production to China slows down. Partly due to the fact that most labor-intensive production has already moved out from [the investment-source] economies and partly due to increases in labor and land costs in the coastal regions, export-processing production has become less attractive in China than in several other Asian countries. (1996b, p. 55)

Moreover, in promoting the "synergy" of foreign capital and technology with low-cost domestic labor and expanding domestic upper-class markets, the Chinese state is furthering its own conversion from an autonomous developmental state into a dependent-capitalist state operating as a junior "partner in exploitation" with transnational capital (Greenfield, 1998a). As pointed out by Joseph Medley:

> The Chinese state is establishing and reproducing political, economic and even cultural conditions to support foreign capitalist production in China and permit transfers of surplus value from China through international capitalist networks. Firms operating out of Hong Kong, Taiwan and South Korea, as well as Japan, the United States and elsewhere, receive direct support from the Chinese state to establish and expand their operations in China. . . . The state is delegating full control of decision-making to foreign firm managements, guaranteeing protection of intellectual property rights and granting access to domestic markets, especially if the foreign firms bring in advanced technology. Foreign firms are allowed to source means, labor and other production imports at competitive market prices. Finally, income from domestic Chinese sales can be readily converted into foreign exchange and freely repatriated. . . . Chinese state imperialism is producing the conditions for the "free market, structural adjustment" model, and, consequently, its residents are beginning to suffer the deleterious effects associated with that model. (1997, pp. 9-11)

From this perspective, China's mass unemployment, growing inequality, and ecological havoc appear not as manageable side effects of healthy growth, but as intrinsic elements of a class-exploitative accumulation process promoted by the Chinese state itself (Greenfield and Leong, 1997; Meisner, 1997; Smith, 1997; Cheng, 1999). It is thus unsurprising that Greater China analyses place great weight on the conflict-management capacities of the Chinese state. Even with "ferocious state repression of labor activists," however, the marketization and privatization of the PRC economy, together with new hyper-exploitative systems of labor control and abysmal work conditions in export enterprises, have met with widespread worker resistance including strikes, demonstrations, and informal workplace protests (Smith, 1997, pp. 9-10).[14] The Greater China approach, like neoliberalism, structural-institutionalism, and flying geese theories, treats such resistance as merely a counter-productive disruption of an economic growth regime whose social integrity is to be uncritically accepted.

With the vision of China as an autonomous and stable national-developmental regime thrown into question, the notion of *Greater* China as an integrated regional-development center is also undercut. While structural-institutionalist variants of the Greater China approach overestimate the developmental character of the Chinese state, neoliberal variants underrate the importance of having a developmental state with a strong regional presence. Here, one may question whether the dynamism and stability of East Asian industrialization can be sustained in the absence of a single dominant regional hegemon. To illustrate this point, China's recent export offensive was supported by the 1994 devaluation of the *yuan* and the subsequent real appreciation of the $U.S.-linked currencies of Southeast Asia; it was thus mirrored by Southeast Asia's dramatic export slowdown in 1996-97. The rate of growth in Thai exports, for example, slowed from over 20 percent in 1995 to less than 1 percent in 1996 (*Economist*, 1997a, p. 24). "Now," however, "China's own exports are likely to be dented as currency devaluations all around East Asia increase the competitiveness of its rivals" (*Economist*, 1997b, p. 41). With direct investment inflows into China down an estimated 35 percent over the first ten months of 1997 (Faison, 1997), and with the weakening of the Japanese yen through the summer of 1998, "many experts" feared that China might "eventually be pressured to devalue its currency, setting off a new round of devaluations and financial crises around Asia" (Kristof and WuDunn, 1998, p. B2).

Without a dominant hegemon to underwrite and enforce agreements, there is little likelihood that such competitive warfare will work itself out in the interest of Greater China—assuming such a collective entity exists— much less the region as a whole. The culture- and family-based networks of Chinese business certainly have not immunized the region against overcapacity, financial crisis, or trade tensions with the United States. The ascendance of the PRC as a competing investment and exporting center was a major contributor to these problems. Their ill effects have already been felt in the main centers of Greater China, with slower growth in the PRC and Taiwan, and a serious recession in Hong Kong—not to mention the sharp downturns of the SEA-3 economies, where expatriate Chinese capital is also prominent (WuDunn, 1998c). Such instability is, of course, an inescapable part of capitalism; the point is that the Greater China approach idealizes capitalism by soft-pedaling the class exploitation, uneven development, and explosive international conflicts working to undermine the region's prosperity.

Chapter 3

The Challenge and the Contradictions of Dependency Analysis

Dependency analysis understands capitalism as a hierarchical system that operates regionally and internationally for the benefit of elites, in particular those from the developed capitalist countries (Dos Santos, 1970). Since the 1970s, dependency analysis has fallen into disrepute even among left political economists. However, this waning popularity is largely due to the changing international political climate and the empirical failure of certain extreme claims made by the most "economistic and mechanistic" dependency analyses (James, 1997, p. 207). Recent history has not reduced the cogency of the theory's basic concerns: the "major discrepancies of power [that] operate across the supposedly open flow of global exchange and interdependence" and the resulting uneven development of wealth and poverty on a global scale (p. 222).

This critical stance on capitalist development makes dependency theory highly relevant to the East Asian experience. The previously discussed approaches have all embraced the capitalist project and sought, in their different ways, to promote it. By contrast, many left activists and scholars have used dependency analysis to challenge the rationality, historical progressivity, and sustainability of capitalist growth "successes" in East Asia. Politically, the most important element of this challenge is its recognition that existing East Asian problems of environmental destruction, income polarization, labor and gender exploitation, and government repression are central to, rather than temporary side effects of, East Asia's export-led growth strategy. But the power of dependency theory's challenge is undercut whenever it downplays the common class-exploitative basis of all capitalist development regimes.

Dependency and Unequal Development in East Asia

Dependency analyses of the miracle economies have disputed flying geese type claims concerning the benefits of Japan's regional economic leadership for the NIEs and the SEA-3.[1] Specifically, they have focused on the development of a hierarchically structured regional system of export-oriented industry featuring grossly unequal distributions of value added between Japanese and peripheral enterprises.

Dependency analyses recognize that the degree and pattern of external domination differ between the NIEs and the SEA-3. One striking difference is the relative absence of a significant import-substitution base in the latter group of countries. But even in South Korea and Taiwan, key manufacturing sectors—including the all-important electronics industry—still rely heavily on imports of essential components and machinery from Japan. Technological and marketing dependence is further manifested in original equipment manufacturing arrangements with Japanese firms, and in the increasing resort to sales in lower-rung markets in other peripheral countries not as yet fully mined by core-country firms (Hart-Landsberg and Burkett, 1998, pp. 99–100).

Dependency is especially severe in the SEA-3, where export-oriented manufacturing was much more the product of the post–1985 explosion of direct investment from Japan and the NIEs than of any national industrialization projects. Extremely high shares of SEA-3 manufactured exports are produced by or under the control of foreign companies. In the case of Malaysia, foreign controlled companies (primarily Japanese) accounted for approximately 99 percent of the exports of electronics goods, over 90 percent of the exports of machinery and electrical appliances, over 80 percent of the exports of rubber products, and 75 percent of the exports of textile and apparel products at the end of the 1980s (Bernard and Ravenhill, 1995, p. 196). Often such foreign-based export operations are notable for their relative lack of linkages with locally controlled firms.[2]

Many developed country industries also rely significantly on imported inputs. The dependency of NIE and SEA-3 firms, however, involves imported inputs making proportionally much larger contributions to final value added per unit of locally produced output. Hence, in response to the flying geese approach, dependency analyses highlight the unequal distributions of value added generated by vertical and horizontal divisions of labor between leading and following countries. As for the vertical divisions, consider the Thailand operations of Jinbao Electronics, a medium-sized Taiwan-based firm:

In April 1990 Jinbao opened a factory in Thailand to manufacture low-end calculators that could no longer be made in Taiwan and exported at a profit. Of its calculators, 60 percent by volume and 40 percent by value are now made in Thailand. Jinbao has been assembling a majority of its calculators for Japanese companies such as Casio and Canon. . . . The innovation behind the product, the brand name, and the marketing are Japanese. All key components for the calculators, such as liquid crystal displays (LCDs) and production equipment in the Thai factory such as insertion equipment, are imported from Japan. All procurement and administration are controlled from Taipei, and the management of the plant is Taiwanese. The labor is Thai. Output from the plant is exclusively for export. In international trade data Jinbao's production is recorded as Thai exports of electronic goods. To purchasers at the other end the products appear to be Japanese. The direct foreign investment statistics indicate a Taiwanese investment. (Bernard and Ravenhill, 1995, pp. 186-187)

Such hierarchical industry structures tend to reduce the acquisition of value added as one descends from the lead country (Japan) to mid-range followers like Taiwan, and then to lower-level locations such as Thailand (cf. Llinqueco, et al., 1989; Bello, 1992; Fallows, 1994). Meanwhile, horizontal industrial divisions among follower countries often operate as mechanisms for their competitive division and rule by the lead country's capital. This has become an increasingly important issue as Japanese corporations develop regional production networks integrating different elements of productive activity across countries.

Mitsubishi Motors, for example, had 12 fully owned parts and assembly plants in Asia as of mid-1995. "Its partners crank out low-cost parts Mitsubishi uses in Japan and elsewhere in Asia. . . . Thailand's MMC Sittipol Co. sends truck frames to Mitsubishi in Japan and intake manifolds to Malaysia's Proton" (Updike and Nakarmi, 1995, p. 51). Similarly, "Nissan's factory in Thailand . . . produces diesel engines and molds for stamped parts, its subsidiary in Indonesia turns out mechanical parts, and its unit in Malaysia provides clutches and electrical parts" (Bello, 1992, p. 92). Toyota is also among the companies having "worked out regional specialization schemes" (p. 92; see Doner, 1993, pp. 180-181).[3] Although "the Japanese firms have appealed to the ASEAN countries' long-time dream of setting up a 'regional car complementation' program," their operations

are not of the sort that would allow the ASEAN countries to develop a truly integrated regional auto industry. The current integration has not been worked out in partnership with governments with a view to maximize technology transfer and other benefits for the participating countries. It is driven, instead, by the efforts of Japanese corporations to cut costs and increase profitability. (Bello, 1992, p. 92)

East Asia's dependence on Japanese business has been reinforced by Japanese aid and lending policies. Besides helping to finance the import bills associated with export-led industrialization, Japan's development aid is—compared to other core countries—highly integrated with the strategic goals of Japanese transnationals in terms of industrial location, and primary product production and importation. It is largely directed towards infrastructural projects supporting Japanese export-oriented operations (Hatch and Yamamura, 1996). Meanwhile, right up until the 1997-98 regional crisis, private Japanese banks played "a major role in the realization of economic integration into a 'yen co-prosperity sphere'" (Hiroshi, et al., 1993, p. 38; cf. Fumio, 1993). Japanese bank loans in Asia (outside Japan) grew from a stock of $72 billion in June 1993 to $116 billion as of June 1996 (Sapsford, 1997, p. A14). Outstanding loans by Japanese banks to the SEA-3 countries totaled $67.7 billion at the end of 1996, compared to $12.6 billion and $49.4 billion by U.S. and European banks, respectively (IMF, 1997b, p. 7).

Their relatively extreme dependence on imported inputs, technologies, and financial resources left the SEA-3 economies with a strong tendency toward rising trade deficits. For example, Malaysia's current account deficit as a percentage of GDP rose from 3.9 percent in 1992 to 8.8 percent in 1995 (Jomo K. S., 1998, p. 31). Even South Korea did not escape this difficulty.[4] Aside from maldistribution of value added, an important element of the problem was that, with marketing channels shaped by the needs of Japanese capital, East Asian exports were largely directed toward the markets of non-Asian core countries (especially the United States). Sustained export success in these markets generated both protectionist pressures in the core countries and demands for the dependent exporting countries to open up their own markets to imports of core-produced agricultural and consumer goods. These pressures and demands not only added to East Asian trade imbalances, but also threatened East Asian countries with a premature stunting of their agriculture and import-substitution industries (Bello and Rosenfeld, 1990; Hart-Landsberg, 1993).

Dependency analyses see structural trade deficits hindering continued East Asian growth in two ways. First, trade deficits produce increased dependence on capital inflows. However, the policies required to maintain these inflows (low wages and low taxes, tight monetary policy) often preclude the public spending on research and development (R&D), education, and other infrastructural projects needed for upgrading local production toward higher value-added activities. And, as newer, lower cost production sites become attractive to foreign corporations (e.g., China, Vietnam, etc.), it becomes more difficult for the NIEs and the SEA-3 to secure the necessary capital inflows.[5] The potential for balance of payments crises and IMF-style retrenchment is enhanced by the relatively low diversification of manufactured exports combined with tendencies toward collective overproduction by the NIEs and newer players in the export-led growth game.

Second, faced with the need to increase foreign exchange earnings by any means necessary, East Asian governments are driven to implement policies designed to super-exploit female and child labor in light-export manufacturing, repress labor organizing, plunder the country's natural resource base (forests, minerals, fisheries, agricultural lands), and to exploit women and young people in sex tourism and expatriate employment activities (James, 1997, pp. 222-223). While such destructive means of hard-currency accumulation are hardly unique to East Asia, their integral role there shows that even the most dynamic and competitive forms of capital accumulation share capitalism's general tendency to erode the natural, human, and social conditions of production (O'Connor, 1998; Burkett, 1999).

Dependency, Development Models, and Class

The dependency approach encourages a critical rethinking of capitalism and of development criteria. However, when not solidly and consistently grounded in a class perspective on capital accumulation, it leads to an overemphasis on international economic domination and resulting structural trade deficits, considered not as symptoms of more fundamental capitalist contradictions but as the primary barriers to continued growth and development.

Not that external payments problems are unimportant; the 1997 currency crises in the SEA-3 and South Korea destroyed prior optimistic projections that capital inflows could indefinitely sustain the East Asian miracles. But insofar as structural trade deficits reflect unequal distributions of value added across countries, they manifest the uneven development of capital accumulation, that is, the uneven development of surplus-value extraction from the direct producers. The international distributions of investment, production, and value added are shaped by the uneven development of corporate-capitalist organization and capital-labor conflicts within and across countries, not by unequal relations between countries as such. Their ultimate basis is the alienation of the conditions and results of social labor vis-à-vis the direct producers, and their conversion into instruments for exploiting these producers, in all countries as a whole. By neglecting or straying away from this holistic class dimension, many dependency analyses tend to slip into a technocratic perspective on problems of East Asian economics and policy. This has the effect of undermining the national, regional, and global class solidarity needed to move beyond capitalism's uneven and unequal development toward a more worker-community centered political economy.

Guided by a concern with structural inequalities between more and less developed nations, many dependency analyses focus on finding, and winning adoption of, those state policies they hope will enable externally dominated nations to break out of their dependency and shape, often in concert with other similarly situated nations, a development trajectory that is less trade dependent, more environmentally sustainable, and more responsive to popular needs. This approach does not, it is important to note, entail an uncritical support for any particular kind of capitalism as opposed to a more democratic, worker-community controlled economy. The problem is subtler than this: in comparing capitalist policy regimes, the analyst ends up adopting a structural-institutionalist type of thinking in which the dynamics of accumulation are treated as if they were largely the result of decisions made by policymakers free to choose from a range of "best practices," rather than a complex outcome of uneven development, class struggles, and factional conflicts, both domestic and international. Such technocratic analysis promotes a confused politics in which rejection of neoliberalism becomes the guiding star and people are in effect encouraged to work, although critically, with existing governments and regional initiatives such as the ASEAN Free Trade Agreement, to strengthen and progressively reorient the dependent-capitalist state's economic planning and redistributive capabilities (Bello, 1996b and 1996c).

The limitations of dependency analysis shorn of class perspective are perhaps best illustrated by the way some scholars have treated Japan.[6] Somewhat ironically in light of their criticism of Japanese policy toward Asia, these scholars find much to praise about the Japanese state and its role in building an internationally competitive economy. In fact, praise for Japan often goes beyond the endorsement of structural-institutionalist claims regarding the industrial policy successes of the Japanese state. Some analysts, echoing the pronouncements of the flying geese theorists, argue that when compared with U.S. imperialism, Japanese imperialism delivers more productive foreign direct investment and a more flexible accommodation of state-interventionist growth in the countries it targets. In fact, these analyses often wind up treating the competitiveness pressures, inequalities, social dislocations, and environmental havoc created by Japanese investment throughout East Asia as inessential side effects of an economic regime the main technical and institutional features of which are worthy of critical popular support. In this way, popular criticism and input tend to be limited—at least for the time being—to demands for ameliorative state actions against these external effects. The basic relations of capital accumulation remain unquestioned; hence the need to envision and fight for alternative democratic institutions to serve as vehicles of worker-community based development remains equally unaddressed.

The formulation of leftist analysis and strategy on the basis of the most "progressive" form of capitalism for (or from) East Asia raises complex problems that go beyond dependency theory as such (see Chapter 4). However, it can be stated up front that such an approach tends to be derailed by the uneven development of capital accumulation, including overproduction crises. A growing number of left political economists have championed Japan, Taiwan, or South Korea—and recently even the SEA-3 and China—as offering development policy regimes and forms of external dependency that are not only competitive and productive but also (given the right political conditions and strategies) accommodative of worker-community needs (see, for example, Tabb, 1992; Lippit, 1993; Amsden, 1994; Goodno, 1996; Goldstein, 1997; Miller, 1997; Lazonick, 1998). Due to the difficulty of separating the authoritarianism of the regimes being trumpeted from their competitive economic successes, this strategy was never very effective. It has been seriously fractured by East Asia's economic crisis.

This crisis has revealed the supposedly long-termist, productivist, and nurturing qualities of the Japanese and East Asian economies to be just so many one-sided idealizations of capitalism. The early 1990s reduction of Japanese direct investment in the SEA-3 countries was a major factor forcing these countries to pursue external short-term capital flows in order to cover their growing trade deficits, setting the stage for the financial crises which triggered the region's recession (see Chapter 12). The withdrawal of speculative Japanese loans and portfolio capital played a significant role in the financial crises themselves, and the recession was accentuated by further cutbacks of Japanese direct investments, especially in the SEA-3 countries (IMF, 1997b; Henwood, 1998). When not firing thousands of workers,

Japanese and NIE-based manufacturing units severely pressured their workers and subcontractors in the SEA-3, Vietnam, and China to produce more at lower wages and prices (Greenfield, 1998b). It turns out that Japanese and East Asian capitalism are just as crisis-prone, and just as likely to redistribute the costs of crisis onto those who can least afford them, as any other kind of capitalism.

Chapter 4

The Use and Abuse of Japan as a Progressive Model

The non-Marxist perspectives surveyed thus far all suffer from faulty conceptions of Japanese capitalism and its international expansion. Neoliberalism and structural-institutionalism both focus on national development-policy options within a given international context. As a result, each provides at most a partial understanding of Japan's crucial influence on East Asian development as a regional whole. Moreover, because they ignore or soft-pedal the class contradictions and uneven development common to all forms of capitalism, neoliberalism and structural-institutionalism underestimate the instabilities and limits built into the Japanese growth "miracle" and its apparent spread to the East Asian NIEs and the SEA-3.

Flying geese and Greater China approaches also idealize Japanese and East Asian capitalism. While rightly emphasizing the importance of regional dynamics, each treats crisis tendencies and popular struggles as inessential, manageable impediments to a predetermined development model. Greater China analyses also underrate the continued shaping of East Asian development by Japanese capital. Meanwhile, flying geese approaches fail to critically analyze the regional division of labor between Japanese capital on the one hand, and NIE and SEA-3 capital on the other. Dependency perspectives have pointed out the unequal distributions of value added—and other extreme social costs—built into this Japanese-dominated division of labor. Nonetheless, many dependency approaches maintain an essentially uncritical stance on the development "successes" of the Japanese economy itself, and in some cases this has caused dependency analysts to voice technocratic support for Japanese-style development and strengthened relations with

Japanese capital (as opposed to U.S. capital) in the NIEs and the SEA-3. All of this suggests that the first step in the construction of a more meaningful perspective on East Asia must be an historical and class-based analysis of Japanese capitalism and its regional expansion. Before turning to that task, however, we consider another important dimension of Japan as an analytical and political reference point.

The fact is that misconceptions about Japanese capitalism are not unique to analyses of East Asian development and crisis. During the 1980s and early 1990s, positive references to the Japanese economy became quite common among progressives searching for new arguments and experiences favoring state-interventionist policies in the more market-oriented developed countries—especially the United States and Great Britain. By highlighting the high productivity and international competitiveness of Japan's more state-interventionist and (supposedly) more cooperative and egalitarian economic institutions, these progressives hoped to craft new programs, and arguments for them, that would prove politically viable in an increasingly conservative political climate.

Three basic claims often appeared in progressive evaluations of Japanese capitalism; indeed, these claims appeared to define a left-liberal consensus (hereafter LLC) on Japan as a progressive reference point. The LLC saw Japanese capitalism as superior to U.S. capitalism because of its greater rate and more efficient allocation of productive investment, more cooperative and efficient approach to labor-management relations, and more humane and efficient approach to structuring international economic relations. In what follows we highlight the arguments underlying each of these claims before scrutinizing them more critically.

Japanese Capitalism as a Progressive Model

The LLC argued that Japan's superior economic performance could, in large part, be explained by the country's rapid rate of industrial capital accumulation, which was itself the result of both a traditionally high rate of household savings and the efficient channeling of these savings into private- and public-sector investments in capital goods, new technologies, and supporting infrastructure. Clinton and Gore (1992, p. 6), for example, in line with the writings of their liberal advisor Robert Reich, noted how in the 1980s "our competitors' economies grew three or four times faster than ours—because their leaders decided to invest in their people and Washington did not." They suggested that a crucial reason why Japan "threaten[ed] to surpass America in manufacturing by 1996" was that the Japanese "were investing more than twelve times what we spend on roads, bridges, sewers, and the information networks and technologies of the future" (p. 143).

Walden Bello made the same point when he used "the Japanese model of state-led capitalism" as a positive reference point for his critique of conservative "Reaganite" economic policies:

> In 1989 Japan invested 23.2 per cent of its GNP in plant and capital equipment and R&D, while the United States invested 11.7 per cent. In non-defense R&D spending, U.S. expenditures as a percentage of GNP in the 1980s came to 1.8 per cent, while the figures for West Germany and Japan were 2.6 per cent and 2.8 per cent respectively. It is hardly cause for surprise then that the United States, which pioneered the development of most high technologies, has lost the lead to Japan in memory chips, semiconductor manufacturing equipment, robotics, numerically controlled machine tools, optoelectronics, and other strategic areas. (1994, pp. 73, 99)

Robert Pollin also praised "Japan's success with a credit allocation-centered planning system" as "the outstanding example of how an economy can use credit allocation techniques to promote financial stability and long-term growth" (1993, pp. 341-342). Others pointed to the relative patience of investment fund suppliers and the shared long-term profit orientation of non-financial firms and their financiers as an important element of Japan's competitive efficiency. For example, when interviewed by *Dollars and Sense*, the renowned Japan scholar Ronald Dore suggested that Japanese "joint venture partners, distributors, banks, and insurance companies" engaging in "cross-shareholding . . . see stock ownership as a long term mutual commitment" (McDermott and Tilly, 1994, p. 20). Such long-term reciprocity was contrasted to the behavior of the U.S. financial system where systemic short-termism and speculative pressures ruled the roost—to the detriment of long-term investments, corporate commitments to propertyless "stakeholders" including workers and communities, and long-term industrial competitiveness (Stanfield, 1994; Goldstein, 1997).

The LLC also credited Japan's more cooperative and efficient approach to labor-management relations for making a significant contribution to the country's superior competitiveness. Rapid productivity growth and cost-effectiveness were ascribed to corporate Japan's less bureaucratic and more worker-participatory structure of production—with worker participation enhanced by a greater security of employment. Once again, exogenous cultural factors—by rewarding values such as patience and cooperation—were said to reinforce corporate "lifetime employment" schemes and other labor-management relationships involving shared responsibility and mutual long-term commitments.[1]

Appeals to learn from and emulate the Japanese labor-management experience were often made by liberal writers. They were clearly evident in Clinton-Gore campaign proposals for "a partnership between business and labor and education and government, committed to compete and win in the global economy"—including measures for "reorganizing the workplace [to] encourage greater cooperation between labor and management" (1992, pp. 69, 126). Ronald Dore suggested that in Japan "the intensification of work" had been bound up with "greater initiative, greater respect for workers, and a greater sense of achievement" (McDermott and Tilly, 1994, p. 38). Similarly, worker-participation advocates David Levine and Laura D'Andrea Tyson included Japan (alongside Sweden) as one of the countries where businesses had, in order to "increase productivity . . . increased worker participation—giving workers a substantive say in the production process, including training new employees, dealing directly with suppliers, setting the work pace, and keeping the firm's financial records" (1989, p. 20).

David Gordon also applauded the fast growth of labor productivity in Japan compared to the United States, explaining this in terms not only of the greater rate and more efficient allocation of private and public investment in Japan, but also of Japan's more enlightened labor-management practices. Gordon suggested that "U.S. corporations are losing ground to . . . Japanese competitors in part because they continue to rely on the stick, not the carrot, in the workplace" (1993a, p. 344). In arguing for "a 21st-century production system"—one based on "visionary corporations which [have] improved their competitiveness by involving their workers"—Gordon highlighted the example of Japanese firms which "are more likely to stimulate their workers with the carrot seeking cooperation rather than conquest" (1993b, pp. 21-22).[2]

The last central LLC claim regarding the progressivity of Japanese capitalism was that it provided a more cooperative, efficient, and humane basis for global economic relations, including relations between developed countries and the third world, than did the inefficient, coercive, and extractive practices of U.S. capitalism. The left variation on this theme was well represented in William K. Tabb's critique of the "vampire capitalism" practiced by "the U.S. ruling class" during the Reagan-Bush years (1992, p. 81). Tabb described vampire capitalism as a "strategy of growth through redistribution—a redistribution from everyone in the world to the U.S. ruling class—based not on the productive capacities of the United States, but on its coercive talents, its military muscle, and its political and ideological domination" (p. 81). He then included Japan among the "nations" which "offer modes of capitalist development that are more efficient, and even kinder and gentler, than our increasingly social-Darwinist version" (p. 83). Going further, Tabb suggested that "the United States should emulate Japan ... in a more productive use of imperial power," and that the left should orient its strategies toward such a "progressive variation of capitalism," that is, a "Reichian approach to competitiveness, based on improving domestic factors of production, [which] could become the conventional wisdom of a revitalized liberal progressivism in the United States and reunite elements of the old liberal social-change constituencies" (pp. 86, 90).

Although we have drawn upon the works of various left and liberal writers to highlight the central tenets of what we believe to be a left-liberal consensus on Japan, we do not mean to equate the politics of the former with those of the latter or to argue that this consensus represented the viewpoint of a consolidated political movement with a common political vision. Most of the left writers we have quoted have made clear in their political writings and work—in sharp contrast to the quoted liberal writers—their rejection of capitalism and their commitment to the creation of a new social order. Nonetheless, many leading scholars, both left and liberal, shared a common perspective on the Japanese experience, even while seeking to advance very different political agendas. By the early 1990s, this shared understanding of the Japanese experience had helped to establish Japan as a positive political reference point for many progressive activists in the United States and other highly market-oriented developed countries. Unfortunately, this understanding was and is seriously flawed and, as a result, politically destructive for building an effective left politics.

A Critique of the Left-Liberal Consensus

LLC advocates applauded Japan's high rate and strategic allocation of productive investment and, by extension, the high household savings rate that helped to support it. But they failed to examine this investment regime in terms of the basic class relations of the Japanese economy.

Such an examination shows that the "traditionally" high Japanese savings rate is partly due to the extremely high housing costs faced by Japanese workers (Bennett and Levine, 1976, pp. 452-453; Horioka, 1990, p. 59). High savings have also been a response to the country's relatively small welfare state, as "private individuals or organizations to a large extent provide for protection against health, unemployment, and old age hazards through their own savings and social resources such as the family and voluntary group association" (Bennett and Levine, 1976, p. 449). As Shigeto Tsuru puts it, "the inadequacy of the social security system, especially for the elderly, necessitates a higher rate of individual saving with precautionary motives than in most other advanced countries" (1993, p. 70). Indeed, it was only "by keeping the prospect of a poverty-stricken old age ever-present" that "the regime stimulated the highest savings rates in the world" (Halliday, 1978, p. 231).[3] "The vast majority of these savings have gone . . . straight to the banks [often via the postal savings system] whence they have been redirected largely to favoured private industry" (p. 231). In sum, "the so-called frugality or austerity of the Japanese may be as much the result of financial insecurity as any devotion to a cultural work ethic or desire to retain austere traditional life styles" (Bennett and Levine, 1976, p. 449). The "tradition" of high Japanese household savings in reality "represents a consistent long-term policy for a specific form of high capital accumulation" (Halliday, 1978, p. 231).

One must also question the LLC's presumption that Japan's greater investor patience and more "efficient" planning for competitiveness had little to do with the undemocratic, pro-capitalistic character of government agencies like the Ministry of International Trade and Industry. The LLC in effect assumed that even if the basic priorities to be served by accumulation and the planning process had been democratically determined, capital would have been just as patient, cooperative, and productive. What seems more likely is that the relative patience of Japanese capital has been based firmly on the relative weakness of the Japanese working class. Indeed, Steven (1990, pp. 12-13) suggests that it was only Japanese capital's complete domination of the Japanese working class that allowed the Japanese state to effectively focus on international competitiveness and management of external economic conflicts in the period after the Second World War.

The LLC has also misunderstood the significance of post–1970s Japanese financial developments. Specifically, it presumed that the 1980s growth of Japan's speculative "bubble economy," and concomitant pressures toward liberalization of the financial system leading to financial instability, were basically exogenous to the more progressive aspects of the Japanese investment regime rather than an outcome of the economy's competitive maturation and accompanying overproduction of surplus value relative to productive and privately profitable investment opportunities (Pollin, 1993; Goldstein, 1997). The LLC ignored the possibility that a selective credit policy . . . designed to stimulate priority sectors . . . represents an approach that, on the basis of its own maturity, will give rise to pressures for liberalization as the masses of capital increasingly begin to demand access to all possible forms of production and financial enhancement. (Macedo Cintra, 1994, p. 45)

Indeed, as Tsuru (1993, pp. 162–169, 188ff) indicates, by the late 1970s the annual accumulation of internal funds in Japanese manufacturing corporations exceeded their domestic investments, and this growing surplus of funds fueled not only expanding foreign investment but also increases in (domestic and foreign) real estate holdings by these "non-financial" corporations. The fact that exploding real estate prices underpinned rising stock prices of many corporations (and vice versa) certainly gives new meaning to the purported "insulation" of these firms from outside speculative pressures (Ziemba, 1991; Oizumi, 1994). Insofar as the banks' relative shift from corporate loans to corporate share purchases resulted from, and contributed to, this phenomenon, we may say that the associated "mutual commitment" of corporate fund suppliers and users was basically a function of capitalist maturity and the attendant shift toward finance-led accumulation—that is, hardly separable from the "bubble economy" (Tsuru, 1993, p. 189). With the 1990s Japanese financial mess appearing increasingly similar to the 1980s U.S. situation, and with the Japanese authorities openly using the U.S. savings and loan bailout and financial-regulatory reforms as a model for their own cleanup operations, one wonders how historically progressive Japanese financial relations were and are apart from the quite normal war-aftermath boom and maturation phase of accumulation after World War II (Sweezy, 1980).[4]

When LLC scholars did recognize the problems of capitalist maturity and the warped priorities of capitalist competitiveness, they usually failed to reconcile them with the purported progressivity of Japanese capitalism. Dore, for example, had the following to say about the Japanese economy:

I'm not sure what potential there is for utilizing their current manufacturing capacity for the domestic market. There's a problem of transition comparable to the conversion problem faced by U.S. defense industries. . . . I doubt if Japan can escape for much longer the consequences of the forces of technological change and imports from other countries that are reducing employment opportunities for people of low learning ability (McDermott and Tilly, 1994, p. 21).

How can Dore find the Japanese model so desirable if it expended its labor and other productive resources (including the region's ecology) to build an industrial structure that outlived its economic usefulness in less than one generation—a structure whose unviability mirrors that of the U.S. military-industrial complex? One irony here is that by not asking any searching questions about the historical progressivity of capital accumulation and competitiveness, LLC advocates surrendered to neoliberal ideology. More specifically, they had no answer to the supposed imperative for Japan to move toward a more moderately paced, free-market driven, and "high consumption" pattern of economic growth—that is, to become more like the United States (Williams, 1994).

For Japanese workers, the Japanese labor-management system has also appeared considerably less progressive than one would gather from glowing LLC accounts. To begin with, "lifetime employment" has never covered more than "30 percent of all workers in Japan, with a concentration of male workers in large private firms and the government" (Takahashi, 1997, p. 59). Even in large corporations, a significant number of employees are classified as "part-time" or "temporary," and are thereby excluded from "lifetime employment," seniority-linked pay, and other corporate welfare benefits. Many of these contingent laborers work as many hours as the full-time "permanent" workers, and in recent years the former have made up a growing fraction of Japan's corporate labor force (pp. 60-61; Watanabe, 1993).[5]

While women are largely excluded from "permanent" jobs with "lifetime employment" (and even more so from managerial positions), they are overrepresented in the "temporary" and "part-time" groups. As of 1992, more than 90 percent of part-time workers and two-thirds of temporary workers were women (Houseman and Osawa, 1995, p. 12). Japanese women have also been disproportionately crowded into low-wage manufacturing and service jobs—especially in the small and family enterprise sectors (Hill, 1996, pp. 137-145). Indeed, "that a sizable proportion of Japanese women are still employed in the traditional sectors of the economy is a feature largely unique to Japan among the more developed countries" (Ogawa and Clark, 1995, p. 295).[6]

Even for "permanent" workers in the big Japanese corporations, "lifetime employment" normally ends with a forced "retirement" between the ages of 50 and 60, followed by many additional years of full-time labor (with reduced wages and benefits) in smaller subcontracting enterprises, contingent corporate positions, or self-employment (Takahashi, 1997, pp. 61-63). Control over the terms of post-"retirement" employment is, in fact, a powerful lever used by management to elicit loyalty and more intensive work efforts from employees (Rebick, 1995; Clark and Ogawa, 1997). Deferred wage payments (in the form of accelerated seniority scales, retirement bonuses, and the like) are also designed to raise workers' "cost of job loss" (Steven, 1988a, pp. 92ff).[7] When reinforced with "team" techniques of hierarchical workplace control, this labor-management framework has forced Japanese workers into long and intensive work hours such that physical and mental exhaustion have become serious problems (Hideo, et al., 1994, pp. 15-25; Itoh, 1994, p. 46). No wonder that when transplanted to North American settings, Japanese management systems have often proved to be untenable—instigating open rebellions among workers (Dassbach, 1993; Hideo, et al., 1994, p. 17; Parker, 1994).

The dependence of core-corporate accumulation on the superexploitation of disposable "temporary" and "part-time" workers, and of workers in smaller subcontracting firms, is not an incidental or conjunctural aspect of the Japanese model. It has been a primary source of capital for the commanding heights of the Japanese economy since the 1920s (see Chapter 6). While LLC advocates applauded the apparent insulation of Japanese corporations from short-term financial pressures, these corporations continued to use subcontractors as a buffer for cyclical and financial pressures (Yamamura, 1967, pp. 160-166; Halliday, 1978, p. 226; Tsuru, 1993, p. 109). In the 1990s, pressures by the big Japanese corporations on their subcontractors reached a historic extreme, producing widespread bankruptcies among small- and medium-sized enterprises despite government loans financed by the postal savings of the working class.

Indeed, pressures on smaller enterprises have now become a prime cause of Japan's growing unemployment crisis. This crisis is not fully appreciated until it is realized that the Japanese unemployment rate has now moved to levels considerably above those found in the United States, once common standards of measurement are used. As Yukichi Takahashi explains:

> The average rate of unemployment reported in Japan corresponds to the Bureau of Labor Statistics U-5 measure, like that used to report monthly and annual unemployment levels in the USA. But if one refers to the more inclusive U-7 measure that takes into account the number of discouraged unemployed and involuntary part-time workers, the total rate, as calculated in an independent analysis by the Management and Coordination Agency, reached 8.9 percent in 1994, three times the officially reported rate. (1997, p. 57)[8]

An important reason for the greater downward bias in Japan's official unemployment rate is that "proportionally more people in Japan than in the USA are regularly self-employed or work in a family enterprise, where people remain on [or are added to] the payroll even when the level of activity declines as business conditions change" (p. 57). Women (and older workers) are disproportionately represented among such disguised unemployed. In fact, "women in Japan have represented a large reserve of workers who have contributed flexibility to overall employment. Japan's low measured unemployment rate . . . has been due at least in part to the large number of women employed in temporary positions, who appear to leave the labour force altogether during business downturns" (Hill, 1996, p. 134). Hence, compared to other developed countries, Japan exhibits a greater "sensitivity of female labour force participation to short-run economic fluctuations"—as "women are employed in greater numbers in economic expansions only to be laid off during downturns" (Ogawa and Clark, 1995, p. 295).[9]

More broadly, the scrap-and-build strategy of industrial accumulation employed by Japanese capital from the 1950s onward was predicated upon, and in turn reinforced, the subjection of Japanese workers to levels of insecurity and competitive pressures unparalleled in the rest of the developed capitalist world (see Chapters 9-10). This strategy required not only secularly high rates of exploitation underpinned by long and intensive workdays, but also a high degree of inter-sectoral transferability and downward flexibility of real labor costs during crisis and capital restructuring periods. What Jon Halliday wrote a quarter century ago about this connection remains true today: "there is no evidence that Japanese business has had difficulty dealing with recessions or other questions (such as accelerating capital accumulation) through manipulations of the labor force" (1978, p. 227).

In short, the patience of Japanese financiers and core corporations, and the relative "insulation" of Japanese corporations from short-term financial pressures, have been gained at the expense of increased insecurity and misery for workers—especially women, the aged, and workers in the smaller subcontracting enterprises. Capitalist patience and corporate insulation largely represent a *transfer* of financial pressures downward in the corporate (and class) hierarchy rather than a reduction per se of these pressures. In treating such structural inequalities in culturalist and technocratic fashion, the LLC bypassed among other things the patriarchal and class-exploitative roots of the "family" ideology that legitimizes capitalist hegemony in Japan (see Chapter 6). LLC interpretations even failed to notice the blatant one-sidedness of "familyism" when applied at the micro level as "enterprise solidarity." While Japanese labor organizations are indeed limited to individual enterprises, "management shows no 'enterprise solidarity.' The simplest evidence of this is the superb trans-enterprise organization of Japanese big business, which has the most powerful federations in the capitalist world" (Halliday, 1978, p. 230). Japanese "group solidarity" is thus largely "an ideological weapon, where the capitalist class operates class solidarity within itself and fragmentation among the working class" (p. 230).

The above observations cast considerable doubt on the LLC view that Japanese capitalism represents a superior basis for international economic relations and for developed country–third world relations in particular. Moreover, as discussed in Chapters 9 and 10, it is by no means obvious that the scrap-and-build pattern of development and international expansionism employed by Japanese capital has been a rational process from the standpoint of Japanese workers and communities, when compared to socially plausible alternatives. It is equally questionable whether Japanese globalization has been straightforwardly "progressive" for working people in the third world. Japanese transnational manufacturing, mining, forestry, fishing, and agricultural operations are known worldwide for the absolute ruthlessness with which they exploit local workers and the natural habitat.[10] Moreover, during the 1980s and 1990s, a large and growing share of Japan's foreign investment was concentrated in financial and commercial real estate activities, including construction of hotels, golf courses, and the like, in connection with the development of vacation spots for higher-income Japanese professionals and managers—with the sex-tourism industry a major beneficiary of such investment. Workers in third world countries (and many workers even in other developed countries such as Australia, where Japanese capital is quite prominent) thus wound up serving the luxury recreational-consumption needs of the Japanese elite before addressing their own basic needs (McCormack, 1991, pp. 130–132).

Some LLC advocates have argued that Japanese capitalism is historically progressive insofar as, unlike U.S. capitalism, it has not depended on militarism to support its internal or external growth—at least not since the Second World War. As discussed in Part II, however, there is a definite historical continuity in the core institutions of Japanese capitalism running from the late-nineteenth century, through Japan's most violently militaristic period ending in 1945, and further on through the post–World War II era when Japan's recovery and high-growth "miracle" occurred symbiotically with the evolution of U.S. imperialism in East Asia and worldwide. Indeed, in order to redistribute the costs of its own hegemonic activities, the United States encouraged and supported Japanese elite efforts to reconstitute its East Asian sphere of influence. This symbiotic development included the massive economic jump start that Japanese capitalism received from U.S. military spending associated with the Korean and Vietnam Wars.

Japan currently possesses a modern military machine based on the second largest military budget in the world. Moreover, developments such as Japan's participation in the 1992 Kampuchean peacekeeping operation (in direct violation of Japanese constitutional law) have justifiably raised fears throughout Asia as to whether this military machine is being prepared for active use (Itsunori, 1994). A full-scale resurgence of Japanese militarism appears doubtful at least for now. Nonetheless, it remains an open question as to whether Japanese capital can continue to profit from (much less dominate) its regional periphery without the supporting military-political infrastructure that has until now been provided by the United States (see Chapter 10). In short, the LLC's notion of economic competitiveness and power without the ability to project military force idealizes a developing contradiction in Japanese (and global) capitalism as simply a "natural fact."

Conclusion

With Japan's growing economic problems in the 1990s, the use of Japanese capitalism as a positive reference point has rapidly diminished—and the progressives who had relied on this strategy now face serious analytical and political difficulties (see Chapter 5). To gain useful lessons from the LLC's downfall, one must pinpoint its basic methodological and political shortcomings. In this respect, the foregoing critique of the LLC closely parallels Rosa Luxemburg's classic response to Eduard Bernstein's more original left-liberal revision of Marxism and of socialism. Luxemburg notes, for example, how Bernstein takes crucial elements of capitalism out of their structural economic context:

> Bernstein's theory does not seize these manifestations of contemporary economic life as they appear in their organic relationship with the whole of capitalist development, with the complete economic mechanism of capitalism. His theory pulls these details out of their living economic context. It treats them as the *disjecta membra* (separate parts) of a lifeless machine. (1970, p. 61)

As a result, says Luxemburg, Bernstein's revisionism has a close affinity with the viewpoint of "the isolated capitalist [who] sees each organic part of the whole of our economy as an independent entity . . . as they act upon him, the single capitalist" (p. 62). Insofar as revisionism limits its analysis to an uncritical acceptance of "the economic facts . . . just as they appear when refracted by the laws of competition," it "is nothing else than a theoretic generalization made from the angle of the isolated capitalist" (p. 62).

Luxemburg concludes that such an ahistorical, nonholistic perspective necessarily "ends in utopia" because it is incapable of seeing how "the contradictions of capitalism mature"; indeed, like the isolated capitalist, revisionism "wants to lessen, to attenuate, the capitalist contradictions" (pp. 60, 63).

Like Bernstein's revisionism, the LLC was based on an understanding of capitalism that "pulls details out of their living context," views the economy "from the angle of the isolated capitalist," and "is guided by the possibility of the attenuation of the contradictions of capitalism" (Luxemburg, 1970, pp. 60-62). The LLC employed an ahistorical and nonholistic "smorgasbord" approach to the study of the Japanese experience. It first associated the progressivity of Japanese economic institutions with their contribution to international competitiveness. These institutions were then torn out of their historical and structural context and used as positive reference points for a progressive economic policy. Elements of the Japanese system that were difficult to define as progressive either went unmentioned or were treated as unrelated to Japanese competitiveness. In this manner, the supposedly more progressive Japanese institutions were deemed transplantable to progressive economic programs designed for other contexts. The contradictions of capital accumulation and its internationalization were thus bypassed, and "progressive" redefined as the most efficient and humane form of capitalist competitiveness.

The political dangers of such a methodology involve more than just its tendency to be short-circuited by uneven development and crisis. LLC-type analyses derive development visions from the requirements of capitalist competition rather than from critical engagement with popular struggles against the exploitation and social costs built into this competition. The LLC's technocratic approach—tearing institutions out of historical contexts and rearranging them into optimally-engineered programs—minimizes the role of popular mobilization while emphasizing the formulation and provision of policy advice in and through academic think tanks, corporate media, and establishment politics. Thus, like Bernstein's old-style revisionism, it ends up in a false utopia concocted by elite intellectuals—a chimerical picture of a capitalism that can be technically restructured in such a way that its major problems can be solved without a revolutionary push beyond capitalism.

To fully appreciate the political limitations inherent in the LLC approach, one has only to imagine what would happen if workers in Japan (or whatever country is the latest left-liberal development fad) were to begin effectively organizing to challenge and transform their system in a socialist direction. Progressive movements in other countries (e.g., the United States), insofar as they have been influenced by LLC-type thinking, would be placed in a most difficult position—unable to explain or even acknowledge such a development, because to do so would undercut their own arguments that Japan's basic economic institutions are workable and superior from a worker-community perspective. In short, LLC logic makes international solidarity difficult if not impossible to build. Finding an alternative to this logic thus ranks as a top priority for any popularly-based perspective on the East Asian experience (see Chapter 14).

PART TWO

Japanese Capitalism:
Development, Crisis, and Ideology

Chapter 5

The Japanese Economy: Crisis and Ideology

The American political and economic establishment is in agreement: Japan's economy is in crisis. The *Wall Street Journal* sums up the consensus as follows: "Japan's once-formidable economy is sliding into the Twilight Zone, with unemployment soaring to record highs, output plunging, bad loans mounting, prices continuing to fall and the yen zigzagging around nine-year lows" (Hamilton, 1998, p. A1).

Mainstream reports on developments in Japan contain more than just analysis of economic trends, however. There is also a clear message: U.S.-style capitalism is now the undisputed champion of the world. In 1989, the establishment celebrated what it believed to be the collapse of socialism and the victory of capitalism. In 1999, it is determined to celebrate the collapse of Japanese capitalism, a capitalism that is allegedly in crisis precisely because of its adoption of socialist-oriented principles and practices.

Many progressives have been thrown on the defensive by Japan's economic difficulties and the mainstream ideological offensive. They had previously embraced Japanese-style capitalism, viewing it as both more humane and more efficient than U.S. capitalism. They had hoped that public recognition of Japan's achievements would build greater support for both state intervention and labor-management collaboration, changes which they believed would help secure full employment and social equality as well as high productivity and international competitiveness. While some progressives continue to argue the superiority of the Japanese system, or at least elements of it, most have withdrawn from the political fray, offering only occasional challenges to the most extreme predictions of gloom and doom for the Japanese people.

This political dead end was avoidable. It was largely the result of the faulty political decision to try and build a progressive movement in the United States on the basis of the alleged superiority of one type of capitalism over another. This mistake was, in turn, compounded by a serious misunderstanding of the Japanese experience. It is time to rectify these mistakes. To do so requires, as a starting point, a critique of shared mainstream and progressive claims that the Japanese political economy was shaped by socialist influences and that its contemporary problems represent another failure for socialism. Only when these claims are rejected does it become possible to construct an effective left response to capitalism's ideological offensive—a response that confidently asserts the need for, and works to advance, an openly socialist movement.

Japan is indeed facing serious economic, social, and political problems. However, these difficulties are not the result of anti-capitalist state, corporate, and labor practices. Rather, Japanese growth was based on clear capitalist principles of profit maximization, labor repression, and expansionism, and contemporary problems stem from contradictions inherent in capitalism *and* Japan's widely celebrated model of export-led growth. The political importance of these points becomes clearer upon closer examination of mainstream responses to Japan's growing economic problems.

Indicators of Crisis

Support for the argument that Japan faces serious economic problems is easy to find. After several years of stagnation, Japan's economy finally fell into outright recession in the fourth quarter of 1997. Real GDP declined at an annual rate of 5.3 percent in the first quarter of 1998—a downturn steep enough to produce, for the first time since the mid-1970s oil crisis, a negative growth rate for an entire fiscal year (WuDunn, 1998a, p. A1). As of late 1998, both private-sector and government economists were predicting an additional decline in real GDP of at least 2 percent for the fiscal year ending on March 31, 1999 (WuDunn, 1998d, p. A5). The earlier government forecast of 2 percent growth had "become something of a joke in Japanese financial circles" (Strom, 1998d, p. C4); and it was further discredited by the subsequent revelation that real GDP had shrunk at an annual rate of 3.2 percent in the fourth quarter of 1998 (Spindle, 1999, p. A15). Hence, when the Japanese government announced that annualized real GDP growth had suddenly jumped to 7.9 percent in the first quarter of 1999 (coincidentally just enough to ensure a positive growth rate of 0.1 percent for the fiscal year), most observers were skeptical (Strom, 1999b, p. B2).

Regardless of its statistical accuracy, the short-term "recovery" of real GDP in early 1999 did nothing to prevent Japan's official unemployment rate from rising to a post–Korean War record of 4.9 percent in June of the same year (Associated Press, 1999c, p. B2). Indeed, the unemployment rate has been moving upward since the mid-1990s. When it climbed to a new high of 4.3 percent in September 1998, for example, 2.95 million Japanese workers were registered as unemployed, up 25 percent from a year earlier (Bloomberg News, 1998b, p. C4). As of May 1998, there were only 53 jobs available per every 100 applicants (down from 55 in April), and this ratio had either declined or remained constant for 17 straight months—as the number of job openings at Japanese companies fell to levels not seen in the previous 20 years (Bloomberg News, 1998a, p. C4). Over a million Japanese received unemployment benefits in June 1998, the first time the total had topped the million mark since March 1976 (Shimbun, 1998). Unemployment was a particularly serious problem for women, young labor force entrants, and older workers.[1] Many of those affected were not counted in the official unemployment statistics. With the official unemployment rate at 3.9 percent in March 1998, for example, "the actual level of unemployment was about 7.2 percent when women who remove themselves from the work force were included in the statistics" (Strom, 1998b, p. C3).

Not surprisingly, the recession and declining employment security have worsened downward pressures on workers' wages. For the first time in ten years, workers even at large Japanese companies took significant real pay cuts in 1997—cuts averaging 1.3 percent (Strom, 1998a, p. B2). Negative wage pressures intensified in 1998 as the recession deepened. In October 1998, the "Labor Ministry reported a 4.8 percent fall in average pay in August, the sharpest drop since 1971, and a ministry official said he expected the declines to continue" (Strom, 1998d, p. C4).[2]

At the other end of the capitalist spectrum, the Nikkei Index of Japan's stock market prices hit a peak of 38,915 in December 1989, after which it fell sharply for several years (Jongsoo Lee, 1997, p. 58). Share prices rebounded in 1996, with the Nikkei climbing above 20,000, but then fell again—reaching "yet another 12-year low" at 13,197 on October 2, 1998 (Strom, 1998d, p. C4).[3] In similar fashion, after peaking in 1986-87, a massive bubble of real estate prices was rapidly deflated, and depressed property values fell an additional 70 percent after 1992 (Oizumi, 1994, p. 200; WuDunn and Kristof, 1998, p. B2). The number of business failures has exhibited an opposite trend, as "Japan's severe recession caused corporate bankruptcies to soar 17.1 percent to 19,171 cases in 1998, the second highest level since World War II" (Associated Press, 1999a, p. A5).[4] Not surprisingly, Japan's banking system is also in bad shape. By mid-1998, the stock market and real estate deflations and corporate balance-sheet problems—in Japan as well as in Southeast Asia—had left Japanese banks holding problem loans amounting to $600 billion by official estimates, with independent analysts placing the figure at close to $1 trillion (Sanger, 1998, p. A1).

An important focus of Japan's worsening economic quandaries has been the international value of the yen. After hitting a high of 79 per $U.S. in April 1995, the yen fell to an eight-year low of 148 per $U.S. in August 1998 (Strom, 1998c, p. C5). Unlike the yen's undervaluation during the prior decades of rapid economic growth, which was very much a conscious policy strategy to support booming exports (Tsuru, 1993, p. 83), its more recent depreciation and volatility were widely viewed as signs of economic weakness and uncertainty. The liberalization of Japan's financial system has made it easier for worried Japanese households and businesses to switch from yen to foreign currency assets. In April 1998, for example, "Japanese investors sent a record amount of capital flowing out of the country. About 3.74 trillion yen, or $25 billion, went into equity and bond investments overseas . . . the largest amount since the Government started compiling such data in 1980" (WuDunn, 1998b, p. C8). Such capital flight could disrupt efforts by the Japanese monetary authorities to use low interest rates as a means of domestic economic recovery.[5]

Everything else equal, a weak yen is still helpful to Japanese exporters. The yen depreciation of 1995-98 meant that companies such as Sony and Canon could "sell their compact disk players and copiers at relatively low prices to American consumers" (Vickers, 1997, p. 4). No wonder the *New York Times* heralded the "weakening of the yen, which makes Japanese products more competitive overseas," as a primary factor enabling the prospective rebound of "Japan's export-oriented electronics and automobile companies . . . from the slump of the last few years" (Pollack, 1997, p. C2).[6] Even with the yen's depreciation, however, Japan's vaunted export machine had begun to sputter—with exports falling for six straight months to June 1998 when they recorded a year-to-year fall of 6.8 percent. The yen's partial recovery vis-à-vis the $U.S. in late 1998 and early 1999 further "threaten[ed] to take the momentum out of Japan's exports," and thereby "prolong Japan's most serious postwar recession" (Strom, 1998e, p. B1). Hence, when the yen appreciated to 108 per $U.S. on January 11, 1999, the Japanese authorities felt they had to intervene in the foreign exchange markets and buy dollars with yen to reweaken the latter currency in spite of the looming threats from domestic financial uncertainty and capital flight (Sesit and Spindle, 1999).[7] More and more, Japan faced a situation where "both rising and falling currency values seem to be damaging" (Wysocki, 1999, p. A1).

As bad as the above developments are, a mere listing of Japan's economic difficulties does not capture the crisis mode of thinking on the part of most mainstream economic analysts. According to the *Wall Street Journal*, for example,

> Government officials and economists around the world are increasingly worried that Japan's accumulated financial and economic problems are pushing it to the brink of a depression, one replete with deflation, bank runs and tremendous unemployment. . . . Outside Japan, worries are growing that the nation's problems could drag down much of the rest of the world, starting with Asia. (Hamilton, 1998, pp. A1, A9)

There is, in short, a widespread feeling that Japan's economic problems represent much more than just a serious recession. The mainstream consensus is that Japan is currently suffering a crisis of world-historical significance.

Mainstream Interpretations of Japan's Economic Problems

As to the causes of the crisis, the mainstream consensus is that they lie in Japan's failed attempt to modify or overcome capitalist market dynamics. Singled out for special blame are Japan's activist state, system of interlocking corporate relations and corporate-bureaucratic links, and highly regulated and socialist inspired labor market practices.

The activist state is alleged to have increasingly turned its attention away from promoting competitive export production to protecting the domestic economy. In an environment of economic globalization and intensifying international competitive pressures, these protectionist tendencies became increasingly expensive and counterproductive, encouraging inefficient investment and labor utilization. The *New York Times* explains the problem as follows:

> In the 1980s, it seemed that Japan had evolved a humane, efficient variant of capitalism. The Government sheltered banks and brokers from failures, while banks bailed out client companies and ailing competitors. Profitability was invariably subordinated to growth and stability. By suspending the cleansing action of the marketplace, the Japanese aimed to soften the rough edges of capitalism. That strategy has now been exposed as a destructive pipe dream. (Chernow, 1997, p. A17)

Business Week makes the same point:

> Some of the best explanations [for the crisis] come from the "revisionists."
> These theorists first explained how the Japanese political economy, operat-
> ing by different rules from orthodox free-market economies, is incompatible
> with global free trade. . . . Today, revisionists point to how Japan's uniqueness
> has gotten the country into trouble. (Neff, 1998, p. 144)

Japan's unique corporate structure is also seen as hostile to free-market
practices and thus to blame for Japan's economic problems. Japan evolved
an economic structure whereby major companies were linked to each
other as well as banks through stock ownership. For example, there are
approximately 2,300 companies listed on the Japanese stock market. Nearly
70 percent of their stocks are held by other corporations, more than half of
which are mutual holdings where companies own each other's stock. Less
than a fourth of the stock is held by individual investors (*AMPO*, 1998, p.
36). As a result, firms "find it easy to tolerate low returns and difficult to
tolerate outright failure. . . . Traditionally, managers have faced little pressure
to improve their return on assets. Most of their capital came from banks
which also held equity in the firm. Troubled firms could stay in business by
borrowing more" (*Economist,* 1998d, p. 23). Indeed, "neither the tax system
nor the financial and social environment create any incentive for Japanese
managers to maximize profits" (*Economist,* 1998e, p. 56). Under no pressure
to improve returns, corporations were thus able to maintain investment and
employment stability with little regard for market signals or efficiency.[8]

The Japanese created their unique political economy in large part, it is
argued, because it was compatible with their country's traditional, socialist-
oriented, value system. As Kristof explains, "to foreigners, Japan often seems
virtually socialist in mindset, profoundly believing in social equality" (1998,
p. A6). And, even though it is now clear that this system is no longer workable, "Japan cannot summon the political will to lay off surplus workers, to
extinguish insolvent banks, to snuff out the hopes of the kindly old ladies
who run rice shops and futon stores" (p. A1). This "anti-capitalist side of
Japan's economy" explains why its economic problems "are disconcertingly
similar to those in the former Communist world" (Kristof, 1997a, p. A1).
The Japanese system is not "real capitalism"; it is, rather,

> marked by a high degree of central planning, presided over by powerful
> bureaucrats confident they can allocate resources better than the free mar-
> ket. Business is highly regulated and often collusive. The economy is biased

toward producers rather than consumers, resulting in first-class steel mills and third-class apartment buildings. And in many cities, the economy seems closer to that of a 16th-century village than that of a modern capitalist country. (p. A1)

The Japanese may not want to change their outmoded system into "a modern market economy"; but, according to the mainstream consensus, they now have little choice (p. A1). Over time, the state interventions and protected corporate culture described above led to a growing misallocation of resources. The effects of this misallocation were overcome, and growth sustained, in large part because of massive increases in public and private debt. Official public debt is said to be about $4.5 trillion, an amount equal to approximately 100 percent of GDP. But the actual public debt is esti mated to be much higher, approximately 250 percent of GDP, "making Japan the most indebted nation in the industrialized world" (Bremner, 1998b, p. 138). This higher figure includes the off budget activities of the Fiscal Investment and Loan Program—known as *zaito*—which borrows from public pension funds and the state-owned Postal Savings system. Significantly, it is estimated that approximately 9 percent of the money lent by *zaito* is sunk into projects that are not generating enough income to ensure loan repayment (p.139).[9]

The government appears to be rapidly approaching the upper limits on its ability to borrow. According to one analyst,

the government is earmarking 46% of its effective tax revenue for servicing the debt. If interest rates rise again, the government borrowing costs will jump, and its ability to cover expenses would deteriorate. . . . if long-term rates were at 1990 levels of 7% or so, the cost of debt servicing would make it impossible for the government to cover its payroll. . . . This scenario has compelled Moody's Investor Service to put Japan's sovereign debt on Credit Watch. 'Japan could become like the Latin American governments of the 1980s, when debt service ate up expenditures,' says Moody's senior analyst Thomas Byrne. (Bremner, 1998b, p. 139)

Moreover, even if the government can somehow ward off its growing debt problems and continue to boost its spending, it is not clear how much impact fiscal policy can have. More than $550 billion has already been pumped into the economy through various spending government packages since 1993. This is roughly twice what Germany spent on reunification, and it was not enough to keep the Japanese economy out of recession (Bremner, 1998a, p. 29). The effects of more recent fiscal stimulus plans, including the record $195 billion package unveiled in November 1998, remain to be seen. But record-low business and consumer confidence have clearly diminished the ability of fiscal policy to induce private-sector recovery (WuDunn, 1998d, p. A5; Strom, 1998d, p. C4). This difficulty motivated the government's desperate attempt to "boost consumer sentiment" and "spur the country's anemic consumption" by handing out $6 billion worth of "shopping vouchers" to Japanese households in early 1999 (Associated Press, 1999b, p. A4).

The Japanese banking system also played an important role in supporting the country's past growth. But, the Japanese corporate culture, which encouraged banks to lend to corporate partners regardless of profitability, has left these banks with bad debts officially estimated to be about $600 billion. The true amount of problem loans is probably closer to $1 trillion (Sanger, 1998, p. A1). Many banks have continued to make loans to insolvent companies who used the money to make payments on their old loans—a practice that allowed the banks to understate the number and value of non-performing loans in their portfolios. The government has attempted to keep a lid on the problem by lowering interest rates below 1 percent, thereby helping banks lower costs and corporations repay loans. Then, in October 1998, the government began implementing a long-term bank "recapitalization" scheme involving 60 trillion yen (just under $500 billion) in public loans to the banks (*Economist,* 1998f, p. 79). Even so, it appears that the recession and the need to meet new solvency conditions associated with the April 1998 Big Bang financial liberalization have left banks with little choice but to reduce their lending. "In a March survey of 1000 companies by the Ministry of Finance, 40% said they were facing far tougher lending terms, and 38% said the scarcity of credit was hurting their business" (Bremner, 1998a, p. 28). Thus, a new wave of bank lending is unlikely to provide the necessary stimulus for recovery. This is the motivation behind the government's "financial environment counter-measure loan system," under which the Japan Development Bank has been channeling billions of dollars in prime interest rate loans ($8.3 billion in the first quarter of 1999 alone) "to companies whose usual bankers have for the first time begun to charge a risk premium to reflect the weakness of their customers' finances" (*Economist,* 1999e, p. 72). However, this socialization of risk and loss threatens to worsen the public debt problem.

Exports had also been an important factor in promoting past growth. That source no longer seems so promising. Approximately 40 percent of Japan's exports go to Asia. With several key Asian countries now in crisis, Japan's exports have been falling. And, with no end in sight to the recessions in South Korea, Indonesia, Thailand, and Malaysia, the situation is unlikely to radically improve. The other main market for Japanese exports, the United States, is limited by that country's already huge trade deficits with Japan and resulting protectionist pressures (see Chapters 9 and 10 for discussion).

In short, with perceived structural limits on government fiscal policy, bank lending, and exports in the face of recession-induced cutbacks in business and consumer spending, most analysts are convinced that "In the months to come, Japan's recession will show how much damage the dysfunctional economy can inflict on the world. . . . It's time, then, for foreign businesses and policymakers to imagine a global economy in which Japan—the world's biggest creditor and Asia's most important player—spends perhaps a further five years in the wilderness searching for a solution to its problems" (Bremner, 1998b, p. 142).

The only solution these analysts can imagine is one where the Japanese finally get serious about reforming their economy. Meaningful reforms, they argue, must involve transforming Japan into a free-market economy. The government must refrain from trying to direct funds, and it must stop protecting domestic industries. It must deregulate and liberalize the economy. Banks must become independent from both corporate partners and government directives, and make loans based on profitability. Corporations must be subjected to market forces and allowed to fail. Above all, "only when managers are rewarded for taking difficult decisions will the economy be put squarely back on its feet" (*Economist*, 1998e, p. 56).

It is recognized, even by their advocates, that these changes will be painful for the Japanese people in terms of growing unemployment, poverty, and instability. Nonetheless, "putting off reform is only making the pain worse" (Katz, 1998, p. A21). As the *Economist* says, "creative destruction will help Japan to raise its return on capital" (1998d, p. 23).

Thus, the Japanese are left with two choices: maintain their existing system and face a deepening crisis, or accept several years of pain on the road to recovery. Most mainstream observers believe that the Japanese have yet to recognize the seriousness of their situation and, as a result, meaningful reform is still years away.[10] However, some are becoming increasingly hopeful that change will come sooner than later. Nicholas Kristof, for example, asserts that "in Japan almost as much as in Russia, there is a consensus that the old economic and political system was ill-suited for the future, and that society must move several steps in the direction of American-style capitalism" (1997a, p. A1). The *Economist* similarly concludes that: "Redundancies and bankruptcies are evidence that the economic adjustment mechanism is working at last. Capitalism, you might say, is finally coming to Japan. Pity it had to be the hard way" (1998d, p. 23).

Political Implications

The attention given to Japan's economic future is no doubt motivated by many factors, including concern for the stability of the world economy. But among the most important reasons is the desire of mainstream analysts to convey the following political message: the Japanese economy has not been run according to "real" capitalist principles—some, as noted above, even say it is socialist—and it is Japan's anti-capitalist values and practices that are responsible for the country's crisis. Like the earlier crisis of Soviet Communism, the Japanese crisis demonstrates that it is not wise to interfere with profit maximization and market forces. In short, Japan's economic problems prove once more that capitalism is the only viable path to economic progress.

This argument strikes at the heart of recent efforts by many progressives to win support for a restructuring of the U.S. economy. Central to their efforts was the promotion of Japanese capitalism as superior to U.S. capitalism (see Chapter 4). According to these progressives, Japan demonstrated that a society could achieve full employment, income equality, and harmonious labor relations and still be highly competitive in the international market place, all without relying on militarism or an aggressive foreign policy. Thus, throughout the decade of the 1980s and into the early 1990s, they used the Japanese experience to justify their call for greater state intervention in the economy to force capitalists to focus on productive rather than speculative activities and to create labor-management partnerships based on employment security and worker participation in production. And while few of these progressives actually called Japan socialist, many did argue that the Japanese system, especially its system of labor relations, did hold valuable keys to how a successful socialist economy might be organized.

This strategy is no longer viable. Having relied on Japan's economic success to legitimate their criticism of U.S. capitalism, progressives now find themselves on the defensive. Japan's economic difficulties have given mainstream commentators all the ammunition they could want to demonstrate the superiority of "free-market," U.S.-style capitalism over any socialist inspired economic system. The *Economist*'s gloating assessment is typical:

> Japan's experiences are salutary for those who think that investment should be encouraged at all costs, or that bureaucrats are better at allocating resources than markets. Some pundits used to claim that Japanese companies

could build long-term profitability—in contrast to American companies, even at the mercy of quarterly results. So much for that theory. (1998c, p. 16)

Disheartened by this turn of events, most progressives have little to say about current developments in Japan. Some have openly retreated in the face of the mainstream ideological assault. For these leftists, too, the crisis demonstrates that the anti-capitalist features of the "Japanese model" were incapable of sustaining economic prosperity in the long run—especially in a hostile global-capitalist environment of slower growth and intensified competition. William K. Tabb, who had earlier championed the Japanese model as a superior economic basis for social-democratic politics in the United States (Tabb, 1992), exemplifies this progressive retreat:

> How did Japan get into such a mess? The answer is somewhat disquieting. The very policies and institutional practices which are credited with Japan's postwar success have turned savagely costly in an era of slow growth and have sabotaged that success by not accommodating to new circumstances. . . . Once the global growth rate slowed, and competition intensified, the very mechanisms which had promoted cooperative and innovative performance instead favored costly collusion and unwillingness to face up to growing problems. (1999, pp. 11–12)

The most optimistic thing that can be said by these retreating progressives is that in the absence of "a real alternative, Japan's best bet may be to continue muddling through, and avoid steps that would further weaken what solidarity and redistribution exists in their system" (Tabb, 1999, p. 40).

Meanwhile, those progressives willing to contest the mainstream ideological onslaught have fallen back to the equally uninspiring position that Japan's economic situation is not as bad as commonly claimed. For example, they point out that many of Japan's large, multinational corporations are still highly competitive in global markets, and they suggest that these core Japanese corporations have continued to avoid harsh U.S.-style "downsizing" in favor of "a strategy of retaining corporate revenues and reallocating the labor force in ways that promote sustainable prosperity . . . the spreading of the benefits of economic growth to more and more people over a prolonged period of time" (Lazonick, 1998, p. 2). But with the worsening of Japan's recession, unemployment, and downward wage pressures—and the growing stream of downsizing announcements by Japanese corporations—such left-wing trickle-down interpretations have become increasingly untenable. It is worth noting in this connection that many mainstream critics of the Japanese economy also point to the continued export successes of selected Japanese corporations—but as evidence of the innovation, efficiency, and growth that could be more broadly enjoyed if the Japanese would only abandon their anti-capitalist values and expose their *entire economy* to the competitive pressure of free-market forces (Vickers, 1997; WuDunn, 1997b). By continuing to assert the relative progressivity of Japanese core-corporate practices in the face of growing contrary evidence, left-wing trickle-down analyses risk strengthening the hand of these mainstream critics. At the same time, by identifying the interests of Japanese workers and communities with the competitive interests of Japanese corporate capital, such left-liberal interpretations lend false credence to the notion that Japanese capitalism—when viewed as a *regionalized corporate system of export production*—is not really in crisis (Terry, 1998).[11]

Whether Japan's economy is in an irreversible structural crisis is an important, although at this point largely unanswerable, question. But from the point of view of the ideological struggle to promote social transformation, it is not the primary question. Whether Japan sinks into a long depression or not, it is clear that it has lost its status as "model economy." Any reasonable examination of the situation in Japan leads to the conclusion that no one will be able to win support for change in the United States on the basis of the performance of the Japanese economy. However, mainstream celebrations to the contrary, this outcome does not mean that it is impossible to imagine, much less advocate, attractive alternatives to capitalism. Rather, it only makes clear the bankruptcy of the progressive strategy.

This strategy was always doomed to failure because it was based on a faulty understanding of the Japanese experience. The reality, as the following chapters show, is that the Japanese economy has never been anti-capitalist or socialist in any meaningful sense. Its current trials do not, therefore, reflect adversely on the feasibility or desirability of socialism.

Chapter 6

Historical Roots of the Japanese Model

This chapter shows how, beginning in the late nineteenth century, the Japanese economy grew rapidly based on a capitalist model that (1) promoted a concentrated and privileged industrial core; (2) stressed production for export; (3) captured overseas markets through military and then economic power; and (4) maintained its competitiveness through the exploitation and repression of its workers, especially women workers. Chapters 7 and 8 will explain how the essential features of this model, after being restored in a modified form in the decade following the Second World War, supported the "miracle" of Japan's economic recovery and decades of rapid growth starting in the early 1950s. Overall, our analysis suggests that Japan's current economic difficulties do not involve any crisis of socialism or even of a relatively egalitarian capitalism. Rather, they represent the exhaustion of the world's most efficient and exploitative version of export-driven capitalism—an economic strategy that mainstream analysts continue to endorse, not only for the third world, but for the United States as well.

Political Conditions of Japan's Early Capitalist Development

The system of Tokugawa feudalism, which ruled over Japan for over 250 years prior to her mid-nineteenth century opening to the West, possessed several features that helped prepare the ground for the country's subsequent capitalist development. Japanese feudalism was a highly authoritarian system, with intensive exploitation and repression of peasants legitimized mainly by an elite ideology of patriarchal "familyism"—not by legal relations of reciprocal rights and responsibilities between exploiting and exploited classes, as was more the case with West European feudalism.[1] The surpluses extracted from Japanese peasants fueled the consumption not only of the big landlords (*daimyo*) and their extended families, but also of the numerous knights (*samurai*), bureaucrats, and higher state officials representing the central government of the Tokugawa *shogunate* (Anderson, 1974, pp. 447, 451). Within Japan's feudal economy, there was a gradual commercialization of agriculture and other rural economic activity (with commensurate growth of inequalities among the peasants), and by the mid-1800s many peasant households were even supplying wage labor (especially that of younger women) to small-scale capitalist enterprises (pp. 449-454; Halliday, 1978, pp. 10-13). Although more tightly regulated, urban merchant and money-dealing capitalists were also quite active—and the Tokugawa tradition of bureaucratic economic regulation left its own imprint on Japanese capitalism.[2]

However, the modern Japanese political economy traces its roots back most directly to the Meiji Restoration of 1868. This event was triggered by growing peasant rebellions; Western imperialism which forced Japan to sign a series of unequal treaties; and tensions within the ruling class, especially over how best to maintain Japan's independence.[3] The combination of "troubles at home, dangers from abroad" led to an alliance of several feudal lords who, with the encouragement of the Emperor Meiji, overthrew the ruling Tokugawa *shogunate* (Beasley, 1995, p. 21).

The new government took immediate steps to consolidate its political position. Tens of thousands of peasants, motivated by economic grievances, had formed armies and fought the Tokugawa military, often following up their victories by establishing democratic governments. The Meiji government had no interest in supporting this development, "launching at once a vigorous counter-revolution against the class which had made the Restoration possible" (Halliday, 1978, p. 23). Peasant uprisings continued to take place until 1873, the year in which the Meiji government formed an expanded army composed largely of conscripted peasants (Beasley, 1995, pp. 61-64).

The new government also faced a series of challenges from members of the aristocracy. Dissident samurai who objected to political and economic changes, especially the forced commutation of their stipends and the creation of a non-samurai army, led several uprisings in the late 1870s before suffering military defeat at the hands of the new conscript army (Beasley, 1995, p. 64). A more serious challenge came in 1881, when members of the aristocracy pressured the Emperor (and the inner circle of feudal lords that guided the Emperor's actions) to accept a constitution and national assembly (*Diet*). While agreeing to their establishment, the Emperor put off their introduction until 1898 in the case of the former, and 1890 in the case of the latter. The ruling elite then used the intervening years to undermine their significance by working to strengthen the social position of the Emperor and create a state apparatus that would be beyond popular reach. Elements of Western state institutions were selectively adapted to Japan in line with this authoritarian goal (Beasley, 1995, Chapters 5-6).[4]

The Meiji government began a campaign, largely through the educational system, to promote "ethics," by which it meant the importance of obedience and loyalty to authority, in particular the Emperor (Halliday, 1978, pp. 40-45; Beasley, 1995, pp. 80-83). This campaign included the introduction of new classes, government-sponsored textbooks, and controls over the activities of teachers. The government also took steps to consolidate its control over the state bureaucracy. As an example, it reorganized Tokyo University into an official training school for bureaucrats. In this way the bureaucracy was positioned to select and train its own bureaucrats (Beasley, 1995, pp. 67, 95). A series of imperial edicts was also passed in the late 1880s that formally declared the bureaucracy and its members to be servants of the Emperor. It was only after this Emperor-centered bureaucracy was in place that the constitution, which had been designed by a bureau under the direction of the Imperial Household Department, was presented to the country as a gift from the Emperor. The widely praised Japanese bureaucracy has its roots in this period, the result of a successful maneuver to limit popular control over the government's political and economic decision making.

State Policies and Imperialism in Japan's Economic Development

The Meiji government also faced the continued threat of foreign domination. In response, it pursued a strategy of building up the country's economic *and* military power. As Paul Baran explained:

> The correspondence of the vital interests of Japanese capitalism with the military requirements for national survival was of momentous importance in determining the speed of Japan's economic and political development after the Meiji Revolution. . . . Neither foreign competition nor foreign aggres-

sion could be deterred by building a few armaments factories or by piling up a stock of weapons. What was called for was the rapid development of an integrated industrial economy capable of supporting modern warfare and at the same time able to meet the onslaught of foreign competition. (1957, p. 161)

This required, among other things, that the state take an active role in directing economic activity.[5] However, such intervention was initially constrained by the unequal treaties signed with the United States and other Western imperialist countries which, among other things, limited the government's ability to raise tariffs. As a result, the Japanese economy developed mainly along two lines—one centered on export-oriented, privately controlled, light-manufacturing activity, especially in textiles, and another centered on military-oriented, state-directed, heavy and chemical industrial activity, especially in munitions and shipbuilding (Halliday, 1978, pp. 52-53, 57-61; Beasley, 1995, pp. 103, 106).

The textile industry rapidly developed in the rural areas from the 1880s onward, taking advantage of the desperation of peasant families who were forced to sell their children, primarily daughters, to labor bosses. The government supported the growth of this new industry through tax policy and state-arranged imports of machinery and technicians, but it was the highly repressive and exploitative labor conditions that enabled it to remain competitive in the face of more advanced Western competitors. Indeed, as late as 1930, the textile industry accounted for over half of all factory workers, over one-third of industrial value added, and roughly two-thirds of manufactured exports (Ohkawa and Rosovsky, 1973, pp. 82-83; Halliday, 1978, pp. 45, 57; Beasley, 1987, p. 126). Meanwhile, beginning in the 1870s, heavy manufacturing and mining received a great boost from Japanese imperialism, as the Meiji government promoted shipbuilding and armaments production in preparation for its regional expansionism. War victories over China in 1894-95 (securing Japanese control over Taiwan and a large indemnity) and Russia in 1904-05 (giving Japan control over Korea and economic concessions in Manchuria) encouraged the government to support the further development of military-related industry. The textile industry likewise gained from access to new markets in China, Taiwan, and Korea (Beasley, 1987, Chapters 4-7, and 9; 1995, pp. 103-104 and 111-112).

In promoting the country's industrialization, the Japanese government also fostered the growth of "a select group of oligopolies . . . which operated across much of the industrial, commercial and banking spectrum" (Halliday, 1978, p. 60). Thus as early as the turn of the century, the Japanese economy was marked by industrial dualism—a small number of large, highly profitable, oligopoly firms, and a large number of small-scale enterprises. The former, known as *zaibatsu*, took the form of conglomerates controlled by a family-owned holding company (Beasley, 1995, pp. 116-117). Not surprisingly, the *zaibatsu* were "integrally connected to the central state-controlled core of the economy, the armaments and shipbuilding sectors. Under the impetus of imperialism, these were the only sectors of heavy industry which were developed to the level of other advanced capitalist countries while, overall, industry remained concentrated in light industry right up to the Pacific War" (Halliday, 1978, pp. 60-61).

World War I provided another major boost to the Japanese economy. Sales of munitions and transport equipment to the combatants, especially Russia, profited the state-*zaibatsu* heavy industrial sector. Even more importantly, the Japanese government took advantage of the fighting to force the Chinese government to yield to a majority of its "Twenty-one Demands," thereby opening new markets for Japanese producers and access to raw materials for the growing heavy industries (Beasley, 1987, pp. 108-115, 122-141).

While Japan's early imperialist ventures were largely advanced for political and military reasons, their success had helped to strengthen an industrial structure dominated by several large *zaibatsu* that were now among the leading advocates of further imperialism. In short, the Japanese economy, in particular its leading sectors, was now dependent on a growth strategy tied to international expansion. And given the overall industrial weakness of the country relative to that of other imperialists, such expansion depended heavily on the use of military force.

The Class Nature of Familyism and "Life Employment"

The fruits of Japan's post-Meiji economic progress were not shared with the country's workers. The state and *zaibatsu* were determined to ensure corporate profitability at all costs. In fact, their success in exploiting the domestic workforce provided another incentive for imperialist expansion: by keeping domestic wage-based purchasing power weak relative to domestic productive capacity, it made rising exports and foreign investments imperative for continued capital accumulation.[6] However, Japanese workers did not accept their situation passively. Although repression made strikes difficult, they did take place in the mines in the 1870s and in textiles in the 1880s. More commonly, workers demonstrated their unhappiness with wages and working conditions through acts of sabotage, and high turnover (Halliday, 1978, pp. 63, 68-69). Firms responded, in part, by attempting to develop what later became known as the "life employment system," a response directed especially at skilled workers. This strategy required that all major firms agree not to employ workers who voluntarily left a job in search of a better one. But given the shortage of skilled industrial workers, especially during the boom economy of the 1890s, few firms stuck to the plan (p. 65).

The state also intervened to help capitalists control labor. The bureaucracy, building on its earlier "ethics" campaign, began promoting the notion of "familyism." The message of this campaign was that as citizens of Japan, the people should embrace their "father," the Emperor, and accept his leadership. And as workers of Japan, people should respect their obligations to their "father," the employer. This campaign marks the beginning of elite attempts to blunt working-class organization through the promotion of an "enterprise family" ideology. Although such familial notions had been an important element of *ruling-class* ideology under Tokugawa feudalism, their adaptation to the capitalist enterprise setting was purely an elite exercise in artificial social engineering in no way indicative of popular "Japanese values" as such. As Halliday points out, the "all-embracing ideology [of 'familyism'] was heavily fostered around the turn of the century, and parachuted in from above by the ruling class in order to try to tranquilize the turbulent labor scene. It was not, as its supporters claimed, a 'traditional' Japanese system at all" (1978, p. 64). Leaving nothing to chance the state, in 1900, also introduced the Public Peace Police Law, which gave it the legal power to break unions. In spite of these actions, a series of bitter strikes broke out in mines and heavy industry plants during 1906 and 1907 (Beasley, 1995, pp. 125-126).

The intense exploitation of workers during World War I—while corporate earnings rose significantly during the war years, real wages fell by approximately 40 percent—led to new uprisings (Halliday, 1978, p. 71). One of the most dramatic was the 1918 "Rice Riots" which lasted several months and involved millions of working people. It was followed by major strikes in 1920 (at the Yawata Iron Works, with more than 20,000 workers involved) and 1921 (at the Mitsubishi and Kawasaki dockyards, where more than 35,000 workers participated). In the latter, shipyard workers launched the country's first "production control" struggle when they took over and began running the docks (pp. 70-72). It was in response to this growing challenge that the owners of the largest and most modern firms finally made common cause in the late 1920s to operationalize their life employment system.[7]

The system offered skilled workers a number of benefits, such as permanent employment status, higher wages, and special bonuses, in an effort to buy their loyalty. According to W.G. Beasley,

> It applied to the major high-technology industries, spreading outwards, it would seem, from ship-building and the engineering trades, though even in those fields it benefited only part of the labor force. Unskilled and semi-skilled workers, who had no scarcity value, lacked the bargaining power to insist on comparable advantages, no matter who employed them. In other words, what was emerging was an elite among workers, similar to the one which the zaibatsu and a few other concerns comprised in the business world at large. (1995, p. 119)

As intended, this new labor system greatly strengthened the power of the owners by dividing workers and increasing overall employment insecurity. In concert with the newly created category of permanent worker—a status individual employees often only achieved after many years of service to a firm—companies created another category, that of temporary worker. Temporary workers were vulnerable to immediate dismissal, were paid less, and received none of the fringe benefits offered to the skilled, permanent workers. In the large companies, as many as 70 percent of the workers might be categorized as "temporary," even though many of them had worked continuously for the same company for over a decade (Halliday, 1978, p. 66). Inequalities between permanent and temporary workers combined with the preexisting (and growing) inequalities between workers in big and small firms to keep core-industry workers insecure and tied to their individual enterprises.[8]

The life employment system also included a new pay regime. Permanent workers received more money the longer they worked at the same enterprise. All workers had salary forcibly withheld until retirement; workers dismissed from the company lost their "savings." Finally, managerial evaluation of work quality became an increasingly important factor in determining overall earnings. All of these changes were explained as part of the corporate commitment to "familyism," in that they were allegedly designed to promote and reward group harmony and loyalty (Halliday, 1978, pp. 65-66). The government added further strength to this anti-worker offensive by introducing the Peace Preservation Law in 1925, which enabled the government to prosecute "anyone who has organized an association with the objective of altering *Kodutai* (national polity) or of denying the system of private property" (Tsuru, 1993, p. 23).

In sum, by the end of the 1920s, the basic outlines of Japanese capitalism's unique features were already clearly visible: a two-track labor relations system (with permanent and temporary workers) promoted in terms of "familyism"; a dual industrial structure composed of a few large core industrial conglomerates (primarily the *zaibatsu*) and a large number of small, peripheral firms; and a powerful state bureaucracy fully insulated from any kind of representative-democratic control—a bureaucracy that actively intervened in the economy to promote an externally oriented accumulation process at the expense of working people in Japan and the rest of Asia.

Militarism, Domestic Repression, and Economic Centralization

During the 1930s and early 1940s, the Japanese state became increasingly dominated by the military and far more aggressive in its imperialism (Beasley, 1995, Chapter 11). This transformation of the Japanese political economy was motivated by several developments. Most important were the economic downturn beginning in the late 1920s that was soon intensified by the effects of the worldwide depression, and a Chinese attempt to restore Chinese control over North China and Manchuria (Halliday, 1978, pp. 122-123). It was the military that took the first action in response. In 1931 it forcibly seized control of Manchuria from China. In the following years the government, military, and *zaibatsu* took steps to expand Japanese influence in North China and to merge that area, along with Manchuria and Korea, into an integrated production base serving the needs of Japanese industry (Beasley, 1987, Chapters 12-13). These actions eventually led to a full-scale Japanese invasion of China in 1937, and then, beginning in 1940, an attempt to gain control over the raw materials and markets of Southeast Asia. It was in the context of this latter push to create a Greater East Asian Co-Prosperity Sphere that Japan decided to attack the United States in 1941, thereby triggering the Pacific War (Beasley, 1987, Chapters 14-15; 1995, pp. 199-208).

Japan's aggressive international actions were supported by a number of domestic policy measures designed to strengthen the Japanese state and *zaibatsu*, especially in relation to the left and labor. For example, the government undertook massive surveillance of, and launched frequent raids on, progressive publications and groups. It also crushed labor activity by outlawing strikes and undermining independent labor unions through violence and intimidation. In 1939, the remaining unions were pressured to disband. In their place the government established two organizations, *Sanpo* (the Industrial Patriotic Society) and *Roho* (the Patriotic Labor Association), both of which were supervised by the police. Each organization was composed of enterprise level groups whose mission was to promote worker-management collaboration under the banner of familyism. The difference between the two was that *Sanpo* enrolled permanent workers while *Roho* included only temporary or part-time workers, thereby reinforcing divisions within the workforce. "In accordance with an ideology in which the enterprise was another embodiment of Japan's unique family system, the *Sanpo* hierarchy paralleled the enterprise hierarchy, with the head of the enterprise being the head of the local *Sanpo* association" (Moore, 1983, p. 10). In short, while *Sanpo* and *Roho* had "some of the trappings of unionism," they were "really a means to control labor for national purposes" (Bennett and Levine, 1976, p. 445).

Given the intensity of state repression and ideological indoctrination, it is not surprising that "from 1937 onward it is impossible to speak of any organized resistance to the regime from the left" (Halliday, 1978, p. 158). Up until the end of the Second World War, labor protests were necessarily limited to informal channels such as workplace absenteeism and sabotage (p. 158). Japan's catastrophic defeat and postwar economic crisis would radically change this situation.

The government also took concrete steps to enhance its ability to control economic activity as well as the role of the *zaibatsu* (Cohen, 1949). For example, it made "domestic manufacturers subject to compulsory cartels, headed by prominent businessmen under the guidance of the relevant ministry, a decision which greatly strengthened the power of bureaucrats and the conglomerates over smaller firms" (Beasley, 1995, p. 192). It also established a number of powerful planning institutions, such as the Ministry of Munitions, to ensure that resources, human and non-human, were mobilized according to the needs of Japanese imperialism (p. 190).

Developments over this period did not, however, represent a fundamental break with the past trajectory of Japanese capitalism. For example, the military did not hijack or overthrow the government, nor did it radically transform the country's main political or economic institutions. Its basic policies of aggression were fully supported by the *zaibatsu* who eagerly and profitably participated in them. Just as in previous economic expansions, the rapid capital accumulation of the 1930s and early 1940s was fueled on the supply side by rising rates of exploitation (real wages lagging behind labor productivity) and on the demand side by rising exports and other sales opportunities provided by Japan's military-industrial complex

(Cohen, 1949, pp. 1-9; Ohkawa and Rosovsky, 1973, p. 119; Minami, 1998, p. 49).[9] What happened, in short, is that the oppressive and imperialist characteristics of Japanese capitalism became more pronounced as the system consolidated itself domestically and expanded itself externally in conflict with Western (especially U.S.) imperialism.

Chapter 7

The Postwar Struggle to Reshape the Japanese Political Economy

J apan's prewar system was in no way socialist, and it did not serve the needs of working people. However, after their country's surrender in August 1945, Japanese workers mounted "a major challenge to capitalist rule" (Halliday, 1978, p. 207). Their valiant struggle to create a new system based on humane and democratic-socialist principles was repelled only by the combined efforts of the U.S. occupation and the Japanese prewar ruling class. As a result, the Japanese government and big business were able to gradually rebuild, although with some significant modifications, the basic system of the past (see Chapter 8). The fact that "labor and capital fought it out, socialism versus capitalism, during the first nine months of reconstruction" is surely an important reference point in any determination of the essential class nature of the contemporary Japanese political economy (Moore, 1997, p. 5).

Initial U.S. Occupation Policy

Japan's defeat in World War II did not lead to the immediate destruction of its system. The reason was simple: U.S. policymakers decided from the very beginning of the occupation to "maintain the Japanese system of government, including Emperor, cabinet, and bureaucracy; and to reject military government" (Halliday, 1978, p. 168). As pointed out by Gabriel Kolko, this "willingness to retain the Emperor and work through many of the existing political organizations indicated the basic ambivalence and flexibility in American policy before the total collapse of China" (1968, p. 545). In order for the United States to remain "preeminent in the Far East . . . with a minimal commitment of resources," it needed "an alliance with a major state of the region . . . China or Japan" (p. 544). China's civil war intensified after the Japanese surrender, with Mao Tse-tung's popular anti-imperialist forces increasingly gaining the upper hand over Chiang Kai-shek's corrupt Kuomintang regime (despite abundant U.S. aid to the latter). The revolutionary situation in mainland China, coupled with upsurging anti-imperialist "resistance movements throughout the Far East," made a stable, relatively self-sufficient, and capitalist Japan "a vital element in thwarting what Washington perceived as the greater immediate danger of the Left in Asia" (Kolko and Kolko, 1972, p. 300). Given this background, one can understand the U.S. decision to "retain the Emperor and operate through the existing Japanese government . . . the symbols and instruments of the old ruling class" (p. 301).[1]

In short, even though there was a large U.S. occupation presence, its ruling body, the Supreme Command for the Allied Powers (SCAP), never truly functioned as the government of Japan. Although the SCAP and its Supreme Commander General Douglas MacArthur formulated policy directives, it allowed the existing Japanese government considerable freedom of action in implementing them. For example, an October 4, 1945 MacArthur directive formally "dismissed all the police chiefs and abolished altogether the elaborate system of secret and 'thought control' police"; yet "the occupation continued to rely on the regular police system" (Kolko and Kolko, 1972, pp. 309-310). The Japanese police "were cooperative and all too efficient in aiding the occupation in keeping order, which soon meant curtailing popular demonstrations and strikes. And the United States Counter Intelligence Corps soon discovered that their most valuable assistants were former officials in the outlawed Japanese secret police" (p. 310).

In the economy just as in government, the SCAP basically left Japan's pre-surrender power structure untouched. As T. A. Bisson, a Special Advisor to the SCAP's Government Section, observed at the time, "the prewar and wartime set of Japanese industrialists and financiers, with minimal exceptions, has continued to control the operation of Japan's postwar economy" (1947, p. 241). "Postwar Japan," in other words,

> continued to function as a *political and economic* unit, both physically and institutionally. Government, control agencies, and business firms were organizationally intact at the surrender and the wide range of measures taken by the occupation has interfered remarkably little with their operational mechanism. All changes have been mediated through regular Japanese government

channels, further ensuring minimum disruption of normal *political and economic* processes. (p. 241, emphases added)

Nonetheless, several early initiatives indicated that the U.S. occupation was prepared to take radical steps to transform the Japanese political economy so as to ensure that it would never again pose a challenge to U.S. hegemony in the Pacific. For example, beyond direct actions against the Japanese military, some U.S. policymakers spoke of the need to break up the *zaibatsu* and deindustrialize Japan.[2] The *zaibatsu* were at the heart of Japan's industrial and war-making power. As discussed earlier, "in Japan there was no development from small corporations to large mergers" such as that which occurred in the United States; rather, "a sector of the feudal ruling class had simply industrialized the nation in a short span of years, and these families controlled the process from the beginning" (Kolko and Kolko, 1972, p. 319). At the end of the war in 1945, the four largest *zaibatsu* accounted for approximately 25 percent of the total paid-up capital of all Japanese corporations, but 50 percent of the total in the financial sector, and 32 percent in heavy industry (Halliday, 1978, p. 180).

Given the close ties between Japan's governing elite and the *zaibatsu*, and given the occupation's strategy of working through the same governing elite, any U.S. thoughts about breaking up the *zaibatsu* were "quixotic at best" (Kolko and Kolko, 1972, p. 322). Simply put, Japan had "no class or group to support a decentralized capitalism"—at least not one capable of governing the country as a stable and reliable partner of U.S. hegemony in East Asia (p. 319). Still, it is interesting to note that many U.S. officials harbored no doubts about the connection between the *zaibatsu* and Japanese imperialism. For example, the November 1945 Pauley Reparations Mission to Japan observed that: "They [the *zaibatsu*] are the greatest war potential of Japan. It was they who made possible all Japan's conquests and aggressions. . . , Not only were the Zaibatsu as responsible for Japan's militarism as the militarists themselves, but they profited immensely by it" (Halliday, 1978, p. 181). The Pauley report thus called for action not only to break up the *zaibatsu* and large firms, but also to ship large parts of the country's industrial plant and equipment to other Asian countries—the Mission's working assumption being "the maintenance of a standard of living and industrial capacity equivalent to that prevailing in 1930" (Kolko and Kolko, 1972, p. 322).

Corwin D. Edwards, head of the January 1946 U.S. Mission on Japanese Combines, described an additional dimension of the close relationship between the *zaibatsu* and Japan's international aggression, noting that "the low wages and concentrated profits of the Zaibatsu system have limited the domestic market and intensified the importance of exports, and thus have given incentive to Japanese imperialism" (Halliday, 1978, p. 178). The U.S. State-War-Navy Coordinating Committee policy paper on Japanese labor, which eventually became the basis for early occupation labor directives, also makes clear the anti-labor underpinnings of Japan's prewar industrialization and aggressive expansionism:

> With relatively high technical efficiency in many lines of production and extremely low labor costs due to the low wages paid to even the really skilled among her workers, she was able to undersell her commercial rivals in a wide range of goods in many parts of the world. This low wage level, it should be understood, was a product of the peculiar political, social and economic forces existing in the country, among which should be listed the violent opposition by government to genuine labor organizations that has already been discussed. Unions were persecuted not only because of their political and social potentials but because it was feared they might be able to force increases in wages. Such increases, by raising labor costs, would have tended to diminish the volume of or the profit margin on Japanese exports, reduce foreign balances, and prevent the importation of those machines and materials vital to Japan's plans for armament and conquest. (Moore, 1983, pp. 64-65)

Of course, Japanese workers did not have to be told that they had been oppressed and needed to organize so as to raise their standard of living. Unfortunately, under postwar conditions, they confronted a major economic crisis which threatened to further impoverish them. This crisis was worsened if not instigated by the actions of the *zaibatsu* and the Japanese state.

The Postwar Economic Crisis

As the war turned against Japan in 1944 and 1945, influential individuals in the country's governing elite became "more concerned with the prospect of revolution than of military defeat, to which they were reconciled" (Kolko, 1968, p. 550). "Ridden by fear of social revolution and apprehensive about Allied intentions, certain members of the civilian leadership had early begun to consult among themselves about how best to meet the coming disaster" (Moore, 1983, p. 3). Among these leaders were former Prime Minister Konoe Fumimaro and future Prime Minister Yoshida Shigeru. Yoshida assisted in the drafting of Konoe's 1945 policy Memorial which, in setting out a strategy for postwar reconsolidation of the Japanese power structure, stated that: "What we have to fear . . . is not so much a defeat as a Communist revolution which might take place in the event of defeat" (Kolko, 1968, p. 550).

With this kind of advance planning, Japanese business and government leaders moved quickly to solidify their economic and political power immediately upon surrender in 1945—taking advantage of the fact that their "apparatus of oppression . . . remained intact at [this] crucial moment" (Moore, 1983, p. 4). Between August 14 and the formal signing of the surrender decree on September 2, the Japanese government "handed out vast quantities of goods [held in their warehouses] and twelve billion yen in currency, mostly to the great zaibatsu concerns" (p. 28). It has been estimated that the total transfer of wealth amounted to "a minimum of fifty billion yen, and its immensity can be gauged by the fact that currency in circulation on 1 August was only 28.5 billion yen" (p. 28). In the succeeding months, the *zaibatsu* received billions of additional yen in government indemnity payments for factories that had been converted to war production. "One account puts the total of the indemnity payments to the zaibatsu in a little over three months after surrender at 26.6 billion yen" (p. 30). Subsequently, the SCAP gave confiscated goods worth over 100 billion yen to the Japanese government to use for recovery; most of these also found their way through backdoor connections into *zaibatsu* hands (pp. 28-29).[3]

Armed with this "war chest," the *zaibatsu* decided to take a wait and see attitude toward the economy; they refused to invest and/or produce. Rather, they were content to sell off their supplies on the black market for considerable profit (Bisson, 1947, p. 243). Indeed, "given the extreme shortages . . . goods were hoarded and sifted into the black market for several years, vastly enlarging the profits of the ruling class during a period when its future was still ambiguous" (Kolko and Kolko, 1972, p. 308).[4] The Japanese capitalist class decided against industrial renewal in part because it feared that a quick economic recovery would encourage U.S. policymakers to break up the *zaibatsu* and ship Japanese plant and equipment abroad as reparations. The "strategy of sabotaging economic reconstruction to gain a soft peace" is only part of the story, however (Bisson, 1947, p. 244). Perhaps even more important was the fear among Japanese business and political leaders that a quick recovery would strengthen the hand of labor and the left. Economic stagnation was seen as the best means of disciplining labor and winning occupation support for the renewal and revitalization of the prewar Japanese political economy. The U.S. occupation's willingness to work through pre-surrender Japanese government institutions (including the police) certainly facilitated this elite strategy of "waiting out" the workers.

Whatever its exact motives, the effects of the "virtual strike of capital" staged by Japanese business were dramatic (Halliday, 1978, p. 208). Industrial activity after surrender fell below 10 percent of the 1935-37 average, rising only to about 13 percent by winter 1945 (Moore, 1983, p. 76). A full year later, industrial production was still only approximately 30 percent of the 1935-37 average (Bisson, 1947, p. 243). In fact, it remained less than 50 percent of that average as late as 1948 (Moore, 1983, p. 78). Inflation compounded the crisis, with the official cost of living index increasing twelve-fold between June 1945 and January 1946 (p. 86). The true jump in the cost of living was much higher, since it was determined largely by more swiftly rising black-market prices for food and other basic household items (Bisson, 1947, p. 243).

Indeed, Japanese workers were (in contrast to the *zaibatsu*) in no position to wait out the crisis. "For while the Japanese elite hoarded or channeled resources into nonproductive but profitable areas, the inflation mounted and wages lagged" (Kolko and Kolko, 1972, p. 324). Average real wages fell to below ten percent of their 1937 level by late 1945, and over the first three years of the occupation they never reached as high as 30 percent (Moore, 1983, p. 86).[5] Unemployment was also a major problem: over the first six months after surrender, the number of unemployed averaged about ten million people out of a labor force of 30 to 32 million (p. 88). With no real system of public relief, many faced starvation—forcing the United States to begin emergency shipments of food beginning in the spring of 1946. Tragically, a good share of this food aid was itself diverted, directly or indirectly, into the black market.[6]

Japan's post-surrender economic crisis clearly cannot be blamed on "normal" postwar disruptions of the economy.[7] Rather, it can only be described as "a crisis engendered by fundamentally vicious economic policies, affecting budgetary expenditures, economic controls, and agriculture, which operated with generalized and damaging effect on the whole economy . . . while an unscrupulous minority waxed fat on it and bids fair to retain control of the nation's tangible assets" (Bisson, 1947, pp. 242-243).

Unionization, Production Control, and Democratic Struggles

While the *zaibatsu* were arming themselves for the class struggle (largely thanks to government financial handouts), the occupation was, although more slowly, forcing the removal of many of the restrictions that had kept the working class in check. For example, *Sanpo*—the state-run quasi-union of "permanent" workers—was dissolved on September 30, 1945. And on

October 4, 1945, SCAP issued its famous directive calling for an end to restrictions on civil liberties as well as the release of political prisoners (Kolko and Kolko, 1972, p. 309). One response to this greater freedom was a surge in unionization. From September through December 1945, union membership rose from 1,177 to 380,677. It then jumped to 902,751 in January 1946 before skyrocketing to 4,849,329 in December of the same year (Moore, 1983, p. 42).

It is true that not all of this growth represented independent unionism; in many cases, workers, out of desperation, agreed to accept a renewal of their past *Sanpo* enterprise units under a new name in hopes of maintaining their jobs. But the same desperation also kindled the fires of a powerful independent working-class movement (Moore, 1997, pp. 12-13). This labor upsurge stunned the occupation authorities, few of whom "suspected that the formal civil liberties, which had never threatened the capitalist social order in the United States, could, in Japan, undermine the foundations of conservative control" (Kolko and Kolko, 1972, p. 303). "Much to the shock of MacArthur and many on his staff, the Japanese masses immediately began to use their new rights in unanticipated ways. The reforms of free speech, assembly, political activity, trade unions, and press were modeled on U.S. laws and the Americans implicitly expected them to be used—or not used—as in the United States, although the setting in Japan was one of potential revolutionary upheaval" (p. 309).

Although initially seeking only to improve wages and work conditions, this new labor movement soon found itself with no option but to broaden its objectives to include the democratization of the Japanese economy. Faced with the threat of unemployment and starvation, the workers quickly realized that strike action would serve little purpose. Thus, beginning in October 1945, a growing number of Japanese workers turned to production control.[8] The first production control struggle took place at Tokyo's *Yomiuri* newspaper when workers took over the entire newspaper operation. Workers at Keisei Electric Railway and Mitsui Bibai coal mine initiated their own production control struggles in December. The following month, workers at 12 Toshiba unions, representing some 30,000 workers, formed a joint struggle committee to engage in production control. From January through May 1946, some 140,000 workers were involved in production control struggles, more than the number that engaged in strikes and slowdowns combined (Moore, 1983, p. 103).

These production control struggles were initially undertaken to secure union recognition; meaningful collective bargaining; higher wages; democratization of work relations; and participation in personnel, production, and investment decision-making. Workers engaged in production control not because they sought to replace management, but to force it to be more responsive. As a result, production control struggles were usually begun without any vision of maintaining permanent control over the targeted enterprise or as part of a broader process to create a new economy. However, capitalist attempts to smother these struggles, by withholding raw materials or payment for goods produced, gradually pushed workers to take more radical action.

For example, in response to financial pressures, the Toyo Gosei workers decided to convert their chemical plant to produce chemical fertilizer needed by farmers. To finance this conversion they sold other chemicals to other workers engaged in their own production struggle. They also worked out an arrangement with a farmers' association, whereby the association raised money from its members to purchase coal and coke, which they traded to the Toyo Gosei workers in exchange for fertilizer (Moore, 1983, pp. 156-160). This kind of process, in which workers made production decisions guided by the needs of the population, and in concert with other workers and popular associations, was a direct challenge not only to those capitalists directly affected by production control, but to capitalism more generally.[9]

The challenge to the logic of capitalist control and rationality was also growing outside the factory, in large part because of food shortages. In February 1946, a number of labor, farmer, and citizen groups formed the Democratic Food Council. The Council, with an estimated membership of 1,500,000, called for a policy of "discovery and control of hoarded goods; acquisition of control over food; setting up of urban people's food committees; a system of voluntary food deliveries by farmers; production of fertilizer and agricultural materials; and democratization of the control associations and government offices connected with foodstuffs" (Moore, 1983, p. 170). In other words, both "urban and rural people were [now] taking direct action at the point of production and distribution" (Moore, 1997, p. 7).

In March, left activists succeeded in forming the Democratic People's League, whose program included demands for "adoption of a new constitution by democratic methods, liquidation of the bureaucracy, democratic planned economy, industrial democracy, democratization of farm villages, relief to small businessmen, democratization of food distribution, liberation of women, reform of education, and an international system based on peace and justice" (Moore, 1983, p. 173). The first concrete action of the League was a People's Rally on April 7, 1946. Some 70,000 people gathered to demand the resignation of the existing conservative government, an end to government and business attempts to suppress production control, faster economic recovery, and more democratic methods for the distribution of food and consumer goods. At the conclusion of the rally some 50,000 people marched to the Prime Minister's residence, broke through the gate, and charged onto the grounds. They were stopped only by the armed intervention of U.S. military police (pp. 173-176).

Japan's 1946 May Day celebrations were perhaps the largest in the capitalist world, with some two million people involved—"again demanding the equitable distribution of food, price controls, and wage increases" (Kolko and Kolko, 1972, p 313). By now, however, the workers' demands clearly encompassed political goals directly infringing upon capitalist state power. As a SCAP report observed, the May Day demonstrators' program included not only "economic" demands such as "people's control of food supplies," the "right to strike and to bargain collectively," and "workers' control of production," but also political demands for "a democratic people's government" and a more thoroughgoing "purge of war criminals" (Moore, 1983, pp. 177-178). Even "reverence for the emperor, the most important ideological buttress of the old order, was evidently giving way" (p. 178).

Hundreds of thousands of Japanese gathered again to demonstrate their opposition to the existing order on May 19, Food May Day. Following the demonstration, groups went both to the Imperial Palace and the Prime Minister's residence where, after being refused a meeting, they began a sit-in. Finally, "when a group tried to gain entry into the Imperial Palace to demand the distribution of hoarded food, the police fired on the crowd" (Kolko and Kolko, 1972, p. 313). No wonder that years later, when describing the months from the fall of 1945 to the spring of 1946, Japan's Committee for Economic Development concluded that business had faced "an unprecedented period of revolution" (Moore, 1983, p. 144).

The Struggle's Final Phases

It was at this point that the SCAP's Supreme Commander, Douglas MacArthur, decided to openly and directly oppose the growing mass movement for change. He made a public statement during the Food May Day sit-in, warning against "demonstrations and disorders by mass mobs" (Moore, 1983, p. 184). "If minor elements of Japanese society are unable to exercise such self-restraint," MacArthur warned, "I shall be forced to take the necessary steps to control and remedy such a deplorable situation"

(Kolko and Kolko, 1972, p. 313). Overjoyed, the Japanese government headed by Prime Minister Yoshida Shigeru began taking a hard line against labor actions. In June, it declared production control illegal and started calling out the police to suppress disputes. SCAP, which supported these actions, called its new hard-line anti-labor policy one of "housebreaking the labor movement" (Moore, 1983, p. 189).[10] Emboldened by these developments, corporations began a rollback of worker gains.

However, even though the workers' initial anti-capitalist offensive had been defeated, they were still "hungry and increasingly restive as wages lagged far behind prices" (Kolko and Kolko, 1972, p. 512). Forced to abandon their production control efforts and more radical visions of social change, workers turned to a new strategy. In August 1946, they formed a new radical national labor federation, Sanbetsu, which enjoyed the strong support of the Japanese Communist Party. The hope was that a broader industrial union structure would enable workers to overcome their weakness at the enterprise level. Toward that end, Sanbetsu led an October offensive involving strikes in the electrical equipment industry, coal mines, and the electrical power industry. Tens of thousands of workers were involved (Moore, 1983, pp. 213-218).

Even as private-sector workers began recouping some of their lost real wages, government workers—who generally earned half the wage of workers in the private sector—began to take a leading role in the labor movement.[11] Led by railway workers, communication workers, and teachers, the Joint Struggle Committee of National Labor Unions, with Sanbetsu at its center, threatened a general strike on February 1, 1947 if conditions for government workers were not improved (Moore, 1983, pp. 229-235). "It was widely anticipated that nearly four million workers, including sympathizers, would participate" (Kolko and Kolko, 1972, p. 512). But, on January 31, MacArthur secured the strike's cancellation by threatening actions against the leaders and their organizations. The effect of MacArthur's intervention cannot be overstated. As Joe Moore describes:

Labor unity and industrial unionism were the two major casualties of the general strike. The discrediting of Sanbetsu permitted the right-wing leaders of Sodomei [a conservative labor federation also formed in August 1946] to reassert their independence, and it brought internal division to Sanbetsu affiliates, making them vulnerable to big-business and government efforts to drive labor organization back within the confines of the enterprise. Sodomei raiding—which went so far as deliberate attempts to split and destroy Sanbetsu affiliates—accelerated this process immensely, since the successor

Sodomei "second" union was almost always an enterprise union. The defeat of the left, therefore, cleared the way for the institutionalization of the enterprise union, that weakened form of workers' organization that replaced the militant industrial unions of Sanbetsu. (1983, p. 243)

Indeed, by 1947, U.S. opposition to the Japanese left and labor had become part of a broader shift in U.S. policy toward Japan—a process that came to be known as the "reverse course" (see Chapter 8).

Lessons of This Period

The events described in this chapter show that, "contrary to the Western stereotype of Japan as the land of capital-labor harmony and worker docility, classes and class conflict underlie labor-capital relations in Japan, just as they do elsewhere in the industrialized world" (Moore, 1983, p. xix). It follows that the repulsion of Japanese workers' postwar upsurge by the combined actions of the U.S. occupation and Japanese ruling class is "fundamental to an understanding of the real history of the Japanese working class [and of Japanese capitalism] before and since" (p. xx). The Japanese system of labor-management cooperation and "enterprise solidarity" is often seen—even by many progressives—as a natural outgrowth of Japanese "family" values. But from the perspective of the immediate post-surrender period, this system and its ideology represent an elite inversion of "the worker collectivism once forcefully deployed against capital" (Rytting, 1989, p. 28). It was only the "violent suppression of labor" that "turned the solidarity of that era inward, so that loyalty stopped at the worker's enterprise," enabling capital "to make worker fealty a structural feature of labor-management relationships" (p. 28).

By not appreciating "the depth of the postwar crisis of capitalism in Japan" and the extremely repressive, class-biased nature of the postwar stabilization, many students of the "Japanese model" have lost "the sensitivity the scholar ought to have to paths not taken and possibilities unfulfilled" (Moore, 1997, pp. 4–5). Instead, "transfixed by the Japanese 'economic miracle,' they have concentrated single-mindedly on finding the secret ingredients in the modernization of Japanese capitalism that took place during the decade and a half following World War II" (p. 4). The implicit presumption here is that development visions—and the socio-economic aspirations of workers and communities—should be constrained by the imperatives of competitive and profitable capital accumulation. This approach bypasses the class and competitive contradictions built into even the most "successful" models of capitalist development. It also relegates popular democratic and anti-capitalist struggles to the trashbin of history, instead of critically engaging with these struggles in order to envision development alternatives that resonate with the needs and capabilities of workers and communities.

Chapter 8

The Renewal of the Japanese Model

U nited States occupation policy was never designed to destroy the power of the prewar Japanese ruling class. Even prior to Japan's surrender, U.S. policymakers had laid plans for working with Japan's economic and political elites to make Japan a bulwark against Communism in Asia (Kolko, 1968, Chapter 21). Japan's postwar labor struggles threatened to disrupt these plans by revealing "the essential vulnerability of the old ruling class vis-à-vis the rest of the population" (Kolko and Kolko, 1972, p. 511). The "increasing costs of the occupation to the United States treasury" and the continued upsurge of revolutionary left movements in China, Korea, and other Asian countries also helped tip U.S. policymaking scales toward those strongly supporting the renewal rather than weakening of Japan's prewar industrial base and capitalist ruling class—even if this meant a reversal of post-surrender political and economic reforms (p. 510; Beasley, 1995, p. 224). Indeed, the overall situation in Japan, China, and the rest of East Asia favored those U.S. government leaders and business lobbyists who were "urg[ing] not simply the revival of the Japanese economy, but a reconstitution of its ties to the Asian mainland as well" (Cumings, 1990, p. 17; cf. Halliday, 1978, pp. 183-184).[1] The policy changes produced by this strengthened commitment to Japan's full-scale capitalist renewal came to be known as the "reverse course."

Policy Changes Under the "Reverse Course"

Domestically, a crucial element of the SCAP's reverse course policy was its backpedaling on the break-up of large *zaibatsu* firms. The occupation had disrupted the formal *zaibatsu* structure in November 1945 when it ordered the break-up of the holding companies that *zaibatsu* owners had used to control their affiliated firms. Interlocking corporate directorates and equity share holdings were also made illegal, and other early proposals had projected the break-up of the large individual *zaibatsu*-affiliated enterprises— but the enforcement of these measures fell victim to the reverse course. The commission in charge of liquidation had identified some 323 companies for dismantlement. That number was quickly reduced to 100, and by the time the commission was dissolved in 1948 only nine firms had been broken up (Halliday, 1978, p. 182; Tsuru, 1993, p. 41).

The reverse course also meant that the punishment of war criminals had to be carefully managed.[2] As it turned out, the purging process focused on the military. Of the 210,288 people who were purged from public life for their war crimes, 79.6 percent were members of the military elite. Less than one percent were members of the business elite, and less than one percent were members of the bureaucratic elite (Halliday, 1978, p. 173). Thus, "numerous key individuals in virtually every field except the military were left in effective power" (p. 170). In fact, the weakening of the military served to strengthen the hand of much the same bureaucratic and capitalist elite that had dominated prewar political and economic institutions.[3]

The pro-capitalist character of the reverse course is clear even from "the only major reform that the Japanese government reinforced after the occupation ended," namely, the agrarian reform initiated in late 1946 (Kolko and Kolko, 1972, p. 318). The reform's stated intent was "to bring land ownership status to as many as possible of the more than four million farm families who cultivated wholly or partly land which they did not own" (Hewes, 1955, p. 59). "In addition, rent ceilings were imposed on land not redistributed; farm cooperatives were encouraged to help farmers buy the fertilizer and other supplies they needed; and a system of farm credit on reasonable terms was established" (Cary, 1962, p. 20). But the underlying motivation for the program was not simply to help the peasantry; rather, agrarian reform "was thought necessary if Japan was to be made safe for capitalism" (Halliday, 1978, p. 191). This concern has been well stated by Wolf Ladejinsky, the famous agrarian specialist "who engineered much of the land reform." Years after the occupation, Ladejinsky recalled the prereform situation of Japanese peasants:

A tenant farmer paid roughly 50 per cent of his crop in rent. . . . He had to pay for fertilizer and other things, too. He could keep no more than 25 to 30 per cent of his crop. Consequently, the Japanese village was full of unrest.

Under the influence of Communist propaganda, it could have been a very serious political situation during the aftermath of the war. (quoted in Cary, 1962, p. 19)

The political impetus behind the agrarian program was amplified by Laurence I. Hewes, another land reform specialist employed by the SCAP:

> Almost the entire history of Japanese Communist activity, most of its aims and ambitions, centered on agrarian reforms. In fact, land reform had for long been the special political property of the Japanese Communists. If the reform were successfully accomplished, it would pull the rug out from under the entire Communist position in Japan. Finally, such a reform conducted in non-Marxist terms and stressing individual rights, private property, and auxiliary capitalist concepts could embarrass the Communist position throughout the world. (Hewes, 1955, p. 88)

This is not to say that the SCAP-sponsored reform was a sham. "By the end of the 1950s approximately five million acres had been resold to tenants and only 12 percent of the land remained leased"—while "remaining tenants were further protected by providing that all rentals would be in cash and would never exceed the value of one-quarter of a year's crop" (Kolko and Kolko, 1972, p. 318). But the fact remains that the reform not only "destroyed the rural appeal of the Japanese Communists," but also "established a still-persisting pattern of electoral support by farmers for the ruling Liberal Democratic Party" (Prosterman and Riedinger, 1987, p. 122).[4] In this way, the land reform

> proved to be a critical safety valve for the industrialists. It in no way encroached on their privileges, but by eliminating the chief grievance in the countryside the conservatives attained a vital political asset that has provided their electoral victories to this day. The agricultural associations have been intimately linked to the Liberal Party, providing the bulk of votes that have assured their control of Japan since the war. (Kolko and Kolko, 1972, p. 318)

The land reform, together with the SCAP's purge of militarists from governing positions, greatly weakened "the landed aristocracy and their military allies" (p. 316). This helps explain why the reform "gained overwhelming support from most of the Japanese population" (Cary, 1962, p. 20). But the reduced power of the big landlords and militarists also undercut the basis for any "struggle of rival elements in the ruling class," and in this sense, "capitalism was [more] firmly entrenched in Japan" (Kolko and Kolko, 1972, p. 316).

Internationally, the restoration of an industrialized and anticommunist Japan required a radical reduction in U.S. reparations demands. The November 1945 Pauley Report had recommended punitive measures to keep Japan's industrial capacity at or below 1930 levels, especially in military-related sectors. But under the reverse course, the United States first pressed the Far Eastern Commission (the advisory group of allied powers that had fought Japan) for a significant scaling back of reparations, and then cooperated with the Japanese government to ensure that "rather less than 30 per cent of the industrial facilities declared surplus by the FEC were dismantled and transferred to other countries" (Halliday, 1978, p. 177).[5] As a result, when the reparations program was finally halted in the spring of 1949, only 160 million yen (1939 prices) worth of plant and equipment had actually been shipped to other countries in Asia—whereas the Pauley Report had projected the removal of 2,499 yen worth of physical capital (Tsuru, 1993, p. 39). The termination of reparations in 1949 was itself closely related to the Cold War rapprochement between the Japanese and U.S. governments. For example, it ensured that no reparations would be paid to the People's Republic of China or the Democratic People's Republic of Korea (Halliday and McCormack, 1973, p. 23).

After the occupation, Japan developed its own "reparations" program; but it had little to do with compensation for war damages. It was, rather, "instigated by big business as a means of pumping taxpayers money back into the hands of industry. It was specifically designed to bring Japanese exports back into most of the former Greater East Asia Co-Prosperity Sphere with which, naturally, it was coextensive (with the exceptions of the socialist states)" (Halliday and McCormack, 1973, p. 21). By financing the regional trade and investment activities of Japanese business, such "second-stage reparations became a key element both in Japan's economic recovery and in the reconstruction of its economic empire in Asia" (Halliday, 1978, p. 177).

Even before the end of the occupation, the United States had decided "to try to cut Japan off from socialist Asia, which meant *relocating* it in a relatively new Asian context" (Halliday, 1978, p. 185; emphasis in original). Through working bodies such as the Johnston Commission, which visited Japan in February 1948, the United States drew up plans "for the reintegration of Japan into the world economy." The Johnston Commission itself suggested "a guarantee of raw materials for Japan, a shift of exports from dollar to sterling and Far East markets, and the reestablishment of Japanese shipping to cut down on the foreign exchange drain" (p. 185). As part of this effort to "relocate Japan in its new anti-communist East Asian structure," the United States "initiated a triangular programme to boost Japanese exports and make the Japanese economy self-sufficient. The U.S.A. put up funds for South-East Asian countries to purchase Japanese exports, in return giving these same South-East Asian countries 'privileges' in the American market" (p. 186; Halliday and McCormack, 1973, p. 15). Also during the reverse course period, the United States began ensuring that "the World Bank and other puppet organizations lavished funds on Japan"; this helps explain why as of 1964 Japan's cumulative loans from the World Bank had exceeded $500 million, second only to India's $700 million (Halliday and McCormack, 1973, p. 14).[6]

Economic Crisis, the Dodge Plan, and *Zaibatsu* Reconsolidation

While the reverse course helped secure the survival of key elements of the prewar Japanese system, initially it did little to reverse the economic decline of the postwar period. "At the end of 1947 industrial production had reached only 45 percent, exports 10 percent, and imports 30 percent of the 1930-34 average. The United States was supporting the trade deficit of $300 million to keep the economy from total collapse" (Kolko and Kolko, 1972, p. 518). Meanwhile, faced with the government's continued refusal to take steps to improve living and working conditions, government workers continued to threaten new general strikes, first in March and then in July 1948, each time canceling them because of occupation threats. In the July case, MacArthur ordered the government to amend the National Public Service Law to make it illegal for government workers to strike or bargain collectively. The government willingly and eagerly complied, even ruling that existing contracts were invalid (p. 521). SCAP and Japanese authorities also collaborated to weaken organized labor by setting up right-wing "democratization leagues" within the unions (Moore, 1997, p. 8).

It was in this turbulent and repressive context that U.S. policymakers finally began a more active effort to promote Japanese economic recovery. The U.S. government hoped recovery would both end the need to subsidize the Japanese economy and undercut working-class radicalism. In its April 1948 report, the Johnston Commission had already concluded that recovery had to be based on exports, which required cutting inflation and limiting domestic wages and consumption (Kolko and Kolko, 1972, p. 519). Another group of American experts traveled to Japan in May. They drew similar conclusions and recommended a nine-point stabilization program whose measures included "balancing the budget, strengthening the tax collection system, wage, price and trade controls, an improved system of allocating raw materials in order to increase exports, increased production of raw materials and manufactures, and more effective means for bringing food from the countryside into the cities" (Halliday, 1978, p. 188). The program "called not only for 'fixed wages,' but also for longer hours and mass layoffs" in both public and private sectors (p. 188). In December, SCAP formally adopted this nine-point program, and Joseph Dodge, a Detroit banker given rank of Minister, was sent to Japan in February 1949 to implement it (pp. 188-189; Tsuru, 1993, pp. 46-48).

Dodge, following the basic logic of the previous missions, pushed for higher prices and reduced quantities of government-provided goods and services to achieve a balanced budget; the promotion of export activities including the introduction of a favorable exchange rate of 360 yen to the dollar; and the dismantlement of unemployment compensation programs, lengthening of the work day, and freezing of wages to lower labor costs (Halliday, 1978, pp. 189-190; Tsuru, 1993, pp. 48-49). The Dodge line produced a decline in inflation, but also a deepening recession (which was to last until the Korean War) and renewed worker resistance. The social explosion came in June 1949 when workers seized police stations, occupied companies, and engaged in demonstrations and wildcat strikes, all in an unsuccessful attempt to force a change in policy. U.S. troops joined with Japanese police to crush the workers' opposition (Kolko and Kolko, 1972, p. 526).

Although from the point of view of Japanese workers, the Dodge line was a disaster, the same was not true for Japanese business, especially big business. First, it provided a context favorable to the reestablishment of the *zaibatsu* system. Although the *zaibatsu* holding companies had been broken up, the individual large firms continued to exist. As the recession deepened, economic survival came to depend on access to credit. The largest banks in the country were banks formerly associated with *zaibatsu* and they, not surprisingly, channeled most of their funds to former *zaibatsu*-affiliated firms, thereby enabling them to overcome non-*zaibatsu* competitors. As Tsuru puts it: "Such was the monetary background, which, in the generally depressed condition of the economy, had the effect of favoring those Japanese business firms with former *zaibatsu* connections and penalizing small and medium-sized independents. It may be said that . . . gradual redistribution of wealth ensued through capital accumulation favoring big business and a solid link came to be institutionalized between the erstwhile *zaibatsu* banks and industrial enterprises" (1993, p. 56). Thus, *zaibatsu* firms began recreating past links, this time around a bank, not a holding company.[7]

Second, "the deflationary policies of the Dodge Plan created lower wages, unemployment, and massive underemployment that further eroded union strength" (Kolko and Kolko, 1972, p. 526). This facilitated capitalist efforts to rebuild the prewar core labor relations systems—including enterprise unionism and the division of the workforce according to employment status. The Dodge "retrenchment" was thus

> extremely important in assisting management to consolidate its dominant position over the working class. The many dismissals naturally made employees more desperate to hold on to their jobs. . . . As jobs became more and more scarce, and unions which would back the workers' interests weaker and weaker, the pressures to compromise with management by acceding to the latter's version of the enterprise union became stronger and stronger. Whereas in the early postwar period an enterprise union had usually contained all the employees in a plant, management now seized the initiative and demanded that the union grant membership only to a limited number of the enterprise's employees—viz., usually the *minimum* work force which the company would want to employ at the period of maximum retrenchment. Workers, desperate to keep their jobs, were obliged to go along with this definition of the union, which thus became limited to so-called "permanent" workers. Correspondingly, there was now a re-expansion of the number of "temporary" workers. (Halliday, 1978, p. 218; emphasis in original)

As a result of the Dodge recession and accompanying anti-labor policies, "the total number of union members dropped from a peak of nearly 7 million at the end of 1948 to 3.3 million by 1950" (Kolko and Kolko, 1972, p. 526). The attack on organized labor also included "an open red purge that put out of action those leftist party and labor leaders who had been putting up the greatest resistance to the reverse course in labor reform" (Moore, 1997, p. 9).[8]

The Korean War and the Further Renewal of the Japanese Model

The foregoing developments meant that the Japanese elite was well positioned to take advantage of the growth spurt stimulated by the June 1950 start of the Korean War. "Literally in a matter of days the U.S. Army turned Japan into a multi-purpose base for its military operations in Korea" (Tsuru, 1993, p. 57). This resulted in a massive increase in the demand for many different types of goods and services, greatly boosting production and profits. "For example, between July 1950 and February 1951 the U.S. armed forces and the U.S. Economic Cooperation Administration placed orders with Japanese firms for some 7,079 trucks worth nearly $13 million; this was key to the revival of the Japanese automotive industry" (Johnson, 1982, p. 200).[9] Such "special procurements," paid for in dollars, exceeded 2.2 billion over the years 1951 through 1953 (Kolko and Kolko, 1972, p. 643). "The category of extraordinary dollar receipts for Japan lingered on until 1955, by which time the aggregate amount was estimated to have reached 3.56 billion dollars. If we take fiscal 1952 as an example, the dollar receipts due to the special procurements amounted to 62 percent of the total dollar intake of Japan's international payments" (Tsuru, 1993, p. 58).[10]

The Korean War itself solidified the reverse course in U.S. occupation policy toward Japan. By intensifying U.S. concerns about Japan's "security and stability," it worsened the repressive red-scare atmosphere faced by Japanese workers. Indeed, on July 8, 1950—just two weeks after the official start of the Korean conflict—the "SCAP called upon the Japanese government to expand the national police to 75,000 men" (Kolko and Kolko, 1972, p. 642). The Korean War also cemented U.S. plans to make Japan "a major industrial supplier of American involvement and aid not only in Korea but in Southeast Asia" (p. 643). Japanese government leaders readily agreed to this arrangement, which was not only directly profitable to Japanese big business but also helped reestablish the East Asian region "as the natural Japanese market and source of supply for its food and raw materials" (p. 643; cf. Halliday and McCormack, 1973, Chapters 2 and 5). By the time Japan regained its independence in April 1952, in the midst of the Korean War, it had already proven itself to be a useful and loyal supporter of U.S. foreign policy.

After independence the Japanese government took further steps to promote the return of the zaibatsu. The ban on the use of former corporate names and trademarks was ended. The anti-monopoly law was also revised to allow manufacturing corporations to hold shares of competing firms. The revision also raised the maximum fraction of a nonfinancial corporation's shares that could be held by a financial institution from five to ten percent. Finally, interlocking corporate directorates once again became legal. Indeed, Tsuru suggests that "the most important move that gathered momentum after the Peace Treaty was the consolidation and realignment of firms along the former zaibatsu lines" (1993, p. 73).[11]

The postwar zaibatsu resurgence received powerful support and guidance from a state bureaucracy that was undergoing its own process of renewal. In 1949 the SCAP, as part of its plan to promote Japan's economic self-sufficiency, had begun yielding authority over economic matters to the Japanese government—and this formal transfer of power encompassed the management of foreign trade and finance. In response, the Japanese government passed the Foreign Exchange and Foreign Trade Control Law, which required all citizens to turn over all foreign exchange earned through trade to the government. It also created a Foreign Exchange Control Board to supervise the use of that foreign exchange. Also in 1949, the Japanese government inaugurated the Ministry of International Trade and Industry (MITI), and delegated it the powers previously wielded by the Ministry of Commerce and Industry and the Board of Trade. In 1952, the government transferred control over international reserves from the Foreign Exchange Control Board to MITI. At the same time, MITI was given the power to supervise and regulate corporate joint ventures and imports of technology. "When these changes were make, MITI came to possess weapons of industrial management and control that rivaled anything its predecessors had ever known during the prewar and wartime periods" (Johnson, 1982, p. 194).

While the United States sought to promote Japan's recovery through the expansion of light manufactures, the Japanese elite was not satisfied with this as a long-term strategy. Japanese business and government leaders correctly understood that reliance on light manufactures would leave the Japanese economy heavily dependent on the United States. Beginning in 1950—in large part thanks to the Korean War—the bureaucracy, led by MITI, was able to take steps to promote the revival of Japan's heavy and chemical industries, which in practical terms meant the large *zaibatsu* enterprises (Allen, 1958, p. 140).

For example, in response to the growing U.S. demand for goods and services, MITI took steps to expand Japanese productive capacity. Although *zaibatsu* banks were directing credit to their former *zaibatsu*-affiliated firms, available funds were still limited. MITI therefore encouraged and directed a process whereby government funds were channeled to the main *zaibatsu* banks which then reloaned them to MITI-targeted industrial firms. Thus, "the Japanese industrial system took on one of its most distinctive characteristics—the pattern of dependencies in which a group of enterprises borrows from a bank well beyond the individual companies' capacity to repay, or often beyond their net worth, and the bank in turn overborrows from the Bank of Japan. Since the central bank is the ultimate guarantor of the system, it gains complete and detailed control over the policies and lending decisions of its dependent 'private' banks" (Johnson, 1982, p. 203). This lending process deliberately supported *zaibatsu* banks and the creation of *keiretsu* (the postwar equivalent of the *zaibatsu*) to the disadvantage of small- and medium-sized firms. Not surprisingly, then, "the 'big six' among the

Japanese conglomerates that came into being during the 1950s were those based on the Fuji, Sanwa, Dai-Inchi, Mitsui, Mitsubishi, and Sumitomo banks" (p. 205; cf. Cohen, 1958, p. 203).

MITI also supported the expansion of bank-based *keiretsu* through its use of newly created state institutions such as the Japan Development Bank and the Export-Import Bank. In fact, the Japan Development Bank (JDB), established in 1951, quickly became one of MITI's key instruments of industrial policy. In 1952, the Japanese government gave the JDB power to raise money with its own bonds. At the same time, the Ministry of Finance reconfigured the postal savings system so that the money deposited in it by Japanese households would form one big money pool known as the Fiscal Investment and Loan Plan.[12] The JDB borrowed from this pool and made loans to companies based on MITI directives. JDB loans were a key source of funds for *keiretsu* firms from 1953 to 1961. Government banks, the largest being the JDB, altogether supplied over 30 percent of all industrial capital from 1953 to 1955 and then over 20 percent on a yearly basis through the end of the 1950s (Johnson, 1982, p. 212). Even when its relative importance as a lender declined, the JDB remained important in that its loans were taken to indicate MITI priorities, thereby encouraging lending by private banks along similar lines.

MITI was able to support *zaibatsu* recovery and direct it according to its desired goal of rebuilding the country's heavy industrial base through other means as well. One important way was through its control over scarce foreign exchange. U.S. "special procurement" spending for Japanese goods was made in dollars, and MITI enjoyed control over those dollars because of its authority over foreign exchange. Not surprisingly, MITI used this control to encourage *zaibatsu* industrial expansion. MITI also helped rebuild the *zaibatsu*'s gargantuan merchant affiliates, the general trading companies (GTCs). The SCAP had broken up the old *zaibatsu* GTCs, but almost immediately after the end of the occupation MITI began working, through tax and credit policy, to reunite them (Cohen, 1958, pp. 196–197). By late 1952, for example, the former Mitsubishi trading companies had reformed into a single GTC, and Mitsui's GTC was restored in 1955 (Johnson, 1982, p. 205). These "two largest Zaibatsu trading companies [had] accounted for 70 percent of Japan's prewar foreign trade" (Cohen, 1958, p. 197).

GTC reconsolidation was, in fact, a logical outcome of reverse course policy. Any *zaibatsu*-dominated recovery of Japanese industry would require massive imports of industrial materials and food, financed by growing manufactured exports. This expanding trade called in turn for large-scale foreign marketing arrangements, loans, and (ultimately) direct investments—all coordinated with both domestic *zaibatsu* industrial operations and with the Japanese government's foreign aid policies (Halliday and McCormack, 1973, pp. 25-31). After their reassembly in the 1950s, the big GTCs (or, as they are known in Japan, the *sogo shosha*), immediately began filling this strategically crucial position in Japanese and East Asian commerce. By 1972, the ten largest GTCs were handling over half of Japan's import and export trade.[13] On the regional level, "between a third and a half of Thailand's foreign trade was handled directly or indirectly by Japanese trading companies in the mid-1970s" (Yamazawa and Kohama, 1985, pp. 442-443). In the early 1970s, over 90 percent of Taiwan's exports and imports were channeled through Japanese GTCs, with the top ten Japanese GTCs handling over half of this trade (Halliday, 1978, p. 289; Young, 1979, p 187). According to McCormack (1978), "over 30 per cent of the foreign trade of South Korea [was] handled by Japanese trading companies" in the mid-1970s (p. 179). Hone (1974) reports data suggesting that in 1972, the top ten Japanese GTCs purchased roughly 30 percent of the combined manufactured exports of six East Asian countries (other than Japan) (pp. 145, 149).[14]

The *sogo shosha* were not only instrumental in the recovery and renewed expansion of Japan's trade networks; they also facilitated direct foreign investments by Japanese companies searching for raw materials and low-wage labor in other East Asian countries. For example, when the Japanese textile industry began to relocate abroad in the late 1950s, the GTCs sought out and arranged suitable foreign production sites and provided necessary finance (Steven, 1990, pp. 70-71). The Japanese government, through MITI and its banking organs, provided crucial support for such foreign investment operations.

MITI also played an important role in the renewal of *zaibatsu* labor-management relations—primarily through its supervision of the Industrial Rationalization Council, which included the leaders of most major industrial enterprises. The council discussed and formulated policies designed to promote the country's rapid industrial expansion, and labor policy was a central concern of these deliberations. As Johnson explains: "Perhaps the council's least known but later most applauded activities were in the areas of the reform of management, the institutionalization of the lifetime employment system, and the raising of the productivity of the Japanese work-force" (1982, p. 216). In this way, MITI supported the elaboration of "a whole series of management measures, some new, some not, . . . into a comprehensive code of worker control: time control, personnel control, efficiency wages, a pay scale tied to 'ability', rigidly hierarchical status rankings for workers, and the shop supervisory system known as *'shokusei'* (literally 'work control')" (Halliday and McCormack, 1973, pp. 179-180). Under this "scientifically" reconsolidated labor-control system, "the unions themselves became increasingly integrated into the supervisory structure of the company, partners of capital, united with private enterprise in helping Japan compete for international markets" (p. 180).[15]

MITI and the Industrial Rationalization Council also oversaw the "scientific" reconstruction of subcontracting relations between the big *zaibatsu* corporations and smaller enterprises. This involved such practices as delayed payments by larger corporations to their subcontractors (the "shiwayose" system) and "just-in-time" inventory management—practices that placed severe pressures on subcontracting workers' wages, work times, and labor intensities (Yamamura, 1967, Chapter 9). Pressures on small- and medium-sized enterprises were reinforced by the Japanese government's discriminatory "low interest rate policy" which, as discussed earlier, systematically favored "borrowers with traditional ties of the zaibatsu type" (Tsuru, 1993, p. 109).

Although the managers of most large *keiretsu*-affiliated firms were already eager to reestablish and improve their labor-control and subcontracting systems—and had been taking steps in this direction since the beginning of the SCAP's reverse course in 1947—MITI left nothing to chance. It "could and did cut off the access to foreign exchange of any firms" that dragged their feet in the implementation of the requisite administrative devices (Johnson, 1982, p. 217).

Interpreting the Postwar Renewal of the Japanese System

In sum, by the end of the 1950s, the basic prewar Japanese system had, although with significant modifications, been restored. The *zaibatsu* structure, built on a divided and weakened working class, enterprise unionism, and a dependent sector of small- and medium-sized firms, had been renewed. A powerful state bureaucracy had also been restored, one that worked in close collaboration with the *zaibatsu* to promote the country's rapid industrialization. The Japanese working class had waged a courageous struggle to restructure this system, to transform it along socialist-oriented lines, but it had been defeated by the combined strength of the U.S. occupation and the Japanese ruling class. Indeed, through its partnership with U.S. imperialism and the reconsolidation of the *zaibatsu* and their trading companies, Japan's governing elite had gone some distance toward reestablishing Japanese economic dominance in East Asia.

Although they did not produce a fundamental change in the Japanese system, the SCAP-imposed modifications to that system were not inconsequential. Most importantly, the occupation severely weakened the institutional basis of Japanese militarism, softened the autocratic nature of *zaibatsu* enterprise management, and expanded and strengthened formal civil liberties. These changes ensured that Japan's postwar expansion would not be quite as openly dependent on exploitation and militarism as in the past. However, that is far different from concluding that Japan's postwar political economy somehow represents or prefigures an anticapitalist model worthy of support by those seeking alternatives to capitalism.

The Japanese system did go on to deliver record rates of growth and industrialization. But the fundamental underpinnings of the system had little to do with socialism. Moreover, while this system powered growth, it contained its own serious contradictions. Today's crisis can only be understood in this context.

Chapter 9

The Japanese Miracle and Its Contradictions

The early to mid-1950s recovery of the Japanese economy to prewar levels was mostly a result of special Korean War procurements arranged by the United States. This followed on the heels of the U.S. occupation's suppression (in cooperation with the Japanese ruling class and its state functionaries) of the postwar radical-democratic, production-control, and industrial union struggles of Japanese workers. Together with the more general "reverse course" in U.S. policy toward Japanese reconstruction, the Korean War boom and repression of the working class enabled Japan's governing elite to reconstruct the basic institutions of Japanese capitalism—the *zaibatsu*, bureaucratic planning, and labor control systems. The accumulation model that emerged after the Korean War was built around large-scale investments in heavy industry supported by rapid growth of light manufactured exports. Export growth was crucial because it helped fill the widening effective demand gap opened by rising rates of exploitation (real wages that increased more slowly than labor productivity).

Export-Led Growth and Heavy Industry

Prior to the Korean War, the U.S. occupation had pushed Japan to pursue an export-led growth strategy based on light manufactures. However, Japan's governing elite understood the importance of building up capital- and chemical-intensive industries to lessen external dependence and ensure future growth. After gaining formal independence from the United States in 1952, the Japanese government immediately began to encourage and direct the expansion of heavy and chemical industries—especially steel, aluminum, electric power, petrochemicals, cement, and shipbuilding. The result was "a huge network of industrial complexes which [were] among the most advanced and most productive facilities in the capitalist world" (Sweezy, 1980, p. 4). To cite just one example, by 1971 Japan's Nippon Steel had overtaken U.S. Steel to become the world's largest steel company (Halliday, 1978, p. 279). Indeed, "as far back as 1965 the share of heavy industry in Japan's industrial output was higher than in any other industrial country" (Halliday and McCormack, 1973, p. 166). "Metals, chemicals, and engineering already represented about 60 per cent by value of the country's gross factory production in 1960, compared with only 30 per cent in 1930" (Beasley, 1995, p. 247).[1]

Even though Japan's post-Korean War growth was largely keyed to investment in heavy industry, exports were a driving force behind the expansion. As Robert Brenner explains:

> Between 1952 and 1960, Japanese exports as a share of GDP rose by 14 percent. But this aggregate figure does more to obscure than illuminate the central place of export growth in postwar Japanese development, because it distracts attention from the fundamental role of exports in underwriting the pivotal, and extraordinarily dynamic, Japanese manufacturing sector. By 1960, the share of manufacturing exports in manufacturing output had grown to 28 percent, and contributed significantly to the increase of the share of Japanese manufacturing output in total output from 19.5 percent to 26.4 percent and of the manufacturing labor force in the total labor force from about 15 percent to 22 percent during the previous decade. (1998, p. 89)

Two kinds of manufactured exports were important during this initial phase of the Japanese "miracle." First, heavy and chemical industry exports helped the *zaibatsu* to profitably utilize excess productive capacity in these sectors. "By about 1965 production of the major heavy and chemical industries far exceeded the level of domestic demand"; hence exports were a crucial means of "solving crises of overproduction" (Halliday, 1978, pp. 279-280).[2] However, until the mid-1960s a second type of manufactured export was of far greater quantitative importance to the Japanese economy, namely, light-industrial products such as textiles, toys, and simple electrical appliances. Textiles were the leading export during the 1950s but were replaced by transistor radios by the early 1960s (Tsuru, 1993, pp. 77-84).

Unlike the heavy and chemical industries, with their predominantly male labor forces, the light-manufacturing sector employed many women workers. Indeed, its labor-intensive operations were internationally competitive in large part because the wages of Japanese women workers were comparable to those of women in other Asian countries even though Japanese male wages were higher. Labor-intensive manufactured goods made up 65.0 percent of all Japanese exports in 1955, and by 1965 they still accounted for 52.8 percent despite the intervening expansion of the heavy and chemical industries (Krause and Sekiguchi, 1976, p. 409). Given Japan's dependence on imported raw materials, fuels, and technologies, the growth of light-manufactured exports was clearly an essential ingredient in the launching of the growth "miracle."

The results of the dual strategy of heavy industrialization and light-manufactured exportation were indeed impressive. From 1950 to 1960, Japan's real GNP grew at an average annual rate of 10.0 percent, while manufacturing output growth averaged 16.7 percent. This growth was driven by a massive investment boom: private investment in plant and equipment rose at an average annual rate of 15.6 percent over the entire decade, and at 22.6 percent from 1955 to 1960. Capital investment in manufacturing averaged a stunning 33 percent annual growth between 1954 and 1961 (Brenner, 1998, p. 79). By the early 1960s, the Japanese economy was already being extolled as an unprecedented success in "creative defeat" (Tsuru, 1993, Chapter 3).

Industrial Restructuring and the Working Class

Japan's postwar growth "take-off" was anything but smooth, however. The country's high-investment, high-export strategy immediately began to generate and confront barriers, and it was largely in response to these barriers that the economic strategy evolved. The most important difficulty—one present throughout the period from the mid-1950s through the 1980s —was that "Japan's rapid economic growth, which involved tremendous increases in export potential and import needs, caused difficulties for other countries through market disruption. . . . The higher the rate of Japanese economic growth, the greater the strain in foreign markets imposed by Japanese export expansion" (Krause and Sekiguchi, 1976, p. 406). As Japan increased its share of the world manufactured export market, her export success began to occur at the expense of other capitalist countries. By 1959, Japan's share in the manufactured exports of the 12 leading capitalist nations was already 6.6 percent, up from 3.3 percent in 1950. Japan's share rose still further, to 7.6 percent, by 1963 (Brenner, 1998, p. 90). Not surprisingly, the governments of the United States and other capitalist countries responded with import restrictions aimed at Japan plus demands that Japan liberalize its own imports.

Initially, these external trade-related pressures largely focussed on the light-manufacturing sector—the main source of Japan's manufactured exports through the early 1960s. A considerable share of Japan's light manufactures was directed at the U.S. market, so much so that U.S. light-manufacturing firms and trade unions began complaining about the flood of "dollar blouses" and transistor radios from Japan in the late 1950s and TVs in the early 1960s. Responding to such complaints, the U.S. government demanded that Japan place limits on its light-manufactured exports, especially of cotton textile products (Tsuru, 1993, p. 198).[3] Then, hoping to use trade negotiations as a lever to open up the Japanese economy to U.S. and European corporations, the U.S. and European governments began pressing Japan hard to speed up its own trade liberalization. By 1963, such pressures were being exerted not only in bilateral trade negotiations but also through multilateral organizations including the IMF, OECD, and GATT. The following year Japan agreed to phase out both foreign-exchange rationing (an import-control device) and export-subsidies (pp. 112-113; Krause and Sekiguchi, 1976, p. 414).

Meanwhile, on the domestic scene, rapid growth of output and employment was generating higher wages even for women workers. By the mid-1960s, these rising wages were making it increasingly difficult for Japan's light-manufactured exports to remain internationally competitive.[4] This internal development, along with the growing external trade frictions described above, made the light-manufacturing sector an unviable basis for continued export growth. The Japanese bureaucracy therefore began encouraging the movement of light-manufacturing plants out of the country. Production of cotton textiles was moved to East Asia (mainly to South Korea, Taiwan, and the ASEAN countries) beginning in the mid-1960s, followed shortly by synthetic textiles (Steven, 1983, pp. 237-240; 1990, p. 70). Not long after came the relocation of labor-intensive consumer electronics production, including radios, TVs, and tape recorders—again primarily to countries in East Asia (Tsuru, 1993, pp. 197-198).

The outward migration of light-manufacturing production was part of a larger process of scrap-and-build. As light manufacturing was being run down and relocated, the Japanese government focused on shifting the main core of manufactured export growth toward the heavy and chemical industries—especially iron and steel, ships, chemicals, and petroleum products (Steven, 1990, p. 9).[5] These industries, which processed large amounts of imported raw materials, had previously grown largely through domestic-market sales; but now they became increasingly export-oriented. For example, the share of steel products that were exported rose from 11.4 percent of total output in 1960, to 20.8 percent in 1970, and to 30.2 percent in 1974 (Tsuru, 1993, p. 83). For steel vessels, the share of output exported rose from 53.1 percent in 1960, to 76.7 percent in 1970, to 88.9 percent in 1974 (p. 84). The shift of Japan's exporting core from light manufacturing to heavy and chemical industries was reflected in the respective shares of labor-intensive and capital-intensive goods in Japan's total exports. According to Krause and Sekiguchi (1976), the share of labor-intensive exports fell from 52.8 percent in 1965 to 43.5 percent in 1973, while the capital-intensive export share rose from 37.5 to 46.6 percent in the same period (p. 409).[6]

The success of this transformation is shown by the continued rapid growth of the Japanese economy. From 1965 to 1970, real GNP rose at an average annual rate of 14 percent while manufacturing output growth averaged 15.8 percent. Private investment in new plants and equipment showed an annual average increase of 21.1 percent in the same period, almost matching the growth rate achieved during the years 1955-61 (Brenner, 1998, p. 112). The new growth surge undoubtedly generated great benefits for the male Japanese workforce employed by the core, heavy industrial enterprises. As Rob Steven observes: "Domestically, these years represented the high point in the development of heavy industry, which symbolized the 'Japanese miracle' and brought unheard of wages and conditions to the male labor aristocracy" (1990, p. 14).

The growth of male earnings in heavy industry was a crucial source of effective demand for the output of relatively new consumer-goods industries such as automobiles and advanced electronics products. The big core production units in these newer industries also mainly employed male labor (especially in their permanent workforces). Hence, it was once again the minority male labor aristocracy that benefited most directly from the late 1960s rapid growth of industrialized consumer-goods production. Of course, the flip side of the whole scrap-and-build dynamic was that many women lost jobs as the production of textiles and simple electronics was relocated abroad. Many of these women workers were forced into the low-wage service and household sectors. Others found jobs, as did many men who could not find core employment, in the growing network of subcontractors that developed to support the new consumer-goods industries. There was also "a massive influx into temporary and part-time jobs by mainly married women" (Steven, 1990, p. 14).

In fact, underwriting Japan's rapid growth and industrial transformation was a labor system based on the oppression of women, the use of temporary workers, and subcontracting. While women made up only 32.4 percent of all employed workers in 1972, they accounted for 57.5 percent of all factory workers and 46.8 percent of all office workers (Halliday, 1978, p. 224). This is important, since women were paid approximately half of what men earned, generally excluded from "lifetime employment," and forced to retire by the age of 30 if not earlier because of marriage. Japanese firms, even core industrial firms, made great use of largely female temporary workforces. These same core firms derived significant additional cost savings from their use of subcontractors. Some two-thirds of all manufacturing workers were employed by small- and medium-sized firms, many of which operated within networks controlled by the larger and more powerful industrial leaders (pp. 225-226).

The anti-labor bias of Japan's growing industrial system is perhaps best illustrated by the trend in labor's share of gross value added. "Labor's share in Japan fell from 39.6 per cent in 1953 to 33.8 per cent in 1966, and an estimated 33.7 in 1970. This compares with figures [consistently] over 50 per cent for Canada, Sweden, Holland and the United Kingdom" (Halliday, 1978, p. 222). Japanese workers also suffered from the longest average work week of any advanced capitalist country. In 1970, for example, the work week averaged 43.1 hours in Japan compared with 39.1 in West Germany and 37.5 in the United States (p. 222).

With its ability to routinely keep real wage increases well below productivity gains, it is not surprising that Japanese industry enjoyed a considerable cost advantage over its international rivals and thus rapid growth and export success (Brenner, 1998, pp. 77-90). Indeed, as industrial capacity grew far beyond domestic wage-based demand, the Japanese system became, out of necessity, increasingly export-oriented. This is reflected in the shift of the economy's main exporting center from the old light-manufacturing sector to the more capitalized and technologically advanced heavy and chemical industries, indicating that export dependence was increasingly penetrating the dynamic core of the Japanese system.

More "Creative Destruction":
From Heavy Industry to Machinery Exports

Despite the initial success of the scrap-and-build strategy, Japan's economic expansion continued to generate contradictions. Domestically, the growth of the heavy and chemical industries created serious pollution problems (Broadbent, 1998, pp. 12-19). Beginning around 1970, "citizens' organizations concerned with mounting evidence of the multiform dangers to the environment . . . mushroomed throughout the country" and pollution became "a central political issue" (Halliday and McCormack, 1973, p. 193). To the alarm of Japanese capitalists and their state functionaries, this "environmental concern gradually became a matter, less of cost-benefit calculation than of human rights" (Tsuru, 1993, p. 137; cf. Broadbent, 1998, *passim*). Along with the environmental movement, increasing land costs also threatened the further expansion of the country's heavy and chemical industries. Indeed, the land-cost problem became more worrisome to capital insofar as environmentalists pushed successfully for regulations on industrial land use.

Internationally, Japan's growing exports continued to create tensions as they invaded the domestic markets of, and constrained the export opportunities available to, other developed capitalist countries—especially the United States. From 1963 to 1971, Japan's share of manufactured exports by the 12 leading capitalist countries rose from 7.6 to 13.0 percent. Between 1964 and 1971, Japanese exports to the United States quadrupled in value, and the share of Japan's total exports destined for the United States rose from 27.6 to 31.2 percent (Brenner, 1998, pp. 113-114).

The United States responded to its growing trade problems in August 1971 by ending gold-dollar convertibility (effectively terminating the Bretton Woods system of fixed exchange rates) and putting a ten percent surcharge on all imports. This led to the December 1971 Smithsonian Agreement, which included a commitment by the Japanese government to raise the value of the yen by 17 percent. Japan had long resisted U.S. demands to revalue its currency, keeping it at the 1949 level of 360 yen per dollar. Unfortunately for Japan, widening U.S. balance-of-payments deficits pushed the yen's $U.S. value up another 12 percent in 1973 (Tsuru, 1993, pp. 179-180; Brenner, 1998, pp. 122-123).

Close on the heels of the yen's revaluation, the Japanese economy took another serious hit with the sharp rise of oil prices beginning in late 1973, followed by price increases for most other primary commodities. The combined impact of these developments was especially severe for Japan's heavy and chemical industries. Since these industries processed large amounts of imported oil and other materials into exports, their profitability and competitiveness was undermined by the exchange-rate and oil-price shocks. The response of Japanese planners was to launch a new round of scrap-and-build.

Even before 1973, Japanese bureaucrats had responded to domestic environmental and land-cost problems by developing plans for the rundown and relocation of the heavy and chemical industries.[7] At the same time, government planners had begun nurturing the accelerated development of several newer industries, including automobiles and advanced consumer electronics. In 1971, the Industrial Structure Council, operating under MITI direction, publicly called for the creation of a new manufacturing core centered in the electronics and machine industries. Singled out for special attention were those industries producing machines controlled by integrated circuits, including computers, office and communications machinery, and robots. By 1973, a new Machinery and Information Industries Bureau had been created that consolidated planning for electronics, computers, automobiles, and general machinery under one administration—enabling the government to more effectively coordinate and integrate their development.

With this administrative infrastructure in place, the Japanese government quickly responded to the external shocks of the early 1970s by initiating the large-scale relocation of the heavy and chemical industries to South Korea and other East Asian countries where governments and local elites were desperate for industrial development even at a high environmental cost. This process was given further momentum by the decade's second oil-price increase, in 1979-80. "Among the largest undertakings were the Asahan Aluminum smelter in Indonesia, the Kawasaki steel sintering plant in the Philippines, and the Sumitomo petrochemical complex in Singapore"—all huge industrial projects built by Japanese capital during the period from 1974 to 1981 (Steven, 1997, p. 202). At the same time, the Japanese government stepped up its domestic promotion of the targeted machinery industries, in particular, general machinery (including office machines), electrical machinery (including TV and radio receivers, tape recorders, and semiconductors), transport machinery (including motor vehicles), and precision machinery. Brenner sums up the outcome of this scrap-and-build phase:

> Over the years 1973-80, output in the advanced electrical machinery and precision instruments industries and in other "processing" industries (including other machinery, transport equipment, and metal products) grew at average annual rates of 15 percent and 6.2 percent, respectively, compared to just 4.6 percent in the "heavy" chemical, petroleum, and metal industries and 3.6 percent in the labor-intensive textile and food industries. (1998, p. 169)

This shift from heavy and chemical industries to machine industries took place, as did the previous scrap-and-build phase, in concert with a restructuring of labor relations. According to Steven,

The onslaught on the domestic working class in this second period included an expansion of the part-time labor force (women, day laborers, contract workers, temporaries) a reduction in the number of regular jobs in government and in large companies, a rationalization of the labor process through new technologies, an extension of the system of subcontracting, and a freeze on the living standards of the less secure two-thirds of the working class. (1997, p. 202)

Thanks to its flexible system of labor relations, Japan was the only major capitalist country that was able to keep unit wage costs from rising during the 1975–80 period (Steven, 1990, p. 15).[8]

However, the use of an expanding web of labor-repressing institutions to ensure the profitable expansion of a new industrial core did little to solve the problem of Japan's growing reliance on exports. The new core industries, such as the automobile industry, had initially been domestically oriented, supported largely by the rising income levels of workers in the heavy and chemical industries. The latter industries were now being scrapped and relocated. The growth of domestic wage-based demand was also constrained by the very system of temporary and subcontracting relations that promoted the competitive success of the new core machinery industries. Indeed, insofar as labor-market and management systems kept real wage growth well below productivity growth, they ensured that the workforce would not have sufficient purchasing power to support the rising level of production.

As a result, the new core industries—and the Japanese economy as a whole—became even more export dependent during this second scrap-and-build phase. Between 1973 and 1980, exports as a ratio to GDP rose from 9.9 to 13.7 percent, while manufacturing exports as a share of manufacturing output jumped from 27.1 to 45.7 percent (Brenner, 1998, p. 170). The growing dominance of the newer machinery industries in this dynamic is shown by the respective shares of general machinery, electrical machinery, and transport equipment in total Japanese exports: these increased by factors of one-half, one-fourth, and one-fifth over the years 1971–81. During the same period, the export shares of chemicals and primary metal products decreased by factors of 30 percent and 25 percent, respectively (p. 170). By 1980, exports of machinery and equipment accounted for 62.8 percent of Japan's total merchandise exports, and their share then rose still further, to 71.8 percent, in 1985 (Steven, 1990, p. 17).

The "High Yen Crisis" and Further Restructuring

Japan's second round of scrap-and-build eventually proved just as problematic as the first. More than 40 percent of all Japanese machinery exports during the 1985-87 period were sold in North America, mostly in the United States; this included over 60 percent of Japan's motor vehicle exports (Steven, 1990, p. 21). Japan's export success in such key, high value-added products was seen by many U.S. analysts as the main factor behind growing U.S. trade deficits and the deindustrialization of the U.S. economy. Views such as this fueled a major escalation of trade tensions between the United States and Japan, forcing Japan to take part in the international negotiations that culminated in the September 1985 Plaza Accord. The Accord tried to use exchange rate adjustments to bring about more balance in trade, and this led to an appreciation of the yen by more than 46 percent against the dollar during the 1985-88 period (UNCTAD, 1993, p. 130). The resulting erosion of Japan's export competitiveness, and the threat this posed to a continuation of Japan's growth "miracle," became known as the "high yen crisis" (*endaka fukyo*) (Steven, 1988b).

The sharp appreciation of the yen hit Japanese producers hard, but the resulting recession did not last long; production resumed its upward trend in 1987. This quick recovery was possible for two reasons. First, Japanese producers were remarkably successful in holding down the U.S. dollar prices of their exports, with less than proportional declines in profits. This was due in part to the cheapening of oil and raw material imports by the higher yen; but it also reflected the relative weakness of Japanese labor that enabled capitalists to "adjust" wages and work conditions. As Steven observes, "instantly effective cost-reduction, wage rises below increases in productivity and docile trade unions are all manifestations of the 'miraculous' power of Japanese capital" (1996, p. 56). However, given the tensions arising from Japan's trade surplus with the United States, such "success" could not lead to long-term stability.

The second force driving Japan's quick recovery was the now infamous "bubble economy," an investment and construction boom driven by an escalating upward spiral of stock-share, land, and housing prices (Ziemba, 1991; Oizumi, 1994). The bubble economy also fueled a consumption boom among Japanese who owned significant amounts of real estate and financial assets. Monetary policy was accommodative, as the government kept interest rates low for the bigger *keiretsu* corporations and other well-connected borrowers.

While the bubble economy picked up steam, Japanese big business and government planners were busy with another major industrial restructuring.[9] Large portions of the motor vehicle and consumer electronics industries were now "hollowed out" and relocated abroad. However, in spite of the domestic economic recovery—and in sharp contrast to the strategy employed during each of the two previous postwar rounds of scrap-and-build—technological limitations and profit concerns blocked any serious attempt to build up a new industrial core (Steven, 1990, p. 40). Compared to U.S. corporations, Japanese corporations did engage in high levels of capital investment in the half decade following the Plaza Accord (Fallows, 1994, p. 260; Brenner, 1998, p. 216). But this investment was partly a figment of the speculative construction and consumption binges generated by the bubble economy. The domestic manufacturing component of corporate investment, driven largely by the need for cost-cutting upgrades of plant and equipment to offset the higher yen, once again lacked a solid basis in domestic working-class consumption demand (Steven, 1997, p. 204). The emphasis on capital upgrading did encourage a major push to modernize facilities for manufacturing producer goods, in particular machinery and advanced components—and here the intended market was other enterprises or subsidiaries (often located overseas), not the ultimate consumers (especially domestic workers). But this orientation toward investment demand and away from domestic wage-based consumption demand only displaced overproduction problems in space and time; it hardly resolved them (see below).

Moreover, the late 1980s investment boom was not confined to Japan. Japanese foreign direct investment, totaling some $47 billion during the period 1981-85, grew to over $170 billion over the following four years (Steven, 1996, p. 73).[10] This boom of outward FDI was driven largely by the Japanese strategy of relocating production of the goods most vulnerable to both the high yen and trade tensions with the United States, although foreign expansion in the areas of finance, real estate, and commercial activities also played a major role (Magdoff, 1992, p. 15; Sheridan, 1995, p. 478).

More specifically, the post–1985 wave of manufacturing FDI involved a two-part overseas investment program by Japanese capital. There was a major push to locate production of advanced consumer products such as automobiles to the other developed countries serving as their target markets. This mainly meant increased direct investment in the United States; but Japanese investments in new European production facilities increased significantly as well (Mason, 1992, pp. 463-466). There was also a major new flow of manufacturing investment into Asia designed to relocate the production of mass consumer electronics goods and less advanced industrial components to lower-wage countries.

Within this two-pronged strategy, the majority of new foreign investment went to other core countries. Nonetheless, Japanese FDI in the third world—especially Asia—rose significantly after 1985. For example, total Japanese direct investment in South Korea, Taiwan, and Hong Kong during the years 1986-91 was (in dollar terms) over 70 percent of the amount that took place in the entire 1951-91 period. Roughly three-fourths of Japanese FDI in Malaysia over the years 1951-91 occurred in 1986-91, while for Thailand the ratio exceeded 86 percent. For Asia as a whole, the ratio was 63 percent (Yue, 1993, pp. 82-83). This post–1985 wave of Japanese investment in Asia was weighted toward manufacturing. From 1986 to 1990, manufacturing subsidiaries made up over half of all new Japanese corporate subsidiaries established in East Asia (outside Japan), compared to only 30 percent in North America and 21 percent in Europe (Hitoshi, 1993). "Japan's investment in manufacturing in other Asian countries in the years 1986-89 exceeded the *cumulative* total for the whole of the 1951-85 period" (Bernard and Ravenhill, 1995, p. 182; emphasis in original). While Japanese manufacturing FDI in Asia was 31 percent of the amount that went to North America over the years 1986-89, it rose to 45 percent in 1990, and 88 percent in 1993 (Steven, 1996, pp. 78-79).

As noted above, electrical machinery was a leading sector in Japan's new Asian investments. This was especially true of Japanese manufacturing FDI in the ASEAN countries—particularly Malaysia and Thailand:

> From 1986 to 1990, this industry was single-handedly responsible for 30% of all manufacturing sector investment in Asia, and research by the Japan Export-Import Bank shows that during that period 55% of all projects went to Malaysia and Thailand. As for the domestic electrical appliance industry (civilian electronic and electrical machinery) the pattern is even more marked: Malaysia and Thailand got 62% of all projects, ASEAN as a whole got 80% (Hitoshi, 1993, pp. 24-25).

During the years 1987-89, "fully one-third of all Japanese manufacturing investment in ASEAN countries was in electrical machinery production, another 11 percent was in general machinery production, while textiles accounted for less than 5 percent" (Bernard and Ravenhill, 1995, p. 182). "By 1990, Toshiba, Matsushita, Minebea, and similar Japanese firms had built some 340 fully owned plants in Southeast Asia. The great majority, including all the plants in Thailand, Malaysia, and the Philippines, had not been there in 1985" (Fallows, 1994, p. 265).

With the third round of scrap-and-build, Japan's manufacturing sector increasingly focused on production of only the most technologically advanced consumer and capital goods and components. The consumer goods were mostly high-end electronics and automobiles, for both domestic consumption and export. The capital goods and components were sold primarily to Japanese-owned production facilities in the other core countries and in Japan's Asian periphery. Japan's new production facilities in the United States and Europe mainly served their host markets (in some cases operating as platforms for exports back to Japan). Meanwhile, Japan's offshore East Asian factories exported mass consumer goods and less advanced components to the United States and Europe. In the past, Japanese corporations would have supported domestic production of machinery products with parts and components produced by domestic subcontractors; now the parts and components largely came from the new lower-cost subcontracting operations being established elsewhere in East Asia alongside the *keiretsu's* larger-scale offshore facilities (Bello, 1992, p. 91; Steven, 1997, pp. 203-204).

Hence, even though no new large-scale domestic industrial core was established, the third phase of scrap-and-build did not make the Japanese economy less export dependent. It merely made this export dependence less domestically based and more indirect. Henceforth, Japan's continued export growth would mainly hinge on sales of the most advanced components and technologies to Japanese capital's offshore facilities. The sales to the offshore *Asian* facilities would derive largely from these facilities' exports to the United States and other developed country markets. This dynamic was reflected in the changing international composition of Japan's overall trade surplus: In 1985, just 3.2 percent of the total Japanese trade surplus was accounted for by Japan's trade surplus with East Asia; as of 1993, this share had risen to 57.2 percent.[11] As noted by Fallows, much of Japan's growing surplus with East Asia "consisted either of capital goods— equipment for new Japanese-owned factories throughout the rest of the region—or industrial components. These components were, in turn, used in Mitsubishi, Matsushita, Toyota, and similar factories in Southeast Asia to make products destined for the United States" (1994, p. 248; cf. UNCTAD, 1993, p. 137).

The combination of Japan's ongoing export dependence and the regional and global production strategy used to maintain Japanese capital's export competitiveness bore adverse consequences for Japan viewed as a national economy, and for the Japanese working class in particular. This became clearer with the end of the bubble economy in late 1989, when the Japanese government finally took action to bring inflation and asset prices under control. The government's monetary policy of managed deflation pushed Japan into a recession, one which lasted with fitful starts toward recovery throughout the 1990s. In response, Japanese enterprises worked to cut production costs—holding the threat of foreign production and domestic deindustrialization over workers' heads to gain acceptance of austerity.

Unfortunately, by pursuing a strategy of "shifting production abroad and cost-cutting at home" (Sender, 1995, p. 48), Japanese capital intensified Japan's economic problems. For example, anytime Japan's trade surplus grew, as it did in the early 1990s under the combined influence of recessionary import reductions and increased exports of advanced products, the yen was forced up again. This, in turn, touched off new demands on workers for wage cuts and longer, intensified work times, as well as new rounds of domestic downsizing and outward FDI by Japanese firms both large and small. While austerity for workers made the economy ever more export dependent by eroding wage-based demand, the downsizing and FDI made the domestic productive structure continually less capable of generating a strong export-led and high-investment recovery. Repeated rounds of this process left "Japan's once-mighty export machine . . . still sputtering, partly because major manufacturers [had] shifted production overseas" (Hamilton, 1996b, p. A1).[12] Meanwhile, Japanese firms operating in other Asian countries were beginning to take advantage of their low unit wage costs to reexport Asian production back to Japan. By 1996, Japan's imports of color TVs were greater than its exports and covered one-half of the domestic market. The same trend existed with VCRs, personal computers, and even ships, cars, and car parts (Kanabayashi, 1996a; Reitman, 1996a; Steven, 1996, p. 194). Terutomo Ozawa aptly refers to the whole sequential dynamic of cost-cutting, increased exports, higher yen, outward FDI and domestic hollowing-out as a "treadmill," and to the resulting end of the growth "miracle" as the "Japanese disease" (1996, p. 486).

The End of the Growth "Miracle": Basic Implications

Our historical analysis has come full circle, to the current structural crisis of the Japanese economy and its implications for capitalism and socialism (see Chapter 5). One now sees this structural crisis in a different light. The breakdown of export-led growth was hardly the outcome of "socialist" elements in the Japanese system (state-based equity and protection of the weak rather than market-based efficiency and rewarding of the strong). It was, rather, the culminating historical dynamic of an extremely exploitative, hierarchical, undemocratic, and expansionist form of capitalism. Far from socialist, Japan's export-oriented scrap-and-build accumulation was a highly competitive variant of capitalistic creative destruction. But the same scrap-and-build process, by creating more regionally and globally structured systems of production in East Asia (as well as in North America and Europe), has led to a hollowing out of the Japanese economy's growth potential and intensified competitive pressures on Japanese workers. As Morris-Suzuki (1996) observes, this structural crisis cries out for a more critical attitude toward the system that generated prior growth "successes":

> Japanese society is now at a crucial turning point. The forces that propelled the rapid economic growth of the postwar decades have exhausted themselves. . . . To understand Japan's present problems and future prospects, it is now important more than ever to go beyond a search for the *lessons of growth* and to pose new questions about the structure of the Japanese system and its relationship to the world economic order. (pp. 289-290; emphasis in original)

Neoliberalism offers a simple solution to this challenge: in order to transform itself into a successful mature capitalist political economy, Japan must give market forces freer rein over both resource allocation (the employment of land, labor, and capital) and the distribution of income and wealth. It must therefore abandon its outmoded "socialistic" institutions, including state planning, government controls over finance and trade, and the "lifetime employment" system. In short, Japan must become economically more like the United States (while maintaining and even enhancing its support for U.S. military and diplomatic leadership internationally). Meanwhile, the progressives who had supported the Japanese model as a superior alternative to U.S.-style "free-market" capitalism no longer have a coherent or politically viable answer to this standard neoliberal solution. They can only reassert the superiority of statist capitalism over free-market capitalism by ignoring the deep-rooted nature of Japan's systemic crisis and downplaying the essentially exploitative, undemocratic, and imperialistic nature of prior Japanese economic "successes." By eschewing a fundamental critique of capitalistic creative destruction, state-capitalist progressivism joins with neoliberalism in limiting the development debate to questions of means rather than ends. In the interest of moving beyond this technocratic and politically sterile debate, the next chapter considers the dilemmas of mature Japanese capitalism more closely.

Chapter 10

Dilemmas of Mature Japanese Capitalism

Japan's postwar economic development was only socialist insofar as one includes under "socialism" all forms of state intervention in the economy. In Japan, state economic activism was designed to enhance the economic power and international competitiveness of capitalist enterprise, not to fulfill the needs of workers and their communities. Its purpose was capitalist development, not human development. Neoliberalism distorts this reality when it blames Japan's current structural crisis on socialist or egalitarian values supposedly embedded in Japanese capitalism. However, it is not enough to expose the flaws in the neoliberal interpretation. One must also provide an alternative account of the basic dilemmas underlying Japan's contemporary crisis—an account that illuminates elements of Japanese reality that are neglected or distorted by neoliberalism.

From a Marxist perspective, the historical limits of any regime of capital accumulation are rooted in the contradiction between production for profit and production for human needs (Burkett, 1999, Chapter 12). This contradiction is constantly reproduced by capitalism's alienation of workers from control over necessary material and social conditions of production. Under capitalism, the means of production (and the producers themselves) are treated as mere instruments of value accumulation rather than as conditions of a sustainable human development. Moreover, as production driven by capital accumulation becomes increasingly socialized and reliant on an ever more broad and deep appropriation of natural resources, human needs and capabilities themselves become more social and ecological; yet capitalism remains a system of private appropriation. In this way, capitalist development intensifies the contradiction between human needs and production for profit.[1] One form this worsening tension takes is the growing difficulty capitalism has in finding profitable and productive investment outlets for the tremendous surplus product it is capable of generating anywhere near full employment. This difficulty underpins not only periodic recessions and prolonged periods of economic stagnation, but also the massive waste of resources on socially unproductive and even destructive pursuits (finance, advertising, artificial product obsolescence, the permanent military-industrial complex, etc.) characteristic of mature capitalism (Baran and Sweezy, 1966; Sweezy and Magdoff, 1988).

Applying the above framework, this chapter shows that Japan's current crisis is rooted in the dilemmas common to all mature capitalist economies; but it also shows how the various forms of the crisis have been conditioned by the specific responses of Japanese capital and its state to capitalist maturity. Driven mainly by the demands of competitiveness and private profitability, these responses have hastened the exhaustion of Japan's cultural, ecological, and even industrial fabric—thereby accentuating the crisis of mature capitalist reproduction while eroding the viability of the institutional mechanisms that have enabled Japan's governing elite to control the Japanese working class. The crisis thus contains the potential for a revival of working-class militancy and a movement for socialism from below. This potential sheds new light on both the dangers of defending the Japanese model and the need to push beyond its limitations which are really the human-developmental limits of capitalism itself.

In what follows, the historical crisis of Japanese capitalism is demonstrated through an overview of industrial hollowing-out as well as sectoral developments in agriculture, finance, the so-called leisure industry, and the military. Makoto Itoh's (1994) contention that the Japanese economy is suffering from a "distortion of its structure by exhausted and weakened working people" (p. 29) is then corroborated and placed within the broader dynamic of Japanese capital's national, regional, and global operations.[2] Before getting into the specifics of Japan's structural crisis, however, it is necessary to establish in a preliminary way that capitalist maturity problems are relevant to the postwar Japanese experience.

Maturation and Overaccumulation in Postwar Japanese Capitalism

Japan's postwar growth "miracle" was driven by high rates of capital investment supported by manufactured exports. But as the economy's plant and equipment were built up, it gradually became more difficult to find productive investment outlets for the growing surplus the system could generate near full-employment and full-capacity production levels. This difficulty was accentuated by the unwillingness of other developed capitalist countries (especially the United States) to accept ever-expanding manufactured imports from Japan. Such trade tensions prevented Japan from using increased exports as a permanent solution to its long-run surplus-capacity problems. The projection made two decades ago by Paul Sweezy thus proved correct:

> History teaches us, I believe, that every big capital-expansion boom sooner or later peters out. The build-up of Department I [plant and equipment production], especially if it is pretty much from scratch as was the case in postwar Japan, is a process that feeds on itself, sometimes for long periods. But when it comes to an end, as it always does, it precipitates a downturn for the system as a whole; and unless some powerful new factor, such as a war or a major innovation, enters the picture the downturn tends to level off onto a plateau of stagnation. (1980, p. 13)

There are at least two strong indications that the Japanese economy experienced a mounting overaccumulation of capital relative to profitable and productive investment opportunities as the growth miracle approached its end. First, Japanese corporations began to accumulate more internal funds than they could profitably invest in Japan. Tsuru (1993) charts the internal funds of Japanese manufacturing corporations (retained profits plus depreciation funds) as a ratio to their gross investments. During the years 1956-60, this ratio averaged 59 percent, but over 1971-75 it averaged 75 percent, and by 1976-80 it was averaging 109 percent. The same internal funds to gross investment ratio averaged more than 100 percent over the entire decade of the 1980s (p. 188). The rate of accumulation of surplus capital was even more rapid in certain key industries of the "miracle" period. Over the years 1960-70, the internal funds to gross investment ratio for construction firms rose from 58 to 146 percent, and for cement manufacturing it jumped from 47 to 107 percent. In the same period, the ratio grew from 34 to 154 percent for the precision machinery industry and from 29 to 109 percent for electrical machinery firms (p. 189).[3]

The second striking indicator of surplus capital relative to *productive* investment opportunities is the growing share of total employment taken up by "tertiary" industries (jobs outside the extractive, manufacturing, and construction industries). Indeed, even during the postwar recovery and growth-miracle periods, tertiary employment grew at least as rapidly as employment in manufacturing and construction. While the share of the employed labor force working in manufacturing and construction rose from 22.3 to 43.3 percent over the years 1947 through 1974, the tertiary employment share increased from 24.3 to 46.7 percent (Tsuru, 1993, p. 88). Although a significant portion of this tertiary job growth involved socially useful government employment (especially at the municipal and prefectural levels), it was mainly "fueled by an explosion of employment in commerce, finance, and services" (Sweezy, 1980, p. 5). The growth of such unproductive activity (the necessity of which stems solely from the capitalist organization of production and exchange rather than from human needs) "is far from unique to Japan"; what is unique is the sheer magnitude and "speed of the process" in the Japanese case (p. 5).[4]

It might be asked why Japan, having successfully built up an industrial base during the "miracle" period, could not move on to a new path of economic development featuring lower manufacturing investment, less reliance on unproductive activities to employ surplus productive capacity, and higher consumption—especially working-class consumption of useful public *and* private goods and services. Although such a transition would inevitably entail some slowdown of total output growth, it would promise broad improvements in living conditions, particularly if the increased working-class "consumption" were to include large-scale reductions in work time. Using a two-department scheme in which Departments I and II represent production of means of production and consumption goods, respectively, Sweezy explains why such a path was not followed:

> Of course theoretically [overaccumulation] can be counteracted by shifting resources out of Department I (those which had been employed in expanding Department I) to Department II where they can be used to increase the output of private and collective consumption goods. A planned socialist society should be able to effect such a transfer without too much difficulty: apart from purely technical problems, what is involved is an overall reduction in the rate of accumulation and a compensating increase in the rate of private-plus-public consumption. . . . But under capitalism the transfer in question would require a basic shift in the class distribution of income from those whose objective is the accumulation of capital (the endless expansion of exchange value) to those whose basic interest and concern are in the quantity and quality of use value. (1980, pp. 13–14)

Sweezy did not think "such a shift in income from the accumulators to the consumers" (and accompanying reorientation from exchange value to use value) was "at all likely" as long as Japan maintained its stature as "the strongest and least challenged dictatorship of the big bourgeoisie in the whole capitalist world" (p. 14). This prediction is corroborated by the analysis in Chapter 9. There it was shown that when the Japanese economy experienced growing surplus-capacity problems beginning in the 1970s, the response of Japanese capital and its state planners was not to attempt a transition to a less investment-intensive and less export-led growth path. Instead, they tried to out-muscle the dilemmas of capitalist maturity by engineering repeated rounds of scrap-and-build, that is, by using the system's abundant surplus funds for outward FDI and for the build-up of newer export-oriented industries on the home front (Tsuru, 1993, pp. 192–195). Here again, such "creative destruction" is hardly unique to Japan. But the relatively great power of capital over labor in Japan, and the resulting "flexibility" of the Japanese labor force, did allow Japanese capital to pursue industrial restructuring and manufactured-export growth more forcefully and on a larger scale than was possible for the ruling classes of other developed capitalist countries (Steven, 1997, pp. 201–204). As a result, despite the growing accumulation of surplus capital—and with due allowance for short-term instabilities—Japan experienced internationally high rates of investment and economic growth up until the late 1980s, when the scrap-and-build strategy was finally exhausted and the "bubble economy" deflated.

Capitalist Maturity and Hollowing-Out

The flying geese approach to development suggests that Japan needed repeated rounds of scrap-and-build to maintain its industrial strength (see Chapter 2). The reality, however, is that the industrial strength of Japan (or of any other individual country) is not the primary concern of Japanese capital. Since the mid-1980s, Japanese capital's overarching strategy has been to create regional operating zones in North America, Europe, and Asia—with production, finance, and trade increasingly integrated over the core and periphery within and across these three zones (Steven, 1996). Although East Asia appears to play a dominant role in this global strategy, especially in manufacturing (see Chapters 11 and 12), this does not preclude a further hollowing-out of Japanese industry. Indeed, Steven suggests that insofar as Japanese capital's "Asia-zone strategy" combines "the quest for lower costs with the quest for secure and growing markets," it is "finally beginning to hollow-out *(kudoka)* Japanese industry on a scale comparable to the United States and the United Kingdom" (1997, pp. 205-206).

This hollowing-out of Japanese industry—largely through the substitution of outward FDI for domestic investments in manufacturing—has often been denied.[5] But there is considerable evidence to support it. According to estimates by the Japan Machinery Exporters' Association, as of 1994 the value of manufacturing production by Japanese companies in Asia was already about one-fourth as high as the value of manufacturing production in Japan (Steven, 1996, p. 76). Takatoshi Ito (1996) provides further details on this migration of production and employment from Japan to offshore manufacturing zones:

> The Asian and North American subsidiaries of the Japanese firms, especially in the automobile and electronics industries, have been expanding rapidly in terms of both employment and sales. From 1990 to 1994, the number of employees in the Asian subsidiaries increased from about 500,000 to 1 million; while in the North American subsidiaries, the number increased from 370,000 to 523,000 during the same period. The sales of these subsidiaries . . . have expanded by 20 to 30 percent in the currencies of their host countries. As key manufacturing firms expand their overseas operations, they cut back production in Japan. Japanese manufacturing employment fell from 15.7 million employees in 1992 to 14.6 million in 1995. (p. 220)

By 1995, offshore production of cars by Japanese corporations had surpassed car exports from Japan. In the same year, Japanese auto companies exported 167,000 cars from their U.S. and Canadian plants—exceeding the 163,000 exported by the "Big Three" U.S. car companies. More than half of the exports from the North American facilities of Japanese car companies were being sold in Japan as of the mid-1990s. At the same time, Honda was already the top-ranked exporter of cars from the United States, with approximately 20 percent of its U.S. production dedicated to exports. Like Toyota, Honda was now producing the majority of its cars outside Japan (Naughton and Borrus, 1996, p. 113).

To see how the offshore migration of large portions of industry has worsened Japan's economic problems, it is useful to consider the country's exchange-rate dilemma. As discussed earlier, the postwar growth miracle was supported by an undervalued yen which (together with low unit wage costs) enhanced the competitiveness of Japan's manufactured exports. Eventually, however, the United States and other developed countries demanded a revaluation of the yen, leading to the "high yen crisis" of the mid-1980s. The higher yen posed a serious quandary for the Japanese economy: while it reduced the competitiveness of domestic production by raising unit wage costs in foreign currency (especially U.S. dollar) terms, it did nothing to increase domestic wage-based demand and thus nothing to reduce the economy's reliance on exports. As Steven (1988b) observed at the time:

> What has become unique to Japan is the combination of two features of Japanese wages which are further consolidating export-oriented accumulation. First, at current exchange rates, Japanese money wages are higher than American wages, bringing to an end the era of Japan *as a cheap* production place and spurring capital abroad in search of lower wages, even to such places as the US. Second, real wages *in Japan* are still at most only about 60% of real wages *in the US*, and Japanese workers have to save massively to cope with the huge proportion of their lifetime earnings which is absorbed by such things as housing, education, old age and health care. The result is that the higher money wages of Japanese than American workers translate into neither higher living standards nor into greater purchasing power for consumer goods. This is why capital also continues to look to high wages countries in North America and Europe to market consumer goods, since in spite of the higher yen, the disposable income of Japanese workers remains too low to sustain accumulation based on the domestic consumer market. Japanese workers thus face the prospect of growing unemployment and even further pressure on their living standards, since their wages are both too high and too low. Capital has less and less interest in them as either producers or consumers. (p. 77; emphases added)[6]

The combination of a stronger yen and weak domestic wage-based demand thus encouraged outward FDI and partial domestic deindustrialization, which in turn worsened Japan's long-run exchange-rate dilemma. From now on the stimulative effects of any yen depreciations would be much weaker given domestic hollowing-out.[7] Indeed, given Japan's growing reliance on imports of both consumer goods and industrial components produced by Japanese capital's offshore operations, a depreciating yen could create as many problems as it resolved (Ozawa, 1996, p. 489). A major weakening of the yen would also raise the effective cost of growing agricultural imports while increasing the risk of capital flight and threatening elite plans to convert Tokyo into a dominant global financial center (see below). All of this helps explain why the large yen depreciation of 1995-98 failed to effectively pull the Japanese economy out of recession, and why Japan currently faces a situation where "both rising and falling currency values seem to be damaging" (Wysocki, 1999, p. A1).

At a deeper level, the dilemmas posed by the exchange rate are a function of Japan's failure to confront the problem of capitalist maturity head-on. In place of an open social discussion and debate about how Japanese society could best use the massive surplus it is capable of producing near full employment, Japanese capital and its state have imposed the priorities of profitability and international competitiveness on Japanese workers and communities. As a result, the surplus has been utilized for a costly scrap-and-build, export-oriented process that has already—within the short span of four decades—exhausted its positive contributions to Japan's economic development. Ironically, the Japanese economy "has now lost much of the productive strength which drove it in quest of foreign markets in the first place" (Steven, 1997, p. 205). In the absence of a popular upsurge that puts a more worker-community centered response to capitalist maturity on the agenda, the outlook is for Japanese capitalism to converge with the U.S. model of semi-industrial, finance-driven, culturally impoverished, ecologically disastrous, and militarized capitalism. This dark prospect becomes clear upon an overview of sectoral developments.

The Sacrifice of Traditional Japanese Agriculture

The gradual running-down of Japanese agriculture can be traced to the Cold War alliance entered into by the U.S. and Japanese governments after World War II. After all, it was "under the U.S. military and food umbrella" that "Japan's economic development jumped into high gear" (Kazuoki, 1997, p. 182). Although the U.S. occupation did respond to postwar food shortages (and popular rural unrest) by sponsoring a serious land reform and other policies to increase domestic food supplies, it did not envision agriculture as a leading sector in Japan's export-led economic revival. Quite the contrary: Japan was to be used as an outlet for the agricultural surpluses of the United States (Steven, 1988b, p. 78).

It was not terribly difficult for Japan's ruling class to accept this arrangement. Even prior to the war, "the promotion of food exports was never considered to be central to [Japan's] national development program" (Jussaume, 1998, p. 404).[8] Moreover, the occupation-sponsored land reform greatly weakened the roles of rural landed property and agriculture as underpinnings of ruling-class power. Capitalist power became more completely centered on manufacturing industry and finance, especially with the full-scale reconsolidation of the *zaibatsu* and the heavy industrialization drive after Japan regained independence in 1952. The running-down of agriculture even resonated positively with this refocusing of ruling-class strength. "By actively promoting the urbanization of the population" and "fostering the social and economic restructuring which was needed to reinsert Japan into the new world imperialist system," it "strengthened the Japanese industrial bourgeoisie" (Halliday, 1978, p. 194). Meanwhile, the postwar land reform and ongoing agricultural subsidies continued to provide a ready base of rural support to the main governing party, the LDP (Liberal Democratic Party) (Halliday and McCormack, 1973, p. 170). Even as Japan became more urbanized, the effective weight of the LDP's rural vote was maintained by the allocation of legislative (Diet) seats according to the rural/urban population distribution as of 1950.[9] This is important because it was the LDP—together with the central government bureaucracy—that maintained capital's political domination throughout the growth-miracle period and beyond.

There are two basic ways in which Japanese agriculture was run down during and after the postwar high-growth era. First, compared to manufacturing, agriculture was simply not a high-priority sector for public and private investment. For a time, the government encouraged farm production with price supports, import barriers, and other subsidies—but such measures were not comparable to the all-out development efforts applied to heavy industry (1950s and 1960s) and to advanced machinery and electronics (1970s and 1980s). This relative deprioritization of agriculture, combined with government promotion of labor-saving farm technologies (so as to free up more labor for employment in urban industries) "led to a decline in the ability of production agriculture to support farm households and local economies. However, because of the small size of farm plots, proximity to off-farm job opportunities, government price support policies, and a cultural predisposition to maintain landownership, there was a dramatic shift from full-time to part-time farming with little reconsolidation of land into larger production units" (Jussaume, 1998, p. 409). Such was the "stagnation of the domestic agricultural system within its protected and controlled confines" (McCormack, 1996, p. 124).

The second main force in the running-down of Japanese agriculture was the growth of agricultural imports. These rising imports were partly a direct result of the immediate postwar arrangement between the Japanese and U.S. governments. Japan's post-surrender food crisis had a "lock-in effect" insofar as it demonstrated the country's potential "as the world's largest and most profitable market for U.S. agricultural surpluses (wheat, corn, soybeans, etc.)" (McCormack, 1996, p. 124). But as Japan's growth "miracle" kicked into high gear and Japanese manufactured exports began flooding the United States and other developed country markets, the demands for Japan to liberalize her agricultural imports took on a life of their own. "Since Japan depend[ed] on GATT for open export markets for its industrial and service exports," for example, "its resistance in the farm sector became more and more difficult to sustain" (p. 113). In the 1960s, "a series of agricultural goods was designated for step-by-step liberalization; coffee beans and cattle in 1960; fresh vegetables and soybeans in 1961; raw silk in 1962; bananas, raw sugar, coffee, and honey in 1963; and so on" (Kazuoki, 1997, p. 182). Then "Japan's encroachments in the 1970s and 1980s on U.S. markets for industrial goods led to and fueled U.S. demands for remaining barriers [on agricultural imports] to be swept away. Swept away they were, in one sector after another, up to citrus fruits and beef (1991)" (McCormack, 1996, p. 124). Even "the final citadel of rice" came under attack during the 1993 GATT negotiations (p. 124).

The low priority of agriculture in domestic development policy has interacted in various ways with external trade-related pressures to worsen Japan's creeping agricultural crisis. For example, the relative stagnation of Japanese agricultural investment and productivity, together with successive upward revaluations of the yen (largely at the insistence of the United States), "increased the gap between domestic and international prices of agricultural products" (Kazuoki, 1997, pp. 187–188). This not only boosted agricultural imports directly, but also increased the cost of the Japanese government's agricultural price supports (especially for rice) to the point where "the Agricultural Ministry turned from encouraging production to attempting to limit it, and, year after year, designated acreages were removed from production" (McCormack, 1996, p. 124). Thus, the growing cost of agricultural subsidies was not simply a result of misguided government protection as neoliberals would argue. The problem stemmed from the marginalization of agriculture in pursuit of industrial accumulation, and from the reactions of the United States and other developed countries to Japan's export successes. It was, in short, "inherent in the Japanese economic structure" (Kazuoki, 1997, p. 186).

This sacrifice of domestic agriculture on the altar of export-led growth has left Japan increasingly reliant on food imports, thereby reducing the country's food security. "Thus from 1985 to 1988 Japanese imports of agricultural products increased 138.4 percent, and Japan became the largest agricultural importer in the world" (Kazuoki, 1997, p. 188). Between 1960 and 1992, Japan's overall rate of self-sufficiency in grains (including grains used as animal feed) declined from 82 to 29 percent, while its self-sufficiency ratio in terms of agricultural calories consumed (including consumption of meat and dairy products) fell from 79 to 46 percent (pp. 183, 197). All this happened *before* the partial liberalization of rice imports as part of the GATT Uruguay Round Agreement of 1993. Japan's reduced agricultural self-sufficiency has "drastically diminished the security of people's livelihood" by exposing them to "an extraordinary degree of vulnerability to market forces beyond their control" (McCormack, 1996, p. 123). This apparent "faith in the continuance of an open and surplus world food market . . . looks increasingly shortsighted and . . . contrasts sharply with the long-term perspective that is often said to characterize Japanese corporations" (p. 141).

Japan's voracious appetite for agricultural imports now threatens the long-run development prospects not only of Japan but of other East Asian countries. Japan consumes one-third of the world's annual tuna catch, two-fifths of its shrimp, and one-fourth of its annual tropical timber harvest—much of it plundered from offshore East Asia (McCormack, 1996, p. 78). The "increase in Japanese imports of fresh agricultural products and semi processed products from Southeast Asia" has been "pushed by the multinational food companies' drive to export to Japan agricultural products produced in countries where wages are low and cheap raw materials are available" (Kazuoki, 1997, p. 188). Indeed, "Japanese living standards" are now "predicated on . . . an ability to continue to monopolize a vastly disproportionate share of the region's food resources" (McCormack, 1996, pp. 141-142).[10] The sacrifice of Japanese agriculture has thus placed Japan in "a relationship with its neighbor countries that combines domination and dependence, contradiction rather than cooperation"—once more betraying the "Asian values" that supposedly underpinned the Japanese and East Asian "miracles" (p. 144).

Meanwhile, traditional Japanese agriculture is increasingly incapable of self-reproduction (Kazuoki, 1997, pp. 189-198). Even part-time farming has become economically unviable in the environment of liberalized agricultural imports and reduced domestic subsidies. As of the mid-1990s, abandoned fields made up 20 percent of the country's useable farmland, and the agricultural population had aged to the point of "leaving only 6.5 percent of farming households with the prospect of an heir" (McCormack, 1996, p. 124). The remaining farmers are under extreme pressure to convert to "modern" agricultural systems of the U.S. type—with greater use of artificial pesticides, inorganic fertilizers, and monocropping systems controlled by transnational agribusiness. Those able to eke out a living in this way do so only at the cost of backbreaking labor and increased health hazards from the increasingly toxic agricultural environment. With the decimation of traditional farm practices, "many Japanese rural areas are experiencing a weakening socio-economic infrastructure" (defunct or moribund cooperative organizations, for example) as well as a "deterioration in community structures and solidarity" (Jussaume, 1998, p. 409). This rural decay "is being accompanied by a national policy push to reorganize agriculture around larger production units that, it is hoped, will make Japanese agriculture more 'competitive'" (p. 409).

In other words, Japan's ruling class has no interest in any effort to recover and improve the tremendous cultural and ecological wealth bound up with traditional Japanese agriculture—if necessary by investing part of the country's considerable surplus in the renovation of traditional practices. Instead, it only sees an opportunity to "solve" the farm crisis by transforming Japanese agriculture along the ecologically and culturally disastrous lines pioneered by the U.S. agribusiness and food-processing industries. Agriculture is to become just one more source of "profit-making opportunities for firms" regardless of the social costs (Jussaume, 1998, p. 409). This is the logical endpoint of any development strategy operating within the parameters of capitalist profitability and competitiveness. The fact is that Japan's ruling class "has chosen to demolish [traditional] agriculture to ensure its own survival, a choice that also satisfies the demands of other advanced capitalist countries, especially the United States" (Kazuoki, 1997, p. 187). This illustrates how, after a certain point, capitalism exhausts any society's reproductive capabilities. To stop and reverse this exhaustion, the use of society's resources must be guided not by exchange value but by use value—by the goal of human development.

The Twisted Logic of Finance-Led Accumulation

It was in the mid–1980s—just as large chunks of Japanese industry were being shipped offshore and the Japanese people began hearing more lectures on how traditional agriculture was an economic liability—that the bubble economy took off. While treating the renewal of domestic industry and agriculture on terms friendly to workers, communities, and the ecology as an unaffordable luxury, mature Japanese capitalism utilized a rising share of its tremendous potential surplus for speculative finance and construction.

This perverse development was not due to any sudden breakdown of Japan's vaunted state-planning apparatus; quite the contrary. The bureaucracy not only accommodated but actively encouraged finance and construction as new leading sectors in Japan's planned economic growth. The government's "low interest rate policy," previously used to promote priority manufacturing industries, now ensured abundant supplies of cheap credit for construction companies and real estate firms.[11] Banks were not just allowed to increase their own real estate and construction loans to dangerously high levels (up to one-third of total bank loans, with real estate firms alone taking up one-quarter of the total). The authorities also took no action to prevent banks from lending their reserves to less-regulated financial institutions specializing in real estate and construction loans. Such "non-bank bank loans" eventually "accounted for as much as 37.8 percent of the total loans the real estate industry secured" (Ozawa, 1999, p. 356). The bubble economy was also underwritten by government subsidies and tax breaks for urban development projects. Together with the deregulation of urban land use, these measures helped accelerate the inflation of land prices while encouraging the further growth of Japan's bloated construction industry (Oizumi, 1994, pp. 201-202).[12]

Japanese business and government spokespersons applauded the bubble economy as the dawn of a "post-industrial" development "firmly grounded in a hard base of construction and civil engineering, whose technology and capital would help confer other significant long-term competitive advantages . . . to compensate for the decline of traditional industries" (McCormack, 1996, p. 30). In reality, the bubble economy signaled Japan's socially irrational movement toward a finance-led pattern of development, due to the absence of more productive *and privately profitable* outlets for the country's burgeoning economic surplus.[13] For example, as the big "non-financial" corporations began "rapidly accumulating . . . their own internal funds," they not only engaged in large-scale land and stock-share speculation on their own, but also became less dependent on bank loans (Ozawa, 1999, p. 355). "Having lost many large manufacturers as their prime borrowers, the banks had to find new customers" and real estate dealers, construction firms, and stock market operators were obvious candidates (p. 355). In this way, "expanding surplus funds went into the stock market and land speculation" (Oizumi, 1994, p. 202).

Insofar as the bubble economy was associated with a partial loosening of government financial controls, the ultimate determining factors were still the overaccumulation of surplus and the failure of government policy to question capitalist priorities. As Japanese corporations and banks used their growing surplus funds for outward FDI and other forms of external expansion, their "successful endeavors vigorously to penetrate foreign product and financial markets generated increasing demands for reciprocity. Japanese money and capital markets had to be opened reciprocally to foreign financial institutions, or Japan would face exclusion from some of the western financial markets" (Raines and Leathers, 1995, p. 363). "The experiences of Japanese financial institutions in the more open money and capital markets of the west served," moreover, "to re-shape their attitudes toward the domestic Japanese system. These institutions became increasingly interested in exploiting new profit opportunities in Japan that would be provided by reductions in both the degree of segmentation and interest rate regulations" (p. 363).

This background helps explain why many economists continued to tout finance as a potential "growth industry" for the Japanese economy even in the post–bubble period, that is, if remaining "restrictive" regulations could be removed (Ito, 1996, p. 244). (The high savings rates of Japanese households also had foreign financial services firms licking their chops.) The prioritization of finance and its liberalization—leading to the Big Bang financial reforms of 1998—was an ironic culmination of Japan's scrap-and-build development strategy. Now the sectoral "upgrading" of the Japanese economy required a severe weakening of the same government planning apparatus that had helped engineer the country's industrialization. For Japan to become a leading international financial center, inflows and outflows of capital as well as domestic interest rates would have to be freed up. "This, in turn, required that the domestic financial system become more flexible" (Raines and Leathers, 1995, p. 363). Above all, "stockholder rights" (the single-minded pursuit of maximum short-term profit regardless of long-run economic and social costs) would have to reign basically unopposed over the Japanese economy if Tokyo hoped to compete with Wall Street.

By the spring of 1999, this finance-led upgrading was already showing definite signs of success. The Japanese stock market was rallying on the strength of rising purchases by Western investors. Global "money managers," previously "skeptical that Japan would take the painful restructuring steps economists feel are necessary," now detected "a real change . . . in government attitudes"—based on the government's apparent willingness to allow "increased corporate restructuring" and rising unemployment to proceed more or less unhindered (Lande, 1999, p. C23). As the *Wall Street Journal* reported:

> Even figures suggesting that Japan's lengthy recession is far from over have been interpreted benevolently by some investors. For example, one U.S. fund manager said that the recent Japanese unemployment data showing that the jobless rate there climbed to a postwar high of 4.6% are a sign of welcome corporate restructuring. "The unemployment rate will probably go a little higher, but that's not necessarily a bad thing," said Bin Shi, who runs U.S. Global Investors' China-Region Opportunity Fund in San Antonio. "If companies are not hiring excess labor, that's good for the bottom line." (Karmin, 1999, p. C12)

With this kind of progress, who knows? Perhaps Japan could eventually experience the same kind of financial domination over industry and labor that the U.S. ruling class had been enjoying since the early 1980s.

The Leisure Industry and Cultural-Ecological Decay

Alongside the running-down of traditional agriculture, Japan's governing elite began to push resort development as a new "growth industry" for economically depressed rural areas. In his definitive account, Gavan McCormack (1996) describes how this "resortification" movement was closely tied to the bubble economy with its "speculation and corruption" (p. 88). "As the Tokyo money spread over the countryside . . . [t]owns, villages, and prefectures throughout the country entered into such intense competition to be designated as resort areas that, as of December 1991, around 20 percent of the entire land area of Japan was designated for resort development (7.5 million hectares, as against 5.5 million for agriculture)" (pp. 88, 92). In this way, resort development "infected the whole country with the vices of speculation and inflation, exacting as heavy a price on the social and moral values of local Japanese communities as did (in many cases) the resorts themselves of the physical environment" (p. 92).

Indeed, despite official references to resortification as a "greening" of the Japanese archipelago, it did not involve the maintenance and restoration of the country's cultural and ecological heritage. Instead, it converted Japan into "a land of chemicalized golf courses, expensive marinas, toll expressways that penetrated the deepest mountains, and resorts that multiplied the ideology and aesthetics of Disneyland, where culture meant consumption" (McCormack, 1996, p. 87). Rural ecological systems now came under a double attack: while traditional farming was being displaced by the energy- and pollution-intensive technologies of transnational agribusiness, the golf courses and other resort facilities began pumping out their own massive toxic soups.[14] In short, the resortification movement testifies to the inability of mature Japanese capitalism to use its tremendous potential surplus in ways that promote a sustainable human development. As McCormack observes:

> The tide of golf courses, ski resorts, and marinas that now arises over the land is striking for its irrelevance to the needs and problems of local communities, many of whom now see the whole process as a contemporary form of enclosure movement, in which public land, forests, mountains, and beaches are enclosed by private interests for corporate profit. While corporate Japan thrives, they say, the people suffer. Hence the recently coined slogan: *fukoku*

hinmin (Enrich the country, impoverish the people). It is a phrase that points to the poverty at the heart of affluence. (p. 106)

Given the concurrent external expansion of Japanese industry and finance, it should not be surprising that the resortification movement itself was rapidly regionalized beginning in the mid-1980s, as "the level of capital flowing out of Japan into tourism and real-estate development around the region grew steadily" (p. 93). Along with Australia and Hawaii, countries like Thailand and Malaysia—where much of the population lived close to or under physical subsistence—became dotted with golf courses and resort hotels frequented by Japanese managers and professionals. Many of these offshore resort facilities were built by Japanese construction companies with the help of Japanese bank loans and other "foreign aid" moneys.[15] The cultural and ecological degradation of the bubble economy and resortification were thus "reproduced through a widening regional and global sphere" (p. 93).

A similar pattern of degradation—in this case the direct physical *and* cultural degradation of human beings, mainly women—is evident in another of Japan's growing leisure industries, namely, the child sex industry. Japan is, in fact, a global leader in both child pornography and child prostitution. On the pornographic front, Japan "probably produces four-fifths of all the videos and magazines that show children in sexual situations" (*Economist,* 1999c, p. 32). As of 1997, over 40 percent of Japan's estimated 3,000 pornographic websites featured images of children (p. 32). "Interpol, the international police agency, has estimated that between 70 percent and 80 percent of the child pornography available on the internet came [sic] from Japanese sources" (Strom, 1999a, p. A6). "Newsstands and bookstores [in Tokyo] stock a selection of magazines featuring glossy photos of little girls in swimsuits or short skirts, with slightly suggestive close-ups of thighs, crotches and buttocks not quite completely covered by panties" (p. A6). Not surprisingly, Japan has been censured by the UN for its "lax attitude to child pornography" (*Economist,* 1999c, p. 32).

Child prostitution is rampant in Japan, and the situation is getting worse. Indeed, Japanese police cited schoolgirl prostitution (along with drug taking) as a prime factor behind the country's 14.5 percent increase in juvenile crime in 1998 (*Economist,* 1999c, p. 32). "Shinji Miyadai, a sociologist at Tokyo Metropolitan University, estimates that 8% of schoolgirls nationwide—and one-third of girls at some schools that aren't geared toward the college-bound—are involved in the sex industry" (Reitman, 1996b, p. A8). While Japan's economic recession has accentuated the problem, it has also been worsened by the cheapening of cellular phones that facilitate girls' participation in the "telephone clubs . . . where men can wait for calls from teenage girls"—such clubs being "one way the girls fall into the prostitution habit" (p. A8). The "sudden growth of *enjo kosai* (compensated dating), a polite expression for schoolgirl prostitution" has also been fed by girls' desires for designer clothing, jewelry, and accessories: "$500 Prada purses and $350 Louis Vuitton wallets are hot teen items" (*Economist*, 1999c, p. 32; Reitman, 1996b, p. A8). In short, the problem reflects not just poverty but also the evisceration of Japanese culture by capitalistic values of hedonistic consumption—a development in which the bubble economy's luxury consumption boom no doubt played a major role.[16]

As with the resortification movement, the Japanese child sex industry is not limited to Japan. "Japanese companies have arranged tours to Asian countries whose overriding aim is to introduce men to children with whom they can have sex" (Strom, 1999a, p. A6). Such sex-tourism operations became much more common during the bubble economy period when they grew in tandem with the development of offshore resorts catering to the recreational needs of Japanese managers and professionals. Indeed, "the great majority of the men who tour the child-prostitution centers in the Philippines, Thailand, and other parts of Asia come from Japan" (*Economist*, 1999c, p. 32). Unlike in Japan, however, the participation of the non-Japanese child prostitutes is often forced or semiforced and virtually always borne of extreme poverty (see Chapter 12).

Another disturbing sign of cultural decay in Japan is the recent wave of sexist, sadist, and just plain stupid TV "game shows." There are, for example, "shows in which men compete to see who can keep from going to the bathroom the longest and in which women play games of Ping-Pong and the loser must strip" (Strauss, 1998, p. B2). One can watch a game of charades "with bad hints punishable by electric shocks," or another program in which "bikini-clad women" are "dunked into scaldingly hot water" and then given the chance to deliver a commercial for the same length of time they stayed in the water. The latter also offers a chance to see the women "rub ice over themselves or jump up and down in pain as the camera focuses on their reddened breasts and legs" (p. B2). A recent program "brought out a young child, told him that his mother had been shot to death and timed him to see how long it would take before he started crying"; in another, "two women [tried] to crush soda cans by putting them in their cleavages and squeezing their bikini-clad breasts together" (WuDunn, 1997a, p. A4).

There are many other examples.[17] The point is that the increasingly money-driven, crass, and hedonistic character of Japanese social life is degrading much of what was most valued in the country's cultural heritage while enhancing its worst patriarchal features. This whole tendency reflects the irrationality of mature capitalism as a system of human development.

The Remilitarization of Japan

To understand Japan's current military position, one must first grasp the tensions built into Japan's postwar security relationship with the United States. Article 9 of the new (1946) Japanese constitution stipulated that "the Japanese people" would "forever renounce war as a sovereign right of the nation and the threat or use of force as means of settling international disputes." Article 9 also stated that "land, sea, and air forces, as well as other war potential, will never be maintained" by Japan. This apparent demilitarization of Japan did carry important advantages for Japanese business. Together with the continued U.S. military presence in Japan (dictated by the 1951 Mutual Security Treaty imposed by the United States), "it reassured Japan's neighbors—most of whom suffered terribly from Japanese wartime aggression—that Japanese troops would no longer follow Japanese investment. The way was thus opened for renewed Japanese economic penetration and domination of the region's economies" (Gerson, 1996, p. 42). At the same time, and for obvious reasons, the United States did not interpret Article 9 as proscribing Japanese economic support for U.S. military operations in East Asia. Thus, Japan's postwar recovery was powered by "special procurements" associated with the Korean War (see Chapter 8). Similarly, the Vietnam War (and Japan's official commitment to the U.S.-client regime in South Vietnam under the 1969 Sato-Nixon communiqué) created important profit-making opportunities for Japanese business.[18] Japan's political and economic participation in U.S. Cold War designs paid an additional dividend: it helped keep the U.S. market open to Japanese exporters.

Japanese opposition to the country's Cold War arrangement with the United States tended to be more consistent and more intense at the grassroots level than among Japanese elites. While Article 9 of the constitution enjoyed broad support due to the deeply-rooted popular opposition to militarism, most of the Japanese people understood the dangers associated with their country's rapprochement with the U.S. diplomatic-military machine. Hence, the U.S.-imposed Mutual Security Treaty of 1951 "elicited intense opposition," as "the majority of the Japanese of all classes were hostile to a separate peace, especially one that would exclude China" (Kolko and Kolko, 1972, p. 530). Popular opposition to the 1960 "revision" of the treaty (which basically renewed it with only cosmetic changes) was even more intense, with large-scale street demonstrations and civil disobedience actions led by students and other peace activists (Halliday, 1978, pp. 252-254).[19]

In fact, the U.S.-Japan alliance has always been "rife with tensions," as Joseph Gerson points out: "Communities truncated by land seizures, and people traumatized by rape, sexual harassment, low-altitude and night-landing exercises, live-fire training, airplane crashes and other military accidents have repeatedly petitioned their government for relief" (1996, p. 42). As an internal colony, Okinawa has been forced to bear the heaviest burden from the ongoing U.S. military presence in Japan. To add insult to injury, the United States has forced Japan to cover a bigger and bigger share of the direct monetary costs of the U.S. military presence. The Japanese government now pays an annual $5 billion subsidy for the 45,000 U.S. soldiers based in Japan—about 70 percent of the cost of maintaining these troops (Bello, 1996d, p. 19).

Those who felt that the end of the Cold War would automatically reduce Japan's military entanglements with the United States were badly mistaken. "In order to maintain trade opportunities especially in the USA, by mitigating trade friction, Japan has become subject to the US demand to share the military costs of keeping the new world order" (Itoh, 1994, p. 49). In other words, the United States is now insisting that Japan step up its support for various U.S. military actions and security arrangements not only in East Asia but worldwide. This includes financial assistance (the more than $10 billion Japan donated to Operation Desert Storm, for example) as well as direct military participation by Japan's Self-Defense Forces (SDF) in U.S. military operations. In short, the process involves an accelerated remilitarization of Japan and of Japanese international relations—with Japan becoming a much more active accomplice in U.S. policing efforts for global capitalism. Naturally, East Asia has a central place in U.S.-Japanese elite plans for Japan's expanded military role (*Economist,* 1999a).

The remilitarization of Japanese international relations was codified in May 1999 when the Japanese Diet approved the new "Guidelines for U.S.-Japan Defense Cooperation." These guidelines effectively killed Article 9 of Japan's Peace Constitution by providing for "U.S.-Japanese military cooperation not only in the event of a direct attack on Japan . . . but also in the event of 'situations in areas surrounding Japan.' The term 'situations' is about as vague as language can get, and the expression 'areas surrounding Japan' is, according to the Guidelines, 'not geographic, but situational'" (Lummis, 1999, p. 14). When the guidelines were passed by the lower house of the Diet on April 27, 1999, a U.S. State Department spokesman, James P.

Rubin, argued that they would "enable the U.S. and Japan to respond quickly and flexibly to any contingencies that might arise" (Kristof, 1999a, p. A5). Three months later, the Japanese government's annual defense report reinterpreted Japan's "right to defend itself" as "including the use of military strikes to prevent likely attacks" (Sakurai, 1999, p. A7).

The new guidelines were the culmination of a long-standing U.S.-Japanese elite campaign to weaken the significance of Article 9 and to bring the Japanese military and Japanese society back into step with international "political realities" as defined by the needs of global capitalism with the United States at its head (Itsunori, 1994, pp. 8–9; Gerson, 1996, pp. 42–44). Previous years had already seen a gradual rebuilding of Japan's military capabilities, and by 1997 the country's annual military budget was the highest in East Asia at $40.9 billion (compared to China's $36.6 billion) (*Economist,* 1999a, p. 24). Beginning in the late 1980s, all three (land, sea, and air) components of Japan's SDF had been reorganized and modernized for operations abroad (Itsunori, 1994, p. 7). The Japanese military is now top-heavy with officers and weapons-production capacity; it would thus be easy for Japan to rapidly expand its military in terms of fully-equipped personnel. Moreover, Japan's "technological infrastructure has been . . . integrated into the U.S. military-industrial complex through joint research on a number of weapons systems, including the FSX fighter and theater missile defenses" (Gerson, 1996, p. 42).[20]

The success of the elite campaign to remilitarize Japan is also evident on the ideological front. Shortly after Japan participated in the 1992 United Nations peacekeeping operation in Kampuchea (in direct violation of Article 9), the traditionally anti-militarist Japan Socialist Party "abandoned its longstanding claim that Japan's military forces are unconstitutional . . . [and] pledged to uphold the U.S.-Japan military alliance, which the party once violently opposed" (Associated Press, 1994). In the spring of 1999 (immediately after the Diet's passage of the new Guidelines for U.S.-Japan Defense Cooperation), the Japanese Cabinet "approved a proposal to make the rising sun flag and a song of praise to the emperor the official national flag and anthem," and the government was hoping that the Diet would approve this rehabilitation of two "emblems of World War II militarism" in its current session (Kristof, 1999b, p. A5). More broadly, the absence of open mass opposition to Japan's growing military cooperation with the United States—the main arms supplier to governments throughout East Asia[21]—demonstrates how successful the U.S.-Japan elite alliance has been in removing all alternatives to the permanent militarization of international relations from the political agenda.

Some observers on the left have argued that the remilitarization of Japan is due to a lack of courage on the part of Japan's governing elite in the face of U.S. power. Walden Bello, for example, criticizes "the timidity of Japanese officialdom" towards the United States, and complains that "Japan does not have the nerve to downgrade the U.S.-Japan security alliance and to decisively lead the region in forging a new multilateral system of peace and security" (1996d, p. 19). However, one may question whether it would be in the interests of Japanese capital and its state functionaries to attempt to forge their own regional alternative to global-capitalist diplomacy, U.S.-style. After all, the postwar recovery of Japanese economic power in East Asia occurred, and is still maintained, under the U.S. military umbrella. And there is something surreal about the image of Japan (the same Japan that profited handsomely from the Korean and Vietnam Wars) pursuing some kind of peaceful Asian way of capitalism together with the same governments that have eagerly armed themselves to the teeth with U.S. weaponry. When one adds Japan's massive trade and financial relations with the United States (not to mention Japanese capital's large-scale North American production facilities), it becomes clear that more than "timidity" or "lack of nerve" underlies the U.S.-Japanese elite alliance.

The real problem here is the contradiction between the conditions of world peace and the conditions of both capital accumulation and the maintenance of ruling-class power. World peace requires an economic system that puts its surplus to use for human development on national, regional, and global levels—and this is not something that capitalism (either U.S. or Japanese) is capable of doing. Instead, capitalism invests its surplus in ways that accentuate the uneven development of countries and regions, and then fuels the resulting international (and inter-ethnic) antagonisms with armaments. Capitalism erodes the conditions of human development and then, when workers and communities rebel, it uses its tremendous resources to forcibly "stabilize" the system on privately profitable terms. The Japanese ruling class and its state functionaries (and the other subordinate ruling classes in East Asia) are part of this system; they could only "opt out" of it by opting out of capitalism itself. Stated differently, Japan's remilitarization merely demonstrates that class suicide is not something that a capitalist class typically does.

Exhaustion of Human Resources

Having intensively exploited its human and nonhuman resources over four decades of industrial creative destruction, Japan should now use its huge productive capabilities to renew and reinvigorate these resources and to create a system of sustainable human development. But the capitalistic dis-empowerment of Japanese workers and their communities prevents them from carrying out the needed transformation. The scrap-and-build pattern of industrial development has alienated the system of production vis-à-vis the needs and capabilities of Japanese workers. This system expends an increasing amount of resources on wasteful and destructive activities (factory-farming, financial speculation, the leisure industry, and remilitarization). Meanwhile, with industrial hollowing-out, rising unemployment, and financial deregulation, the competitive pressures on Japanese workers show no sign of abating and may in fact be worsening. For example, the record official unemployment rate of 4.9 percent in June 1999 translated into a 6.4 percent decline of nominal wages and earnings compared to one year ear-lier. Homeless workers living on the street are now a visible feature of Japanese cities—and the problem is no longer limited to ghettos of foreign workers (*Economist,* 1999g, p. 80 and 1999b, p. 53).

Makoto Itoh has even argued that the Japanese economy now faces a long-run crisis of "exhausted and weakened working people," that is, a sit-uation where "the very success of Japanese capitalist firms in getting their employees to work harder is destroying their social foundation in terms of the necessity to reproduce a healthy labour force" (1994, pp. 29, 46). His argument is based not only on the long daily average work times of Japan-ese workers (see below) but also on the growing evidence of work-related exhaustion and tensions (e.g., the estimated 23,000 Japanese workers between 30 and 60 years of age who die suddenly each year) (p. 46).[22] And Itoh is not the only observer to detect a worsening human-resource crisis in Japan. A decade ago, Keisuke Aoki noted that the "perennial use of over-time, long work hours, and work intensification are not consistent with the model of Japanese-style management that depends heavily on the 'human factor'" (1991, p. 62).

Itoh's dark picture of human-resource exhaustion clashes with the pop-ular image of Japan as an egalitarian, nurturing society unwilling to abide by capitalism's "survival of the fittest" rules. As previous chapters have shown, however, the popular image is more myth than reality. Japanese eco-nomic growth has always been fueled by intensive exploitation of labor, and the post–World War II era was no exception. The most obvious indicator of this exploitation is work time. Indeed, the Japanese Marxist economist Koji Morioka refers to "the combination of a technologically advanced position and long working hours" as one of "the most striking characteris-tics of the Japanese economy" (1991, p. 12).

According to the Japanese Ministry of Labor, the average annual work time in Japan was 2,168 hours per worker in 1988, which translated into an average work week of 43.2 hours compared to 38.5 hours in the United States and 35.9 hours in West Germany (Kates, et al., 1992, pp. J3, J5). However, as pointed out by Gavan McCormack, these official figures greatly understate the relative length of Japanese work time insofar as they exclude a large amount of what is euphemistically called "voluntary overtime" in Japan. He cites estimates that when such unpaid overtime is included, the measured annual average work time of Japanese workers (as of 1991) may have been "as high as 2,617 hours for men and 2,409 hours for women" (McCormack, 1996, p. 80).[23] Not surprisingly, "fewer than 20 percent of Japanese workers enjoy a two-day weekend" (p. 80). To these extended work times must be added the extremely long commutes suffered by many Japanese workers, partly due to the inflation of land and housing prices at locations nearer to workplaces. Workers' average commuting time is "about two hours round trip in the metropolitan areas" (Morioka, 1991, p. 24), and "over 20 percent of the Tokyo workforce commutes for more than three hours per day" (McCormack, 1996, p. 105). In short, "many of Japan's 'corporate soldiers'" live a life mainly composed of "leaving for work at seven in the morning, quitting around nine at night, and getting home at ten or eleven" (Morioka, 1991, p. 24). No wonder that in "a recent survey of Tokyo families, 10% of parents said they did not talk to their spouse at all, and another 51% said they spent 30 minutes or less in conversation with each other each day" (*Economist*, 1999d, p. 48).

Japan's egalitarian image also clashes with the reality of real wage growth lagging far behind the growth of hourly production per worker. Every major expansion of the Japanese economy since the late nineteenth century has featured a widening gap between labor productivity and real wages (see Chapters 6 and 9). In the last two decades this tendency has, if anything, become more extreme. "For instance, in Japanese manufacturing labour productivity increased 2.17 times from 1975 to 1985, almost as fast as in the period of high economic growth, whereas real wages increased only by 5.9 per cent in the same 10 years. Even in the phase of expansion in 1986-90, the disparity was wide between the 33.9 per cent increase in labour productivity and the 8.7 per cent increase in real wages" (Itoh, 1994, p. 45).

Japan's egalitarian reputation is even more puzzling in light of comparative international statistics on the distribution of household income. Carefully surveying the available evidence, Bauer and Mason (1992) conclude that "the overall distribution of income in Japan is probably less equal than often claimed and similar to the distribution in other OECD countries," even though "Japan's lowest income groups are relatively better off than those in many other industrialized countries" (p. 407). The latter finding may partly reflect the undercounting of foreign "guest" workers in the official Japanese statistics. Bauer and Mason also note that income equality "did not increase during the economic boom of the late 1980s, despite the upsurge in business activity." The reason? "Increased income from interest, dividends, and capital gains generated by rising stock prices . . . offset further wage gains" (p. 408). An earlier study by Ishizaki (1985-86), based on data for the late 1960s and early 1970s, found that "the income distribution is somewhat less equal in Japan than the average of the OECD countries," partly because of Japan's larger wage differentials by firm size and worker age,[24] and partly because "the concentration of property income in the high-income group is much greater in Japan than in the [other] major OECD countries" (pp. 41, 44). Ishizaki also found that "in Japan, the proportion of property income in personal income is considerably larger than in the [other] major OECD countries" (p. 44). Considering further that "wealth in Japan as in other countries, is much less equally distributed than income," and that the "rapid appreciation of the stock market and land prices during the late 1980s led to greater inequality in the distribution of wealth" (Bauer and Mason, 1992, pp. 415, 403), one really has to wonder where Japan's egalitarian reputation came from.

From a Marxist perspective, it is not surprising that Japan's distribution of income and wealth is at least as unequal as in other developed capitalist countries. Specifically, this finding reflects the successful efforts of Japanese capital and its state functionaries to stifle any militant classwide organization of the country's workers. And despite Japan's reputation for participatory corporate labor relations, this disempowerment extends into the labor processes of individual enterprises. Admirers of Japanese management often speak as if workers' control over production decisions is something that can be technocratically engineered rather than struggled for on a classwide basis. This has led them to confuse the *appearance* of greater worker autonomy and control with the *realities* of continued hierarchical management and the use of "teams" and other "cooperative" intra-enterprise techniques to obtain workers' consent "in the escalation of their own exploitation" (Hoogvelt, 1995, p. 721; cf. Dassbach, 1993; Hideo, et al., 1994). As pointed out by Tatsuo Naruse, "post-Fordist" conceptions of the management practices employed by Toyota and other large Japanese corporations tend to downplay the fact that in these systems

> improvement in labor productivity does not mean reduction of the standard
> input quantity of human labor per hour—the usual meaning of improve-

ment in labor productivity on the basis of production technology—but rather increase of input; in other words, it means improvement in productivity through increased intensity of labor. . . . It is therefore not correct to regard it as a new production system with a revolutionary technology surpassing the Ford system and thereby achieving a new level of productivity. (1991, p. 45)

Naruse argues further that:

Some writers who regard the Japanese production system as post-Fordist assert that multifunctional workers and [quality control] circle activities mean restoration of craft work, workers' autonomous control, and workers' return to the position of master over the machine system. But such assertions seem to overestimate or misunderstand the real situation. Under the present-day Japanese production system, the scope of transfer of management authority relating to production control to lower grades is very limited. It is barely possible to transfer the authority to define product design, manufacturing lot size, or manufacturing and process speed. Transfer of authority is mainly limited to factory layout for the purpose of improvement in work environment, maintenance and inspection of machinery in the manufacturing process, and activities relating to quality control. The multifunctional worker concept does not imply a skilled worker, as in the age of general machinery, before assembly-line production. (1991, pp. 45–46)

In short, "the idea that the Japanese production system is flexible and suited to human nature is based on a lack of understanding about the conditions of workers. . . . Disregard for or underestimation of the suffering that lies behind high efficiency and flexibility leads to a misunderstanding of the realities of the Japanese production system" (pp. 33–34). Perhaps the most important of these realities is that "enterprise unionism, in which membership is restricted to a firm's [permanent] employees, predominates in Japan" (Benson, 1996, p. 372). The strictly limited power of Japanese workers, both in the workplace and in wage negotiations, is largely based on the inherent weaknesses of the enterprise union form. Tsuru and Rebitzer (1995) provide a useful summary of these weaknesses:

Enterprise unions, by their very nature, allow management and labour to reach agreements that are well suited to the particular needs of an enterprise. The identification of the union with the enterprise, however, limits the willingness of the union to seek wage gains that might hinder the competitive position of the company. Should profits come under pressure (as happened in Japan as a result of the oil shocks in the 1970s and the *heisei* recession in the 1990s), it is natural for enterprise unions to adopt an accommodating position. Declining wage premiums [then] reduce the incentives of non-union employees to form unions. Enterprise unions, whose membership is guaranteed by union shop clauses, will feel only limited pressure to respond to declining interest in union formation at non-union firms. (p. 482)

Given these tendencies, it is not surprising that Japanese union membership as a share of the employed Japanese labor force declined from 35.4 percent in 1970, to 28.9 percent in 1985, and to 24.2 percent in 1993 (p. 463).[25] Besides hampering domestic recruitment, enterprise unionism has weakened international solidarity between Japanese and other East Asian workers—which is again not surprising insofar as the main confederation of Japanese enterprise unions, Rengo, "is robustly corporatist . . . and resolutely rejects industrial militancy and analyses based on social class" (Hoogvelt, 1995, p. 725). Rengo and its member unions are more concerned with promoting the international competitive interests of their "parent" enterprises (e.g., assisting in the regional diffusion of Japanese management practices by "impressing upon visitors the positive and attractive aspects of the Japanese way of doing things") than with building cross-border associations that increase workers' collective regional power. Even in their relations with workers in other countries within the same firm (or the same family of keiretsu firms), the Rengo unions have been "largely unwilling to engage in any activities which might consequently disrupt relations with their parent company" (pp. 725-726). But by acting as "ambassadors for management, Japan's unions are . . . digging their own grave" by worsening the competitive pressures from "the transplantation of Japanese domestic industry abroad (especially in the East and South East Asian region)" (p. 724).[26]

Overall, Itoh's (1994) argument that Japan faces a worsening human-resource crisis due to "exhausted and weakened working people" seems quite plausible once one realizes the true extent of worker disempowerment built into the Japanese political economy and its external expansion. This human-resource crisis is also a crisis of human development—one rooted in the inability of mature capitalism to put its productive resources at the service of human needs. As such, it manifests the historical limits of production for profit as a vehicle of human production and development. Japan's popular egalitarian and anti-capitalist image is based more on the ideological evasion of these limits than on the realities of the Japanese system.

Japan and Capitalist Maturity: A Question of Priorities

The end of Japan's postwar growth "miracle" spawned an interesting debate in the West concerning the strength and effectiveness of Japanese state planning institutions. Neoliberals argued that whatever their past successes in promoting heavy industry, Japan's planning agencies (especially MITI and the Ministry of Finance) had shown themselves to be incapable of managing Japan's movement toward a more service-oriented and high-consumption economy. This task could only be handled through greater reliance on free-market forces, especially private financial markets and institutions (Bussey, 1995; *Economist*, 1998c). Another view, popularized by Karel van Wolferen, was that Japan was suffering from the absence of "any centre of accountability" in the bureaucracy and the rest of the political system (1993, p. 16). For van Wolferen, Japan's economic quandaries did not stem from planning and bureaucratic power as such, but rather from the irresponsibility, incoherence, and creeping paralysis of planning when it "is not ultimately regulated by law, or guided by leaders who are held accountable for what they do" (p. 17). Others suggested that Japan's economic problems had been overestimated and that the country's planning apparatus was still quite effective. Eamonn Fingleton (1995), for example, asserted that "the Japanese economy . . . emerged from the early 1990s stronger than ever," and that it was still "one of the most carefully and intelligently structured hierarchies in history" (pp. 70, 81).[27] Some flying geese theorists gave a regional twist to this optimistic line, arguing that with the recent expansion of outward FDI and offshore production networks controlled by Japanese corporations, the effective locus of Japanese bureaucratic planning had been broadened to incorporate other East Asian countries. Those holding this view tended to see Japan's domestic stagnation and even the East Asian crisis of 1997-98 as momentary bumps on the road toward the successful regionalization of Japan's state-capitalist regime (Terry, 1998).

What is interesting about this debate is how all its participants studiously avoided the question of the priorities to be served by Japan's future development. In focusing on the institutional mechanics of resource allocation, the debate bypassed the basic questions: planning for what and for whom?; markets for what and for whom? In comparing the economic potentials of state activism and private decision-making, the fact that Japan's development would continue to be capitalist was taken for granted. In this way, the debate ignored the true source of Japan's worsening socio-economic dilemmas: capitalism itself with its prioritization of exchange value over use value, of capital accumulation over human development. The possibility was never considered that bureaucratic planning might achieve its goals, and markets efficiently regulate private supplies and demands, *within* a system of capitalist exploitation and competition that continued to exhaust Japan's human, social, and ecological fabric. In the post–Cold War, "end of history" era, the idea that even a successful capitalism might be a failure in human-developmental terms could not be broached let alone pursued to the point of envisioning non-capitalist alternatives.

By contrast, this chapter has argued that Japan is suffering from a crisis of human development that can only be adequately understood as a crisis of economic priorities. As with all mature capitalist economies, Japanese capital and its state are unable to utilize society's tremendous potential surplus for human-developmental ends. Instead, this surplus has been wasted and utilized in ways that have actually exhausted Japan's reproductive potential as understood in economic, cultural, and ecological terms. At the same time, the foregoing critical overview detects an important kernel of truth in neoliberal thinking: as long as capitalist priorities of competitiveness and profitability are not fundamentally questioned, the Japanese government will increasingly be driven to adopt neoliberal policies of domestic deregulation, free trade, and free capital movements. In this case, the Japanese political economy will indeed become more like the United States—a cultural and ecological disaster increasingly reliant on domestic repression and external military force to support an irrational process of finance-led development.

Regardless of how Japan's future economic policies evolve—and whatever their success in terms of profits and GDP—they will not solve the country's crisis of human development as long as they remain within a capitalist framework. Such a solution can only be achieved through a struggle by workers and communities for a democratic socialization of production and its material conditions. The Japanese working class must rekindle its historical legacy of anti-capitalist struggle, especially the unrealized potential of the democracy, industrial union, and production control movements immediately after the Second World War (see Chapter 7). And now, more than ever, Japanese working people will only be able to construct a more democratic and human-developmental political economy by uniting with workers and communities in the other East Asian countries that have come under the sway of Japanese capital—countries now confronting their own development crises.

PART THREE

Contradictions of Capitalist
Industrialization in East Asia

Chapter 11

State-Capitalist Development, Crisis, and Class Struggle in the NIEs

Part I of this book examined mainstream perspectives on the East Asian growth experience, including the recently popular flying geese theory of development. Drawing on aspects of neoliberalism and structural-institutionalism, the flying geese theory shares their positive view of capitalism's power to promote industrialization in a smooth, non-contradictory, and egalitarian fashion. It differs in crediting regional economic relationships and dynamics, in particular those shaped by Japanese foreign direct investment, for enabling the SEA-3 to follow Japan and the NIEs in a sequentially structured takeoff into sustained growth and development.

The popularity of the flying geese approach, as analysis and ideology, stemmed from its empirical plausibility. At first sight, it was difficult to look at the postwar economic history of Japan, then Taiwan and South Korea, and more recently, Thailand, Malaysia, and Indonesia and *not* conclude that global capitalism was working some growth magic. First one country, then another, and then another seemed to be duplicating Japan's successful model of development. The conclusion seemed to follow that global capitalism, if supported and encouraged by appropriate national economic policies, can produce a win-win situation for developed and less-developed countries.

The flying geese approach explained the process as follows: competition and state industrial policies lead firms in advanced countries to shift to higher value-added industries and, through capital mobility, help countries at lower stages of industrialization develop their own industries. Japan helped South Korea and Taiwan, and all three countries then helped the SEA-3. Thus growth spreads and continues throughout the system, with workers in all countries benefiting as countries specialize in areas and at technological levels at which they are most competitive.

One can only agree with the flying geese perspective's general emphasis on the importance of the regionalization of economic activity, in particular of Japanese and NIE capital in the SEA-3 growth process; yet the approach has a crucial weakness: it fails to recognize that international product cycles and resulting diffusions of industrial activities are conducted within class-hierarchical structures of corporate-capitalist control (Hymer, 1979). As a result, the development of products and the location of industrial processes across Japan, the NIEs, and the SEA-3 are not determined according to the requirements of integrated industrial development in each country or region, but rather in line with the profit interests of Japanese capital and of subordinate NIE and SEA-3 capitalist classes. The flying geese approach also ignores the many downsides of the intensive competition among peripheral, semiperipheral, and even core countries for the investments and technologies controlled by transnational corporations. This competition produces a most uncongenial environment not only for integrated and sustainable *national* industrialization efforts, but also for the development of *regional* and *global* productive structures that can serve the needs of workers and their communities in East Asia and elsewhere.

As shown in Part II, Japanese capital's regionalization was a response to the class contradictions of Japanese capitalism itself. As a result, this investment dynamic has worked to undermine popular living and working conditions in Japan. The present chapter and the next show that similar contradictions appear in heightened forms in the region's semiperiphery (NIEs) and periphery (SEA-3). It is shown that the contradictions of export-led accumulation have been accentuated by the integration of South Korean, Taiwanese, and SEA-3 capital into a regionalized production and class structure under the dominance of Japanese capital.

This chapter discusses the emerging East Asian system of regionalized industrialization from the standpoint of the NIEs, focusing on South Korea and Taiwan. Although the foreign direct investment activity of NIE firms did contribute to the SEA-3 growth environment, a critical examination of the causes of this investment, and its consequences for South Korea and Taiwan, makes clear the contradictions inherent in the East Asian export-led growth strategy. Chief among these are the contradiction between national economy (continuation of national development projects) and nationally based capital (with its increasingly internationalized investment and competitiveness imperatives) and the more fundamental contradiction between the needs of capital and the needs of workers and communities.

Chapter 12 then examines the underpinnings and dynamics of export-led growth in the SEA-3 countries. It is shown that the SEA-3 "miracles" exhibited, in magnified form, the essential characteristic of the Japanese and NIE "miracles": reliance on intensive exploitation to generate an unsustainable pattern of economic growth that does little to satisfy the long-term development needs of workers and communities. And, as might be expected given the existing economic hierarchy, the contradictions noted above are found to be most visible and acute in the SEA-3 countries.

State, Industry, and Exports in South Korea and Taiwan

As structural-institutionalists have argued, it was the state, rather than market forces, that played the central role in structuring the economy and shaping growth in South Korea and Taiwan (Amsden, 1989; Wade, 1990). In South Korea, the major post-1961 investment and resource allocation decisions which powered industrial transformation were made by the state, not private entrepreneurs, and in response to government-formulated growth priorities, not profit-maximizing market signals. Furthermore, production itself was highly centralized as a result of state policy and organized by a few large family-owned conglomerates, called *chaebol*. Control over the country's financial system was perhaps the single most important factor enabling the South Korean state to successfully direct the economy. Government planners were able to use their control over both the allocation and cost of money-capital to direct firm activity into areas considered strategic for industrial development.

By the mid-1960s the government had decided upon exports as a priority activity for all firms. Byong-Nak Song, an economist with experience at both government planning agencies and research institutes, explains:

> Under the government export promotion strategy, "survival of the fittest" among competing firms was not determined in the market-place, but through discretionary government actions. "Fitness" was judged in terms of the ability to expand exports, rather than based on profitability. If determined "unfit," firms were likely to face bankruptcy. Such firms were under constant threat of tax investigations and other punitive sanctions. On the other hand firms that efficiently used their government-backed loans to expand exports were implicitly considered fit and favored with even further support. (1990, pp. 101–102)

The government's commitment to exports did not, however, signify a commitment to free-trade principles. The state made regular use of a variety of techniques to control and limit imports. Even goods listed as "automatically approved" for import were subject to a maze of special laws, regulations, and hidden taxes which the government used to restrict their entry.

Equally important, government export promotion was undertaken as part of a comprehensive effort to promote national industrial development. While most international development experts routinely advised countries that they must choose between either an export-oriented or import-substitution-oriented development strategy, South Korea used both strategies simultaneously. The government regularly targeted new areas for development by encouraging the establishment of domestic firms to replace imports. These new firms were protected by both trade restrictions and strict limits on foreign direct investment and, when judged capable, were required to export as well as meet domestic needs.

An excellent example of this development approach was the government's 1973 program to establish new heavy and chemical industries for both import substituting and export generating purposes. The government directed firms into these targeted areas with, among other things, subsidized capital. Subsidized loans grew from approximately 30 percent of total credit over the 1965-70 period, to over 43 percent over the 1971-75 period, to an estimated 80 percent of manufacturing loans in 1978 (Michell, 1988, p. 53). The governments' success is illustrated by the fact that these newly established industries increased their share of total South Korean exports from approximately 13 percent in 1970 to nearly 60 percent by 1985 (Bello and Rosenfeld, 1990, p. 59).

The government itself was also not hesitant about undertaking key investment activities through public enterprises, as in the petroleum, chemical, and iron and steel industries. As a result, investment in public enterprises rose from 19 percent of total investment in 1970 to over 33 percent in 1975 (Song, 1990, p. 118). In the latter year, 12 of the 16 biggest firms in the country were government-owned (Michell, 1988, p. 91).

The government did eventually decide, as part of its heavy and chemical industrialization program, that production should be primarily carried out by private firms. The resulting market environment, however, had little in common with mainstream visions of free-market competition. As part of the decision to establish new capital-intensive industries and launch new exports in areas such as automobiles, shipbuilding, and computers, the government selected a small group of *chaebol* to dominate production. Supported by government licensing and credit subsidies as well as foreign trade and investment restrictions, the combined sales of the top ten *chaebol* relative to GNP soared from approximately 15 percent in 1974 to over 67 percent by 1984 (Amsden, 1989, p. 116). By 1988, the combined revenues of the top four *chaebol*—Samsung, Hyundai, Lucky-Goldstar, and Daewoo—equaled approximately 47 percent of Korea's total GNP (Bello and Rosenfeld, 1990, p. 63).

The general situation in terms of the role of the state was similar in Taiwan. But, Taiwan's specific experience differs from that of South Korea largely because the Taiwanese state and ruling Kuomintang Party (KMT) was dominated by Chinese who fled the mainland in 1949, not by those already living in Taiwan. Fearful of sharing economic power and thus undermining their own political power, the ruling KMT elite chose to emphasize direct state production rather than the promotion of Taiwanese owned conglomerates.

As a result of this policy, state enterprises accounted for almost 60 percent of Taiwan's industrial production in the early 1950s. Although that percentage has since steadily declined, state production still dominates the country's strategic industries, including petroleum, steel, railways, electric power, shipbuilding, and telecommunications. A true picture of the state-party hold on the economy, however, also requires including the economic contribution of some 50 important companies owned in one form or another by the KMT itself. Combined state and party assets have been estimated as being equal to approximately half of the country's total corporate assets (Bello and Rosenfeld, 1990, p. 232). The government also controlled the financial sector through its ownership of almost all the country's banks. Operating through this state-controlled system, the Central Bank of China was able to direct a large share of funds to the big state and party owned enterprises; state enterprises alone received some 30 percent of all bank loans in 1983 (p. 232).

Exports have, as in South Korea, played a leading role in spurring Taiwan's growth. They were encouraged by the government in two different ways. By deliberately denying the great majority of small- and medium-sized Taiwanese businesses access to credit or the domestic market, the government left these businesses with no choice but to export. At the same time, the government actively used tax, labor, and credit policies to attract export-oriented foreign multinational corporations. In fact, the Taiwanese government often combined these two approaches by actively encouraging the creation of original equipment manufacturing (OEM) arrangements, under which Taiwanese firms produced products specified and marketed by foreign buyers like KMart, Sears, IBM, and General Electric.

Again, as in South Korea, support for exports did not mean that the Taiwanese government operated on the basis of free-trade principles. Only exporters enjoyed a relatively open trade regime, normally being allowed to import the equipment and materials they needed at world market prices. More generally, the government used an extensive system of trade management to control imports.

Structural-institutionalists have applauded the policymaking strength and autonomy that enabled the South Korean and Taiwanese governments to formulate and carry out their respective industrialization and export plans; but they have been much less eager to highlight the key role of state strength vis-à-vis labor and the external sources of this strength. In both countries, military dictatorships supported national export efforts with brutally repressive anti-labor policies to maintain low unit labor costs.[1] The wages of female workers were kept especially low, and "Korea's gender earnings differential for all education groups actually grew larger during the 1970s and early 1980s" (Van Der Meulen Rodgers, 1998, p. 745). Such gender-wage discrimination was instrumental in maintaining the competitiveness of both countries' light-manufactured exports (Seguino, 1997a, 1997b). Moreover, the industrialization of both South Korea and Taiwan depended heavily on favorable external relations with the United States and Japan (McCormack, 1978; Hart-Landsberg, 1993, Chapter 7). In terms of the United States, these relations included generous financial support, relatively open access to the U.S. market, and permission to deviate from U.S. free-market orthodoxy. In the case of Japan, they involved sizable and timely financial assistance as well as access to Japanese technology and components (Nakajo, 1980; Castley, 1996). Continuation of this external support hinged on the maintenance of "security and stability" by the South Korean and Taiwanese governments. Indeed, the entire arrangement was largely a product of the Cold War.

Contradictions of Export-Led Industrialization

By the late 1980s, both South Korea and Taiwan were routinely praised by most economists for their economic record—and South Korea in particular was promoted as an economic model whose development strategy should be followed by countries throughout the world. It was also during this period that both South Korean and Taiwanese corporations began investing in other third world countries, especially in the SEA-3 and China. This investment was taken as added proof of the maturity of the

NIEs and their ability to play a positive role in supporting the development of less advanced countries.

Significantly, it was also during the latter half of the 1980s that contradictions in the NIE growth strategy became visible.[2] In South Korea, years of growth left the large *chaebol* too big and central to the economy for the state to continue directing their activities as it wanted. In part this was the result of their export success over the 1986-1989 period, which gave them significant financial independence and the freedom to engage in highly profitable land and stock market speculation. The industrialization process also generated increasingly organized resistance to dictatorship and militant labor movements in both South Korea and Taiwan. In South Korea, mass demonstrations forced the military dictatorship to allow the direct election of the president beginning in 1987. In addition, some 7,000 labor actions took place between 1987 and 1990, leading to a 70 percent increase in wages over the period (Hatch and Yamamura, 1996, p. 89). In Taiwan, the KMT was forced by popular protests to end martial law in 1987. And although the labor movement in Taiwan was less organized and militant than in South Korea, approximately 3000 labor disputes took place in 1987 and 1988, leading to a 60 percent increase in manufacturing wages from 1986 to 1989 (p. 91). Not surprisingly, these developments took a toll on the export competitiveness of the NIEs. By 1990, for example, South Korea's trade balance was back in deficit.

Equally important as obstacles to continued NIE growth were U.S. and Japanese responses to NIE export successes. The United States had reacted to Japan's export offensive by forcing a revaluation of the Japanese yen beginning in late 1985. Initially, the higher value of the yen enabled NIE corporations to enjoy a significant price advantage over their Japanese competitors, thereby allowing them to increase their exports to the United States at Japanese expense.[3] By 1988, however, the United States had turned its anger on the NIEs (Cho, 1994, pp. 164-170). U.S. government pressure forced both South Korea and Taiwan to substantially raise the value of their currencies. In 1989, all the NIEs were removed from the list of countries receiving tariff breaks under the General System of Preferences. The United States also began employing the newly created Super 301 section of its Omnibus Trade and Competitiveness Act of 1988 to force countries designated as "unfair traders" to open their markets to greater U.S. exports and foreign investment; both South Korea and Taiwan were targets.

The Japanese also took action, slowing down their technology and component transfers. As a case in point, "in 1990, the Japanese government decided to ban the export of 200 ultra-modern technologies to Korea until 1995" to ensure that "Japanese firms will have exploited much of the market potential of the technologies" (Bello, 1992, p. 88). Perhaps even more damaging was the Japanese regionalization strategy. Japan's post–1985 Asian-bound foreign investment was initially directed mainly to the NIEs, but as political and labor activity increased, and higher currency values took effect, it was quickly redirected toward the SEA-3 (and later China). Indeed, "in 1988 Japan's ASEAN-bound investment overtook NIE-bound investment," and "the gap has been widening ever since" (Hitoshi, 1993, p. 22). This investment, by helping to build up a significant export base in the SEA-3, seriously threatened the competitiveness of NIE producers.[4] To understand how these developments led to the breakdown of the NIE growth strategy, however, one must consider the regionalization of South Korean and Taiwanese capital more closely.

The Regionalization and Restructuring of the NIEs

South Korean and Taiwanese overseas investments grew rapidly beginning in the late 1980s. Over the period 1968 to 1980, *cumulative* South Korean outward foreign direct investment was less than $250 million; but in 1989 and 1990 *annual* outward direct investments by South Korean firms amounted to $0.5 billion and $1 billion, respectively (*Business Korea,* 1996, p. 19). Approximately 40 percent of the 1990 total was destined for other third world countries (Bello, 1992, p. 89). Taiwan-based firms invested even more abroad in 1990, over $6 billion, although only $1.2 billion was officially registered; Southeast Asia was one of their favored destinations (p. 89). In fact, the NIEs collectively invested more in Malaysia, Indonesia, and the Philippines during the 1989-92 period than either the United States or Japan (Steven, 1996, p. 97). The outflow of investment from both South Korea and Taiwan continued to grow rapidly after 1992. South Korean businesses increased their FDI to approximately $3 billion in 1993. "Between 1993 and 1996, Korea's overseas direct investment posted a phenomenal annualized growth rate of 53 percent on average. In 1996 alone, the amount of Korean firms' overseas direct investment reported to the government totaled $6.22 billion" (Kwak, 1999). Moreover, in late 1995, the "top *chaebol*—Daewoo, LG Group, Hyundai, and Samsung— . . . announced plans to invest at least $20 billion overseas in the next five years" (Nakarmi, 1995, p. 58); Southeast Asia was among the most attractive locations mentioned.[5]

This explosion of FDI from the NIEs could easily be interpreted as a replay of Japan's earlier domestic industrial restructuring and foreign investment activities. After all, South Korean and Taiwanese capital were facing a challenge similar to that faced only a few years earlier by Japanese firms: sustaining export-led growth in a situation of appreciating currency, rising wages, and trade frictions with the United States. And, their response was similar: they engaged in FDI to protect profits, with a growing focus on the SEA-3 and then China. Despite these similarities, however, the regionalization of NIE capital is qualitatively different from the regionalization of Japanese capital. NIE capital, and the NIEs themselves (it must be emphasized that these are not the same thing), *are being regionalized in subordinate fashion* as part of an emerging Japanese-dominated system of production and investment in East Asia. The subordinate status of NIE capital becomes clearer when one considers the *interconnections between* Japanese and NIE capital regionalization.

One such interconnection is the direct competition between Japanese and NIE enterprises. By combining their advanced technology with cheap Southeast Asian labor, Japanese firms place less technologically advanced South Korean and Taiwanese enterprises still producing on their home turf at a decisive competitive disadvantage. Looking at electronics, for example, Bernard and Ravenhill note how the establishment of electronics production in SEA-3 countries competitively displaced much NIE production from the Japanese market:

> Some of the fall in the imports of consumer electronics products from Korea and Taiwan that occurred in the Japanese market in the late 1980s was the result of their displacement by imports from Japanese subsidiaries in Southeast Asia. Imports of color TVs from Korea and Taiwan, for example, fell from 1.6 to 1.3 million units in the years 1989–91. In the same period imports from Malaysia rose from 2,000 to 385,000 units. By the latter date Malaysia had replaced Taiwan as Japan's second most important source of imports of this product and was also the single largest supplier of radio cassette recorders to the Japanese market. (1995, p. 198)

A second interconnection stems from the fact that many NIE firms operate as subcontractors for Japanese producers. In such cases, shifts in Japan's regional production and investment strategies naturally necessitate corresponding regional shifts on the part of NIE enterprises. Here again, the responses of NIE firms to rising costs and trade frictions often are more conditioned and constrained by the regional production strategies of Japanese enterprises than by the continuation of the NIEs' national projects of export-led growth and late industrialization.

This undermining of national development models can also be observed from the Japanese standpoint. The purpose of the Japanese strategy of establishing a regionalized production base in East Asia is not to destroy all competitors; that would be impractical both economically and politically. Instead, Japanese capital is trying to incorporate potential competitors into a regional production structure that is supportive of Japanese interests—one that limits intraregional challenges to those interests. This requires the *integration* of NIE and SEA-3 capital into hierarchical production and investment systems that allow Japanese capital to use its technological, financial, and marketing dominance to set the terms for maximum profit creation and its distribution among competing enterprises on different (core, semiperipheral, and peripheral) levels of the hierarchy.

Hatch and Yamamura explain: "By building *keiretsu*-like production networks that embrace and even smother local entrepreneurs, technicians, and workers in Asia, Japanese TNCs carefully control the pace of technology transfer. In effect, they lock it up in the vertical, quasi-integrated networks they control" (1996, p. 102). As a case in point, in 1994 Japanese firms such as Hitachi, Toshiba, NEC, and Oki Electric Company agreed to share new manufacturing processes and chip designs with smaller chip makers in Taiwan and Singapore in exchange for a predetermined share of their output. A spokesperson for Hitachi stated: "You don't have to make all DRAMs (memory chips) in order to sell all DRAMs" (Hamilton and Goad, 1994, p. A11). Once integrated in this fashion, NIE and SEA-3 capital may try to renegotiate the exact terms on which they participate in the Japanese-dominated production hierarchy. But they will not be able to question the hierarchy itself.

From Contradictions to Structural Crisis

What does this hierarchical competition among increasingly regionalized firms mean for the NIEs, considered as national economies and societies? Increasingly, the answer seems to be premature industrial hollowing out, rising inequality, and intensified competitive pressures on working people whose work and living conditions remain far below core standards. In both South Korea and Taiwan, the movement of light-manufacturing industries abroad has already intensified downward pressures on wages—especially among the female workers previously crowded into these industries (Seguino, 1997a). As Rudy Hung (1996) observes, "the massive relocation of labor-intensive production to mainland China and elsewhere could mean job losses and reduced leverage for Taiwan's low-skilled labor, but big profits for the employers" (p. 151). The spread of regionalization and outward FDI from light- to heavy-manufacturing industries can only worsen such regressive pressures on employment, wages, and work conditions.

A basic problem facing the NIEs, as noted by Schuman, et al. (1996, p. A9) when discussing South Korea, is that their "industry churns out products that aren't as technologically advanced as Japanese and U.S. goods, and yet it has higher labor and logistics costs than rising Southeast Asian nations." This problematic situation manifests more than the still relatively undeveloped technological and marketing capabilities of NIE enterprises and the corresponding dependence of the NIEs on imports of core-controlled components, technologies, and services. It is true that import dependence reinforces the export imperative. Nonetheless, the "necessity" of the treadmill of export-led growth, under which initial export successes do nothing to alleviate competitiveness pressures on workers and communities, is based on the class-exploitative distribution of purchasing power, which precludes explicit pursuit of a more domestic wage-based growth strategy.

Like Japan before them, South Korea and Taiwan tried to develop their domestic economies using a combined export-promotion and import-substitution approach based on state industrial planning and trade controls, with heavy reliance on low productivity-adjusted wages— all enforced by military repression. Although they made considerable progress in aggregate growth terms, recent developments call into question the ability of their domestic growth strategy to survive a regionalized accumulation process. Naturally, the strongest South Korean or Taiwanese *corporations* may profitably participate in this regional process through their subordinate positions vis-à-vis Japanese capital and their advanced positions vis-à-vis SEA-3 capital. Nevertheless, the key point for present purposes is that NIE industries have not succeeded in technologically replicating Japanese capital's core of innovative industries, especially components and machinery industries.[6] "Japan's technological embrace of Korea is reflected in the numbers: Japanese high-technology parts and components have accounted for 20-30 percent of the value of Korean automobiles, 35-45 percent of the value of Korean machine tools, 60 percent of the value of Korean computers, 65 percent of the value of Korean printers, and 85 percent of the value of Korean televisions" (Hatch and Yamamura, 1996, p. 179). The situation is no different as far as Taiwan is concerned. As one Taiwanese specialist explained: "If the Japanese refuse to sell equipment, you're lost" (as quoted in Bello, 1992, p. 87). This is no exaggeration, since about 90 percent of Taiwanese imports from Japan are components, machinery, and parts (Fallows, 1994, pp. 398-399).

Japanese firms developed their own technology by absorbing and improving on the work of others and also created their own advanced marketing networks based on brand recognition. In contrast, South Korean and Taiwanese enterprises continue to rely heavily on original equipment manufacturing. According to Bernard and Ravenhill: "In consumer electronics, apparel, and steel . . . a Korean Trade Association report indicates that OEM exports exceeded 80 percent of total exports" (1995, p. 191). Excluding OEM arrangements, NIE firms' exports are increasingly—given problems of lack of brand recognition, low quality, and technological unsophistication—limited to lower-rung markets in third world countries. This subordinate technological and marketing position explains South Korea's tendency to run larger and larger trade deficits with core countries that cannot be offset by trade surpluses with the rest of the world: its 1995 trade deficit with core countries was $29 billion; its trade surplus with non-core countries was $19 billion. The South Korean trade deficit just with Japan stood at $15 billion in the same year (Sah, 1995). South Korea's overall trade deficit grew to a record $20.4 billion in 1996. As a result of these trends, South Korea's foreign debt also grew rapidly, from $44 billion in 1993 to approximately $120 billion in 1997. Although the country's economic collapse in late 1997 pushed the 1998 trade balance into surplus, the long-term picture remains negative.

On the export side, South Korea will be hard pressed to maintain past growth rates given the likely intensification of competition from Japanese, and even peripheral, capital as overproduction proceeds among export powerhouses new and old (Engardio, 1996). More specifically, South Korea's exports are increasingly concentrated among five major industries—semiconductors, automobiles, steel, shipbuilding, and petrochemicals—and this concentration has been steadily rising since the early 1990s. This has become a serious problem since "unit export prices of the heavy and chemical industries, including the five big industries, have declined 46.3% over the past three years. As the prices have fallen by half or so, exporters have lost income despite increasing export volume" (*Business Korea*, 1999, p. 22). The main cause of these price trends is not hard to find: Japanese-promoted export activity in Southeast Asia. As a journalist for *Business Korea* reports: "What galls Korean exporters is the fact that developing countries are in pursuit of Korea in many product areas. Competition is getting tougher as export industries in Malaysia, Thailand, the Philippines and other developing countries shift from labor-intensive industries to heavy and chemical industries like electronics and machinery. For example, Korea's export similarity index with Malaysia in the Japanese market nearly doubled from 1990's 21.2 to 45.2 in 1995" (Kim, 1997, p. 15). And insofar as South Korean capital increasingly orients itself toward peripheral markets by relocating production to them (partly in response to competitiveness pressures), this strategy is likely to worsen overall trade-deficit pressures on South Korea.

Pressures may even be greater on the import side. To become a member of the OECD, South Korea was forced to eliminate its import source diversification system, which effectively blocked the import of Japanese consumer goods, and open its economy wider to direct foreign investment. The U.S. government also continues to press South Korea to open its markets to greater consumer goods imports, even though the United States has been enjoying a substantial surplus in bilateral trade (Kim, 1999).

The price declines in key export products, coupled with growing import-generated domestic competition and continued labor resistance to lower wages, left the *chaebol* struggling with falling profit margins and rising debt loads despite the country's rapid economic growth over the 1994-1996 period. In fact, "the forty-nine largest business groups had total profits of just $32 million on combined sales of $274 billion [in 1996], a return of just over 0.01 percent" (Moon, 1997, p. 57). Thousands of firms went bankrupt in the first half of 1997, including some of the country's largest enterprises. These bankruptcies, in turn, threatened the solvency of South Korea's banking system. Thus, the South Korean economy teetered on the brink of crisis even before the July 1997 collapse of Thailand's currency triggered the wider East Asian meltdown. South Korea's economic collapse in late 1997 was not simply the result of short-term difficulties brought on by Southeast Asian instabilities and hot money flows; its economic problems are structural in nature (Jeong and Shin, 1998).

South Korean government acceptance of greater import and foreign investment liberalization, as recommended by the IMF, will provide additional encouragement to the large South Korean enterprises to further uncouple their fortunes from the South Korean market by intensifying their pursuit of foreign expansion. These enterprises long relied on profits from high-margin sales in captive home markets to finance the new product lines and predatory pricing strategies that enabled them to penetrate developed country markets. In exchange, they acceded to government regulation of their activities in line with state industrial policies. However, liberalization of imports and rising domestic production costs have seriously damaged this quid pro quo from one side, just as *chaebol* internationalization and domestic hollowing-out have eroded it from the other side (Schuman, 1996). A likely outcome of this unraveling of the South Korean growth strategy is the reperipheralization of the South Korean economy.

The Limits of Export-Led Development

The policy dilemmas outlined above all derive from a more fundamental tension built into all export-led accumulation regimes: production for maximum sales and profit rather than for the producers and their communities. This tension, and the accompanying problem of worsening dependence on export growth, are not temporary side effects of competitive success. Capitalism is a class-exploitative system where firms compete by cutting unit labor costs and accumulating the profits extracted from labor. However, by installing more advanced technologies that reduce unit labor costs, firms expand productive capacity beyond the extent of the market— a market ultimately limited by the purchasing power of the direct producers. This explains why capitalist competition takes the form of a struggle for *export* markets in which firms from different countries compete for shares in the total value added that can be realized within the limits of the global market.

Given the technological and marketing advantages possessed by core-country firms, the only possible means for semiperipheral firms to succeed in this competition are: (1) comparatively low wages and high labor intensities; (2) the purchase of technologies and marketing devices from core-country firms; (3) the ability (through government subsidies) to cut export prices by selling at low or even negative profit margins.[7] The first method worsens export dependence by constraining wage-based demand relative to total production; the second produces the same result by increasing foreign exchange requirements and drawing semiperipheral firms into the export-oriented operations of core-country TNCs. The third method places the exporting country on a treadmill where it must produce more and more commodities to acquire the same amount of value added (see Freeman, 1996 for a detailed analysis). And, as discussed earlier, such a continuous expansion of export volume must eventually run into the barrier of competition from lower-wage countries.

It is clearly a *necessary tendency* for rising living standards of workers to appear as a constant threat to continued export-led development. Under such a regime, capital and state planners feel justified in expecting workers to continue laboring long hours under unsafe conditions at unacceptable wage levels in perpetuity and to thank capital for the opportunity to remain forever "competitive." It is this logic that leads unbelievably wealthy *chaebol* capitalists like Hyundai group chair Chung Se-Yung to argue with straight faces that "we can't do business anymore in Korea" due to "an increase in costs" and because "without globalization of our operations, we cannot grow as much as we would like" (Nakarmi, 1995, p. 58). And *this* is the "flying goose" whose development the SEA-3 countries were supposed to emulate.

Chapter 12

Imperialism, Exploitation, and Uneven Development in the SEA-3

While mainstream economists and international organizations like the World Bank had praised the economic performance of Japan, the NIEs, and the SEA-3, it was the last group of countries that received the greatest acclaim. There were several reasons for this. First, economic growth in the SEA-3 easily eclipsed the average of all developing countries over the period 1988-1995 (IMF, 1996, pp. 121-123). Second, this growth was the result of a broader industrial transformation. For example, Thailand's export to gross domestic product (GDP) ratio increased from 24.3 percent in 1980 to 36.8 percent in 1990; the share of manufactures in Thai exports also rose over the same period, from 25.2 to 63.1 percent (UNCTAD, 1993, p. 128). Third, and perhaps most importantly, growth in the SEA-3 appeared to be based more on unregulated market activity and foreign direct investment than in Japan, South Korea, and Taiwan, and was therefore more in line with neoliberal theory and its political agenda (World Bank, 1993, p. 1).

It is indeed the case that an important factor driving SEA-3 growth was foreign investment. For example, the U.S. dollar value of net FDI inflows into Malaysia ($5.5 billion), Thailand ($6.9 billion), and Indonesia ($4 billion) during the years 1981-90, dwarfed the net inflows occurring over the prior two decades that totaled $4.5 billion, $1.2 billion, and $2.2 billion, respectively (Yue, 1993, p. 73). Moreover, for both Malaysia and Indonesia, approximately half the net inflows occurring during the 1981-90 period took place from 1988 to 1990; for Thailand the share was 73 percent.[1] FDI inflows as a percentage of domestic capital formation in Malaysia rose from 8.1 percent in 1985 to 21.9 percent in 1990, and in Thailand from 1.8 to

7.9 percent (Yue, 1993, p. 74). Even though these figures are for all FDI rather than manufacturing alone, they establish FDI as an important factor entering into the recent SEA-3 growth experience. In fact, it was the FDI-led character of SEA-3 growth that led some economic theorists and international organizations to embrace flying geese perspectives on East Asia's development (UNCTAD, 1993, p. 131).

In contrast to this celebratory view of capitalism and capital mobility, Chapters 9–11 have argued that the Japanese-led process of SEA-3 restructuring was motivated largely by contradictions inherent in Japanese and NIE capitalist dynamics and that it has undermined not only national development projects but also living and working conditions for the great majority of working people in Japan and the NIEs. The present chapter examines the significance of this restructuring for the SEA-3 countries themselves. The main finding is that FDI- and export-led development has integrated SEA-3 workers and resources into a highly exploitative and unstable regional accumulation regime. Because they occupy the most dependent and vulnerable location in this regime, SEA-3 workers have, as a group, suffered the most from its breakdown.

Regionalization of Capital and SEA-3 Industrialization

When examining the SEA-3 experience, it is important to be aware of the "pull" factors that help explain the openness of SEA-3 elites to their emerging position as peripheral participants in a Japanese-dominated system of regionalized East Asian capital.[2] In the mid-1980s the SEA-3 suffered from serious balance-of-payments problems owing to declining primary commodity export prices, rising external interest rates, and reduced official capital inflows. In response, SEA-3 governments aggressively initiated a variety of new programs (including generous tax policies) that allowed Southeast Asia to "become one of the most attractive investment locations in the developing world and attract a disproportionately large amount of FDI, particularly in the 1987-1991 period" (Yue, 1993, p. 60). However, the explosion of FDI in, and manufactured exports from, the SEA-3 was not only due to the "pull" of economic desperation, but also to the "push" of capital regionalization from Japan and the NIEs in response to the internal and external contradictions of their own export-led growth models.

While Japanese and NIE foreign direct investment did trigger an industrial transformation of the SEA-3, there are strong reasons to challenge the conventional conclusion that the resulting SEA-3 export-led growth was largely a remake of the NIEs' late industrialization, which was said to be in turn a remake of Japan's earlier industrial experience. One important reason is that, "unlike the experience of Korea and Taiwan, the recent move to manufacturing for export in Southeast Asia did not build on an experience of successful import-substituting industrialization. Rather, the new exporting industries have been grafted onto economies whose small manufacturing sectors are notable for their histories of rent seeking and inefficiency" (Bernard and Ravenhill, 1995, p. 196) The lack of indigenous import substitution means that developments in the SEA-3 represent a kind of "ersatz capitalism" (Kunio, 1988). Hatch and Yamamura (1996) point in this connection to the low number and low density of linkages forged by Japanese capital with local firms: "For example, as of 1992, Tan Chung Motors, a Nissan affiliate in Malaysia, still imported 65 percent of its automobile parts from its Japanese parent. . . . In Indonesia in the early 1990s . . . electronics firms and automobile assemblers were still importing up to 90 percent of their parts and materials" (p. 159). This paucity of local linkages also applies to most of the industrial facilities in the SEA-3 that are owned by NIE-based firms. As an example, "Korean electronics manufacturers at overseas sites," largely in the SEA-3, "have brought 62 percent of parts and components from home for finishing their production," while "only 17 percent of parts was supplied by local producers" (Moon, 1995, p. 24).

Japan's role in the growth of SEA-3 manufacturing export activity has been central. In 1992 the Japanese share of the *total* stock of manufacturing FDI "ranged from 73 per cent in Malaysia, [and] 68 per cent in Thailand . . . [to] 33 per cent in Indonesia" (Yue, 1993, p. 84). By 1994, approximately 7 percent of all Thai production workers were employed by Japanese firms, and the Matsushita electrical company alone accounted for some 4 to 5 percent of Malaysia's GDP (Hatch and Yamamura, 1996, p. 11). Until the early 1990s, these Japanese–controlled operations produced very little in the way of return flows of manufactured goods back to Japan. "In fiscal year 1989, for instance, only 10.4 percent of the sales of Japanese subsidiaries located in ASEAN were to the Japanese market," while "exports to other markets accounted for over 25 percent of sales" (Bernard and Ravenhill, 1995, p. 204). However, the progressive hollowing out of Japan's productive structure under the influence of scrap-and-build accumulation has tended to increase the role of Southeast Asia (and China) in serving the Japanese market (Steven, 1996, p. 193).

In a further evolution of this development, Japanese corporations are moving beyond using particular Southeast Asian countries as export platforms serving core-country (including Japanese) markets, to develop regional production networks that integrate different elements of productive activity taking place in different countries—networks oriented toward sales throughout East Asia as well as to the United States and Europe (Terry, 1998). As part of this process, "many of the big Japanese enterprises migrating in the latest wave are accompanied by their small-size suppliers and contractors, resulting in the recreation in Southeast Asia of the same *keiretsu* clusters or conglomerate alliances [as] back home, often to the detriment of local suppliers" (Bello, 1992, p. 91).

This trend has often been misread by economists, in that the resulting rise in "localization" seems to suggest a growing domestic integration of Japanese producers with local suppliers. But, quite the opposite is true. "Toyota Motor Thailand, to cite one example, boasts that it gets 54 percent of its passenger car parts and 66 percent of its commercial vehicle parts from local suppliers. The fact is, however, that 75 percent of these 'local' parts come from Japanese suppliers in Thailand" (Hatch and Yamamura, 1996, p. 160). Sony corporation provides another good example. "It reports that affiliates spread across the [Asian] region obtain about 90 percent of their audio parts and about 50 percent of their video parts from local suppliers. But a Sony official in Japan admits that 'virtually all' of such locally supplied electronic components come from affiliates of Sony and other Japanese MNCs in Asia" (p. 160).

This developing *regional* production system differs from the traditional flying geese conception of peripheral industrialization as a replication of the integrated *national* development patterns previously followed in the core and semiperiphery (Seki, 1995, p. 14). The SEA-3 may export products previously exported by Japan and then the NIEs, but SEA-3 growth does not involve the same kind of indigenous project of late industrialization. Instead, the SEA-3 embarked upon export-led growth in a period when the capital regionalization process was beginning to undermine national development models even in the sense of *indigenously formed adaptations* to external forces or "industrialization by learning" (Amsden, 1989). As Bello (1996b) puts it, the "process of corporate-driven horizontal and vertical integration has resulted, over the last decade, in the creation not of a regional economy with plural centers but in the regionalization of the Japanese economy."

The Costs of Export-Led Growth on East Asia's Periphery

Focusing on their high growth rates, the overwhelming majority of economists unhesitatingly declared the SEA-3 to be genuine success stories. After all, they were growing rapidly by selling internationally competitive products. But while this growth did produce lower poverty rates and a growing middle class, it came at a high cost for the great majority of SEA-3 working people.

The SEA-3's main export market was the United States. But although each country ran large surpluses in its trade with the United States, the dependent nature of their respective economies meant that each ran far bigger deficits in its trade with Japan. In 1992, for example, Thailand ran a $2.9 billion trade surplus with the United States and a $8.3 billion trade deficit with Japan, while Malaysia had a $4.2 billion surplus with the United States and a $5.8 billion deficit with Japan (Bernard and Ravenhill, 1995, p. 202). And the faster these countries grew, the larger were their overall balance of payments problems. Malaysia's current account deficit as a percent of GDP grew from 5.0 percent in 1993 to 8.8 percent in 1995. Thailand's grew from 5.1 to 8.1 percent over the same period (Jomo K. S., 1998, p. 31).[3]

Faced with major trade deficits, SEA-3 governments remained under constant pressure to generate more foreign exchange; failure meant the collapse of their economies. Thus, despite high rates of growth, they found it necessary to smash workers' attempts at unionization, encourage the inflow of migrant workers to keep wages low, and continue the high-speed exploitation of natural resources.[4] Not surprisingly, then, most of the gains generated by the workings of these "miracle economies" went to political and corporate elites.

The experience of Thailand, considered by many economists to be the most successful of the new "miracle" countries, provides an excellent illustration of the enormous social costs of "successful" export-led growth.[5] The regionalization of Japanese industry molded a new pattern of hierarchical industrial trade relations with Thailand (with Japan selling high value-added components, technologies, and services in exchange for Thailand's low-wage labor embodied in the final goods) onto a traditional neo-colonial trade pattern (with Japan selling manufactures to Thailand in exchange for primary products). True, the composition of Thailand's trade with the United States also changed, in this case in favor of manufactured exports, especially of electronics goods. But this largely involved a re-exporting of the value added captured by Japanese capital through its control over necessary technology, components, and business services. This unequal division of labor explains why Thailand's trade deficits with Japan overwhelmed its trade surpluses with the United States and Europe.

These structural trade deficits carried with them the constant threat of IMF-style retrenchment in the event of adverse "external shocks"—a threat that became all too real in the wake of Thailand's July 1997 financial crisis. They also heightened the pressure to remain competitive in manufactured export markets, and this translated into a greater government willingness to sacrifice workers' living and work conditions as well as protection of the environment and natural resources. For example, the Thai state followed a policy of depressing agriculture prices to force rural workers, who make up the majority of the Thai population, to seek employment in the urban-based export industries. The resulting rural poverty also enabled "landowners and money lenders to exploit small farmers and accumulate capital," thereby helping to cement the ruling coalition of exploiting classes (Petras and Wongchaisuwan, 1993, p. 35). It also gave rise to another major source of inequality and human misery, the country's huge, foreign-exchange earning, sex-tourism sector, which employs some 13 percent of the total female labor force (p. 36). Thailand's epidemic of HIV and AIDS is directly connected to this hypertrophied sex-tourism industry (Robinson, 1993).

Thus, even during the years of rapid growth, there were especially large increases in poverty and inequality in less urbanized areas outside Bangkok, with poverty rates running up to 38 percent in the Northeast even when measured according to meager government standards. In Bangkok, over one million people were forced to live in crowded slums, producing a striking contrast "between the rich and poor" (Goodno and Miller, 1994, p. 27). According to the Thailand Development Research Institute, the wealthiest 40 percent of the population received 77 percent of all income in 1994 (Gill, 1995). By the mid-1990s, Thailand had joined the ranks of the top five countries in the world in terms of wealth inequality (Sivaraman, 1997). These high rates of poverty and inequality, far from being an accidental "side-effect" of export-led capital accumulation, were a basic condition of this accumulation.

The country's rapid industrialization has also led to environmental destruction with serious consequences for the health of the people. In addition to the severe noise pollution and traffic congestion resulting from competitive industrialization and anarchic urbanization, Thailand suffers from serious air pollution, "estimated to be responsible for as many as 1,400 deaths per year" (Howard, 1993, p. 9). Thailand's water resources are also being degraded by export-led accumulation. For example, the "Chao Phraya River around Bangkok is seriously polluted, with oxygen levels in some areas close to zero" (p. 10). Chemical pollution from both industry and agriculture is also a growing problem (Komin, 1993, p. 261). The air pollution in Bangkok is so bad that "after pouring investment into Greater

Bangkok in the late 1980s, Japanese firms shifted elsewhere [Malaysia and China] in the 1990s" (Fallows, 1994, p. 409).

While there are great social and environmental differences between each of the SEA-3 countries, the human and ecological costs of export-led industrialization in Indonesia and Malaysia are qualitatively similar to those in Thailand (Budiardjo, 1993; Howard, 1993). This should not be surprising. The drive to exploit labor and the environment for growth is an essential feature of capitalism (Burkett, 1999); and this drive is arguably worsened by the export-led development strategy. With its extreme dependence on imported components, technologies, and business services from the core and semiperiphery, the export-led strategy forces peripheral countries to increase exports and other foreign exchange earnings by any and all available means. Rather than treating workers, communities, and the environment as the ends of development, it places them on an unsustainable treadmill of growth.

From Contradictions to Crisis in the SEA-3

Even if one were willing to overlook its human, social, and ecological costs—considering them to be an unavoidable price of growth—the SEA-3 growth strategy was *economically* unsustainable. The underlying problem was that the dependent, export-driven economies of the SEA-3 occupied a subordinate position within a regional production system that increasingly suffered from uneven development and overproduction.

The most obvious threats to continued SEA-3 growth stemmed from the evolving trade pattern as structured by the regionalization of Japanese and NIE capital. More specifically, while the SEA-3 needed ever greater foreign capital inflows to finance their rising trade deficits, they faced growing competition from even lower cost export producers in other countries, especially China. An additional threat was generated by regional dynamics. The East Asian growth strategy, underpinned by ever increasing rates of exploitation (which pushed productivity up faster than real wages), led producers to become, by necessity, ever more dependent on exporting outside the region. But the resulting collective overproduction of increasingly similar exports was bound to undermine their individual profitability and the region's economic stability. As *Business Week* warned in late 1996: "Overcapacity looms [in East Asia] in such key areas as petrochemicals, consumer appliances, passenger cars, and chips." Yet, "in petrochemicals, Indonesia, Thailand, China, Taiwan, and South Korea all are sinking billions into sprawling complexes. . . . A similar situation is shaping up in autos, another export status symbol for aspiring Tigers. . . . An edifice complex also afflicts Asia's semiconductor industry, where manufacturers are scrambling to find the talent to staff their plants. . . . The world cannot absorb this much capacity" (Engardio, et al., 1996, pp. 61-62).

Up until 1990, the SEA-3 countries succeeded in covering their growing trade deficits in large part because each year brought increased Japanese FDI. In the early to mid-1990s, however, Japanese FDI in Thailand and Malaysia began to decline. In the case of Thailand, this investment fell from $2.4 billion in 1990 to $578 million in 1993 (Bello, 1997).[6] It was not that Japan was giving up on Asia. Rather, Japanese corporations were shifting their focus to China and Vietnam, countries with even lower wages and bigger domestic markets. NIE capital, motivated by the same benefits as well as competitive pressures, made a similar decision (see Chapter 11).

Left short as a result of this shift in Japanese and NIE investment priorities, the Thai and Malaysian governments, followed by the Indonesian government, aggressively pursued other sources of foreign exchange. Their timing was good. Stagnation and low interest rates in the developed capitalist world generated substantial interest on the part of investment houses and international banks in the "emerging" markets of Southeast Asia. Leaving nothing to chance, the SEA-3 courted these investors by dropping their foreign exchange controls, opening their stock and bond markets to foreign investors, pegging their currencies to the dollar, raising interest rates, and creating new opportunities for foreign banks to make dollar-denominated loans to local businesses.[7]

Thailand again offers a good illustration of the results: net portfolio investment (involving the purchase of Thai stocks and bonds, especially by U.S. mutual and pension funds) rose from an average of only $646 million in the period 1985-89 to $5.5 billion in 1993 and even higher in the following years.[8] Considerably more money was raised through the Bangkok International Banking Facility, which was established in 1993. This conduit enabled Thai finance companies and banks to borrow approximately $50 billion over a three-year period from foreign (primarily Japanese) banks in Bangkok. Thus, the rapid growth rates of the past were sustained, but at a cost, as the country's foreign debt soared from $21 billion in 1989 to $89 billion in 1996. It is worth emphasizing that the IMF and World Bank had no complaints about these developments (which also encouraged and rewarded cronyism and corruption); they confidently concluded that as long as the financial transactions were being made by private as opposed to public agents, market forces would ensure the appropriate level of debt and efficient use of funds.

The borrowed money did not go into productive investments. Thai finance companies and banks relent a large percentage of the money to property developers. By late 1995, as might be expected given the unbalanced nature of wealth in Thailand, there was a glut of both commercial and residential units. By the beginning of 1997 almost half of all loans made to property developers were nonperforming. Thai finance companies and banks began to default on their foreign loans.

Foreign investors now wanted out of Thailand. Adding to their concern was growing uncertainty over whether the Thai central bank had sufficient dollars to cover investor withdrawals at the pegged exchange rate. This concern was fueled by the fact that Thailand's export offensive was losing steam; its export growth rate fell from approximately 25 percent in 1995 to an absolute decrease of almost two percent in 1996, largely because regional overproduction drove down export prices (Jomo K. S., 1998, p. 31). As foreign investors raced to unload their stocks and bonds (driving down the respective markets) and call in their dollar loans, it became clear that central bank reserves would not be up to the task. Speculators soon joined in the run on the *baht*. The government jacked up interest rates and ran through its reserves, but it could not slow the rush for dollars. Finally, on July 2, 1997, the Thai government abandoned its pegged exchange rate; the *baht* fell by 18 percent on that day alone. That fall, in turn, stimulated more selling and speculation, pushing domestic stock and bond markets and the *baht* down still further.

As Thailand was being tested, investors and speculators turned their attention to other countries in the region. Malaysia and Indonesia had also engaged in substantial foreign borrowing, recorded large and growing current account deficits, established dollar-linked exchange rates, and allowed their finance companies and banks to commit a high percentage of loans to glutted property markets. They had also suffered the effects of regional overproduction of exports. For example, Malaysia's export growth rate slowed from 20.3 percent in 1995 to 6.5 percent in 1996 (Jomo K. S., 1998, p. 31). Not surprisingly, investors and speculators began pulling money out of these countries as well. Stock and bond markets fell, and before July was over the Malaysian *ringgit* and the Indonesian *rupiah* were both headed downward.

Finally, to avert a complete economic meltdown, Thailand (in August 1997) and Indonesia (in October 1997) were forced to ask the IMF for assistance and, in return, accept an IMF structural adjustment program. Malaysia, as it had done in the mid-1980s, designed its own structural adjustment program.

The effects of this economic disaster could not be contained within Southeast Asia. South Korea, as we saw in the previous chapter, was suffering from its own economic problems, including the bankruptcy of large *chaebol* firms and an ever growing current account deficit and foreign debt. As the financial panic swept through Southeast Asia, foreign investors became increasingly concerned about the creditworthiness of South Korean firms and banks and the adequacy of the Bank of Korea's shrinking foreign exchange holdings. They began selling stocks and calling in loans; by mid-November, the South Korean *won* was in free fall and the country was facing its own major foreign debt crisis. Reluctantly, the South Korean government agreed to an IMF program in early December 1997.

The combination of collapsing currencies and government responses to them brought a swift end to the East Asian growth "miracle." The SEA-3 and South Korea went into deep recession in 1998: Indonesia's GDP fell 13.7 percent, Thailand's fell 7.7 percent, Malaysia's fell 6.3 percent, and South Korea's fell 6.1 percent. While each country has experienced some growth in 1999, "unless there is a sustained recovery in private sector demand, economists say, the first rays of recovery could turn out to be as illusory as the first day of an English spring. Most forecasts suggest that at best, the crisis-stricken countries will manage only marginal growth [in 1999]" (Montagnon, 1999, p. 17). No one is forecasting significant reductions in poverty, unemployment, or inequality. Moreover, and more fundamentally, neither the crisis nor the bounce back from it promise any significant change in the underlying structure and orientation of these economies. Focusing on the SEA-3, Japanese affiliates operating in these countries have largely responded to the crisis by buying out their local joint venture partners and further redirecting production to export. In August 1997, for example, Mitsubishi Motors "raised its stake in" its Thai subsidiary "from 48 percent to 98 percent," and it "also became the first Japanese auto maker in Thailand to [take advantage of the country's low exchange rate and] pump up exports" (Terry, 1998, p. 3).

Lessons From the Crisis

Malaysian Prime Minister Mahathir quickly blamed the crisis on Western speculators and called for tougher capital controls. There can be no doubt that speculators played a role in driving down currency rates and that capital controls are useful. But Mahathir's claim missed the mark. As the discussion above makes clear, the crisis was generated by the very workings of East Asia's growth strategy. For example, the decision to drop financial controls and open up financial markets was made by Southeast Asian governments themselves, because they needed to attract funds to cover widening current account deficits. And these deficits were caused, in large part, by the dependent nature of their export industries (as well as the consumption desires of the wealthy). National trade problems were intensified by the fact that growing numbers of Asian countries were trying to export the same basic products. In short, the reality is that the export-based growth strategy is no longer able to deliver sustained high rates of national growth, with or without capital controls.

The IMF continues to blame the East Asian crisis on cronyism and corruption, arguing that free markets and independent public regulatory agencies would have prevented banks from recklessly funneling money to well connected but poorly managed businesses for ill-conceived property developments and investments. But while such cronyism and corruption is a serious problem, the crisis was triggered most immediately by government-initiated financial and industrial deregulation (which in turn encouraged cronyism and corruption) Moreover, its fundamental roots were in East Asian structures of production, not finance.

Even more importantly, IMF structural-adjustment policies will do nothing to promote economic development. East Asian governments found themselves without enough foreign exchange to enable their corporations and banks to pay foreign creditors. Seeking to help East Asian elites avoid default, the IMF offered an immediate infusion of foreign exchange. In exchange for these funds and the promise of more to come, the governments of Thailand, Indonesia, and South Korea each agreed to an IMF structural-adjustment program The programs were designed to ensure that these countries would open themselves more fully to international business as well as give priority to earning the foreign exchange necessary to pay international debts. Acceptance of such programs is supposed to encourage international lenders to extend new credits, thereby enabling existing regimes to avoid a prolonged depression and social chaos.

More specifically, the IMF programs required the Thai, Indonesian, and South Korean governments to: maintain high interest rates to attract funds and defend currencies, cut spending and growth to reduce incomes and imports; weaken labor rights and unions to lower labor costs and promote exports; and privatize, reduce tariffs, and end restrictions on foreign ownership of financial and non-financial businesses to attract foreign investment. Malaysia, while rejecting IMF oversight, has imposed similar policies, although with less gusto than the other countries.[9] The IMF line will make the targeted East Asian countries even more dependent on exports and foreign capital than they currently are, and in the process further lower wages and undermine working and living conditions for the majority of their citizens. It is also likely to further intensify trade imbalances throughout the world, encouraging reactions that are bound to lead the global economy closer to a more generalized crisis of overproduction.

History has shown that IMF "neoliberalism" does not work, except in the narrowest sense of defending capitalist interests, and progressives are right to resist it as an answer to East Asia's problems.[10] However, in their desire to demonstrate the failure of neoliberalism and build resistance to it, some progressives have rallied around existing East Asian regimes, calling for a strengthening of state-directed, export-driven growth. Unfortunately, this strategy leads to a political dead end. The East Asian experience, especially that of South Korea, does demonstrate that there is an alternative to the free market; but East Asian state capitalism contains its own contradictions. And even during its period of rapid growth, working people suffered greatly.

The real lesson of the East Asian experience is that popular and progressive development alternatives cannot be derived from the competitive "successes" of capitalist development regimes. Rather than being limited to policy proposals that are consistent with the predetermined capitalist framework, progressive economic visions must always be informed by popular struggles *in and against* this framework—struggles pointing toward a worker-community driven transformation of development itself. What is required, in short, is bold new thinking about the institutional changes necessary to create more stable, democratic, and socially and environmentally responsive political economies.

PART FOUR

East Asia and the Crisis of Development Theory

Chapter 13

Mainstream Responses to the East Asian Crisis

The 1997-98 economic collapse of Thailand, Indonesia, Malaysia, and South Korea came as a shock not only to government and business leaders, but also to development economists.[1] Even after the assault on Asian currencies moved into full swing in mid-1997, the Asian Development Bank's chief economist still predicted that "these economies should be growing again at a fair clip in the second half of 1998 and thereafter" (Gargan, 1997, p. C15). However, the end of the year found them all in a tailspin, with all relevant economic and social indicators in sharp decline.

Prior to the crisis, mainstream discussions of the East Asian economic experience had largely been limited to a debate between two opposing theoretical views over the factors propelling the region's rapid growth. The dominant view, neoliberalism, was championed by the IMF, the World Bank, and the U.S. government. It credited East Asia's economic successes to fiscal and monetary discipline, the allocation of domestic resources in response to trade-revealed comparative advantages, and—especially in the case of the Southeast Asian economies of Thailand, Indonesia, and Malaysia (SEA-3)—foreign direct investment (FDI). The minority view, put forward by structural-institutionalist economists (hereafter structuralists) with support from some Japanese and other regional government officials, emphasized the positive role played by activist state policies in developing industrial capabilities and competitive advantages (see Chapter 1).

Despite this disagreement, neoliberals and structuralists shared a crucial common ground. Both agreed that East Asia's economic successes demonstrated the ability of capitalism to promote third world development.

Indeed, both actually embraced the ideology, which has become so familiar in the years following the collapse of the Soviet Union, that "there is no alternative" (TINA) to capitalism.

The East Asian crisis has thrown both versions of mainstream development theory into crisis precisely because it threatens this shared vision. The chant of "there is no alternative" rings increasingly hollow, as it becomes clear that the only alternative offered *by capitalism* is "discipline" and "stability," terms that increasingly carry anti-societal, and anti-human developmental implications. In fact, the East Asian crisis threatens to echo the "TINA" notion back onto capitalism as: "This is no alternative!"

This chapter critically examines neoliberal and structuralist understandings of, and responses to, the East Asian crisis. It is shown that neither theory is able to recognize, much less confront, the real problems facing East Asian workers and communities—problems generated by the inner dynamics of capitalist development. Accordingly, new socialist-oriented development visions have never been more needed than they are today.

Neoliberal Responses to the Crisis

Neoliberals usually blame third world economic problems, especially balance of payments deficits and currency depreciation, on overly expansionary macro policies and resulting wage and price inflation. However, most did not blame the East Asian crisis on such policies. The simple reason was that fiscal and monetary policy had not been particularly expansive in South Korea and the SEA-3. In fact, most neoliberals had previously credited East Asian macro-policy discipline and the resulting macro-stability for the region's economic success. In addition, any focus on economic "overheating" as a cause of the crisis would have drawn attention to the negative role played by capital inflows, something that neoliberals were reluctant to have happen since openness to foreign capital had also received credit in their explanations for East Asia's successes.

Determined to place blame on East Asian policymakers rather than capitalist market dynamics, conservative neoliberals therefore redirected their fire away from policy decisions affecting *aggregate demand* toward those involving resource *allocation*. They argued that the primary cause of the crisis was too much government intervention in economic activity, leading to misdirected and inefficient investments in both public and private projects. This intervention, largely made possible because of government control over bank lending decisions, was said to have been motivated by misguided state planning efforts and, perhaps even more importantly, corruption. In this way, government interference with market forces was linked to East Asia's financial crises.

Although some conservative neoliberals were willing to concede that state planning, as supported by state authoritarianism and other so-called "Asian values," had once played a positive role in East Asian industrialization, they believed it had now become counterproductive because of changes in the international economic and political environment. Among the most often cited changes were the globalization of finance, the emergence of new competitors in the manufactured export-led growth game, and the end of Cold War–related insulation of state capitalist development from market pressures. For example, Meredith Woo-Cumings (1997) argued that the prior successes of South Korea's industrial planning efforts were crucially dependent on periodic infusions of United States and Japanese aid. She even suggested that "throughout the past 30 years the Korean financial system was vulnerable to exactly the sort of calamity that has now occurred." In other words, the end of the Cold War spelled the end of the state capitalist development option.

Left-wing neoliberals, while sharing the conservative goal of transforming East Asian countries into open, liberal political economies of the "Western" (and especially United States) variety, nonetheless had a somewhat different understanding of the crisis. Instead of blaming East Asia's financial problems on government meddling in bank lending decisions, they pointed to *inadequate regulation and supervision* of financial institutions as the root cause of the region's problems. This position was argued most forcefully by Joseph Stiglitz, the World Bank's chief economist, who observed that: "Inadequate oversight, not over-regulation, caused [East Asia's economic] problems. Consequently, our emphasis should not be on deregulation, but on finding the right regulatory regime to re-establish stability and confidence" (1997, p. A19).

This emphasis on inadequate financial regulation also led left-wing neoliberals to part ways with their more conservative colleagues on a number of other issues. For example, left-wing neoliberals were critical of IMF-imposed austerity policies, arguing that since East Asian countries "do not have spendthrift governments, but rather huge private-sector debt problems, . . . austerity adds to economic pain without solving the debt problem" (Kahn, 1998, p. C8). They also tended to view corruption differently, as a *consequence as well as a cause* of the inadequate supervision over financial institutions. Finally, they also worried more about the unfair distributional consequences of the IMF-organized bailouts. Paul Krugman, for example, "wonder[ed] whether it would not have been better to let South

Korea declare a moratorium on foreign debt repayment while it moved swiftly to cleanse the balance sheets of the banks and conglomerates" (quoted in Passell, 1997, p. C2).

Problems with Neoliberal Responses

There was an unmistakable air of unreality about conservative neoliberal reactions to the crisis. One reason was that their explanations for the crisis directly contradicted their prior analyses of East Asian economic successes. Even the neoliberal Jeffrey Sachs detected "a touch of the absurd in the unfolding drama, as international money managers harshly castigated the very same Asian governments they were praising just months before" (1997).

The limits of the conservative neoliberal position are perhaps best illustrated by an examination of its treatment of corruption. According to conservative neoliberals, the corruption which brought East Asian growth to a sudden halt was an outgrowth of East Asia's authoritarian governments and regimented societies. Yet this authoritarianism, regimentation, and corruption had been validated economically for decades by exports, FDI, and short-term capital movements. The main reason was that authoritarianism helped to repress labor and other popular movements, thereby lowering (or socializing) the costs of industrial accumulation. Repression also ensured support from powerful external actors such as the United States and Japan, both of whom sought regional political stability and attractive opportunities for their transnational corporations (TNCs) and financial investors.

Naturally, such authoritarian regimes also provided a congenial environment for corruption. Significantly, however, even though this corruption was eventually bound to disrupt growth, it was only *after* East Asian countries partially liberalized their financial systems and reduced restrictions on short-term capital flows (at the advice of conservative neoliberal agencies) that financial-sector corruption began to rage out of control. Moreover, conservative neoliberals were never able to explain how the funneling of billions of dollars of capital into such corrupt systems was consistent with the purported wisdom and discipline of liberalized markets.

The only real attempts by conservative neoliberals to address the contradictions between their pre-crisis and post-crisis accounts involved appeals to changed circumstances. This meant admitting that state interventionism had indeed provided a viable path towards industrialization and growth in the past, especially in South Korea, but then noting that things were now different. However, such responses generated new problems for conservative neoliberals. No matter how positively phrased, they implied the progressive narrowing of development options in the global capitalist economy. After all, if South Korea's authoritarian industrialization had depended on special Cold War circumstances, how likely was it that other third world countries could generate similar growth in a less hospitable global capitalist environment.

Left-wing neoliberal explanations of the crisis were also inadequate. As noted above, these tended to blame East Asia's problems on bad loans caused mainly by inadequate banking regulations and too easy access to short-term foreign capital. Accordingly, the preferred left-wing neoliberal response included measures to strengthen financial-sector regulatory regimes and reduce speculative short-term capital movements; FDI and other long-term capital flows, on the other hand, were still to be encouraged.

This emphasis on questionable lending practices and volatile capital movements did promote a more accurate understanding of the region's crises. It also focused attention on important issues such as the role capital controls played in shielding China and Taiwan from the worst of the regional instability. Nonetheless, left-wing neoliberals failed to move beyond conservative TINA-type thinking.

Insofar as left-wing neoliberals blamed East Asia's weak system of financial regulation on authoritarianism and corruption, their analysis was vulnerable to the same criticism directed at conservative neoliberals. Left-wing neoliberals also failed to consider whether "sound" financial regulations might prove impossible to sustain in a world marked by intense financial-sector competition. This seemed a likely possibility given that foreign investors had willingly poured billions of dollars into these imprudently managed financial systems.

Left wing neoliberals also conveniently overlooked the more general question of why so much core capital had been available for short-term investment in East Asia—a question that might have led them to doubt the wisdom of capitalist "market forces." After all, the accelerating flows of core-generated money capital into domestic and third world speculation, and the growing weight and even dominance of financial activity in total core economic activity, had developed despite an abundance of unmet economic and social needs in the core countries. The movement of huge sums of money capital into speculative activities in East Asia, where many workers and communities lacked basic goods and services, was also hard to justify, at least from a social as opposed to a purely bottom-line point of view.

Left-wing neoliberalism's dichotomous treatment of short- and long-term capital flows was also problematic. Short-term capital inflows were viewed as unstable and thus dangerous; long-term capital movements were seen as stable and thus desirable. Left-wing neoliberals therefore encouraged East Asian countries to discourage the former and promote the latter, especially FDI. In reality, however, the crisis had already shown that reliance on FDI carried its own dangers.

Sizeable inflows of foreign direct investment had enabled East Asian countries (especially the SEA-3) to maintain overvalued exchange rates. Although such exchange rates had helped keep inflation under control, they also increased East Asia's vulnerability to speculative attacks. Moreover, it was the reduction in FDI, as Japanese, South Korean, and Taiwanese transnational corporations began redirecting their operations to other lower wage countries (especially China), that had forced the SEA-3 to aggressively pursue short-term capital in order to finance their growing trade deficits. Most importantly, these deficits were themselves largely the result of transnational investment which had created highly import-dependent structures of export-oriented production in the SEA-3. Here again, the only answer neoliberalism could offer was that "there is no alternative."

The inability or unwillingness of left-wing neoliberals to move beyond TINA-type thinking was also evident in their truncated concern with distributional issues. For example, their alarm over the regressive distributional consequences of IMF-U.S. bailout plans was never extended to include the regressive nature and limits of export-led growth itself. They refused to recognize how the competitive "success" of East Asian export-led growth had been based on low hourly wages, long and intensive work times, acceptance of high industrial accident rates, the severe exploitation of young female workers, and the plundering of natural resources and destruction of the environment.

Structuralist Responses to the Crisis

As noted above, structuralists, in contrast to neoliberals, emphasized the role of state intervention and industrial policy in East Asia's economic successes, especially in South Korea and Taiwan. Not surprisingly, then, structuralist post-crisis writings have focused on South Korea rather than the SEA-3.

Structuralists have blamed South Korea's crisis mainly on the state's overly rapid liberalization of the financial sector and abandonment of industrial policy. According to Alice Amsden and Yoon-Dae Euh, "it was the government's decision to allow banks and other financial institutions to borrow without interference that created the current crisis" (1997, p. A23). Ha-joon Chang (1997) argued that once the government stopped playing "its traditional role of coordinating investments," it was natural that firms would begin to make questionable use of domestic and foreign loans. One result was the emergence of excess capacities "in industries like automobiles, shipbuilding, steel, petrochemicals and semiconductors," which in turn reinforced "the fall in export prices and the accumulation of non-performing loans" (Chang, 1997). Once the South Korean currency began to depreciate, the foreign debt burdens of South Korean banks and industrial firms grew commensurately larger in local currency terms, driving even more companies into default.

Structuralists shared many common understandings of the crisis with left-wing neoliberals while advocating somewhat different responses. Economists from both perspectives agreed that the crisis was mainly financial, not reflecting adversely on the fundamental "soundness" of the South Korean economy. As a result, both structuralists and left-wing neoliberals favored tighter financial regulations and measures to reduce short-term capital flows.[2] For structuralists, however, such actions were more than a means to stabilize the country's banking system, they were also necessary steps to restore the effectiveness of industrial policy. This explains why structuralists were much more likely to strongly support *selective* credit controls and *stringent* controls on short-term capital flows.

Structuralists and neoliberals also agreed on the need for upgrading production and investment into higher value-added sectors. Significantly, structuralists did not even dissent from the neoliberal call for the gradual removal of trade protection in *pre-established* industries. However, structuralists did part ways with left-wing neoliberals in their *consistent* advocacy of trade protection and export subsidies, as necessary weapons in the industrial upgrading process. Most neoliberals, even the left-wing ones, advocated a more "natural" upgrading, with government support limited to the provision of "public good" facilities (education, basic research, transport, communications) and the establishment of the stable domestic environment required by domestic entrepreneurs and TNCs.

Finally, both structuralists and left-wing neoliberals strongly opposed IMF-type austerity policies, believing that such policies would only intensify existing credit crunches and recessions. Indeed, both groups of economists worried that imposition of IMF-type austerity was likely to generate major political backlashes with uncertain consequences.

Problems with Structuralist Responses

Both structuralists and left-wing neoliberals understand development as the outcome of technological and managerial improvements in production on micro and macro levels. Despite the structuralists' preference for a more activist state engineering of industrialization, they share the neoliberal allegiance to "modernization" on capitalist terms. This helps explain structuralism's general disregard of contradictions, including the generation of liberalization pressures by state capitalist development itself.

Especially in regard to South Korea, structuralists tended to treat economic liberalization as a symptom of a lack of will among state managers. In reality, the *chaebols'* growing power vis-à-vis the South Korean government followed inexorably from the formers' growing economic importance as dictated by the government's centralized and authoritarian development strategy. Hence, the eventual loosening of financial controls over the *chaebol* was hardly exogenous. Moreover, "external" pressures to liberalize capital flows and domestic finance were a natural response to successful *chaebol* forays into U.S. and other core-country markets. And, as the structuralists themselves emphasized, the semiforced opening of the domestic financial system seriously weakened the South Korean state's financial controls over domestic business operations and sectoral investment planning efforts.

The structuralists' technocratic focus on *national* industrial policies also caused them to ignore the systemic roots of regional and global overproduction with its disruptive effects on export-led growth. More specifically, the regionwide competition for export markets led national governments to seek advantage through lower unit labor costs, which led to limited domestic wage-based demand, and even greater national export dependence. By 1996, the resulting regional growth in export capacity, combined with the limits of core-country markets and growing competition from lower wage countries (especially China), had produced falling export prices and steep declines in export growth rates for South Korea as well as the SEA-3. Making matters worse for these countries, with the end of the Cold War, the United States no longer had an overriding interest in promoting new industrialization success stories (and potential competitors) in East Asia or anywhere else. Thus, U.S. actions contributed to the growth of disruptive liberalization pressures, and the effective reduction of statist policy options. In sum, structuralists have evaded the most important implication of the crisis, namely, the closing off of development possibilities within capitalism.

Beyond TINA

The foregoing survey of mainstream responses to the East Asian crisis reveals not only their theoretical and practical bankruptcy, but also that this bankruptcy is symptomatic of a global capitalist system which is increasingly incapable of accommodating national development efforts even on its own terms of competitiveness and growth. The East Asian crisis is beginning to sweep away contrary illusions about the opportunities for "modernization" within the capitalist framework—illusions that had largely been created by the special circumstances of the Cold War and by the relatively strict subordination of financial capital to industrial capital in the immediate post–World War II era. With these circumstances no longer present, "successful" capitalist growth now—even more than before—hinges on individual countries' ability to keep unit labor costs internationally competitive, that is, to keep working-class living conditions below international standards for labor of comparable productivity. This systemic bias not only makes any development "success" inherently self limiting, it also creates a powerful tendency toward global overproduction and further downward pressures on worker and community conditions on a global scale.

Given the evident foreclosure of sustainable and human-developmental paths within capitalism, now is not the time to lose confidence in the ability of workers and communities to create a far better economic system. Such a system will no doubt require the construction of new representative-democratic structures of economic governance on local, national, regional, and global levels. However, in developing our socioeconomic visions, we must keep in mind the dialectic of ends and means—above all the principle that "every step of real movement is more important that a dozen programs" (Marx to Wilhelm Bracke, May 5, 1875, in Marx and Engels [1975, p. 278]). In short, new approaches to development based on worker-community empowerment, solidarity, and ecological sustainability can and must be forged out of the growing struggles in East Asia against the marketization of human existence.

Chapter 14

Beyond TINA: Toward Worker-Community Centered Visions of Development

This book has examined competing non-Marxist theories of East Asian growth and crisis, and found them wanting on both theoretical and practical grounds. In the process, it was also argued, both theoretically and through a Marxist-inspired analysis of East Asian dynamics, that Marxism provides a superior framework for understanding the East Asian experience. More specifically, the previous chapters have shown that the East Asian crisis is a crisis of capitalism and that a solution that is responsive to the needs of workers and their communities will require challenging both the logic of capitalism and the power of capitalists.

This is no small task. However, as this final chapter shows, the devastating effects of the crisis have already motivated working people to fight back on many fronts. And, while there are no simplistic formulas for building an effective response to the crisis, a Marxism that critically engages with these popular defensive struggles does offer valuable political and ideological weapons. Both strategically and programmatically, a Marxist orientation can strengthen worker-community resistance to neoliberal restructuring while advancing the movement for the needed social transformation of East Asian political economies.

The Devastating Effects of the Crisis

While international organizations, the region's governments, and the mainstream media acknowledge the existence of the economic crisis, they have generally understated or ignored its negative impact on working people.[1] For example, official poverty, unemployment, and income figures are severely biased downward (see below) by misleading definitions and inappropriate measurement procedures (Chossudovsky, 1999). The media has also been more concerned with highlighting efforts to stabilize currency and stock markets and promote multinational investment, than in documenting the deterioration of people's living and working conditions.

Still, the terrible consequences of the crisis cannot be hidden.[2] In Indonesia, the official unemployment rate reached 21 percent in 1998. Per-capita income plunged from $1200 in mid-1997 to $400 in mid-1999 (Shari, 1999, p. 53). *Forbes* magazine explained the severity of the situation this way: "When you think 'recession' in Western countries, you think worry. Here recession means hunger. Combine recession with runaway inflation and you have a recipe for disaster—and disaster looms. . . . Some 140 million Indonesians, 66% of the population, could slip below the poverty line by the end of 1999, says the International Labor Organization" (Weinberg, 1998, p. 53).

In Thailand, the government claimed an unemployment rate of 4.4 percent in 1998, with over three million unemployed. However, as in Indonesia, these figures were far from reliable. Thailand, like Indonesia, has no unemployment benefit system. Thus, in Thailand, "government figures were based on surveys of companies, those no longer paying social security and numbers of people appearing at the Ministry of Labor, asking for advice. Worse still the actual definition of someone in work, according to the National Statistics Office, is anyone who is aged 13 and above who has worked *at least 1 hour in 1 week!*" (Ungpakorn, 1999, pp. 18–19, emphasis in original). The misleading picture of a "limited" rise in official unemployment is also countered by the reality of a "sharp drop in incomes" for the majority of Thais (Friedman, 1999).

In both Thailand and Indonesia, newly unemployed urban workers were told by their respective governments to go back to their rural homelands. This was hardly a reasonable response: "The chief of Thailand's irrigation department announced on January 2 [1998] that the irrigation system would not be able to cope with the expected number of people returning to farming as a way of survival. In Indonesia, drought has devastated rural Java, making a mass influx of sacked workers even more insupportable" (Jones, 1998).

In Malaysia, the unemployment rate for 1998 rose "from the pre-crisis figure of 2.7 percent to 6.4 percent or an additional 300,000 workers unemployed." However, these numbers significantly understate the extent of the unemployment problem since "the government figure relies on compulsory reporting of retrenchments by employers and does not include the number of contract, casual and temporary workers laid off. The figure also does not include the number of documented and undocumented migrant workers who have returned home as a result of the crisis" (Chandran, 1998, p. 23). As in Thailand, more revealing of the widespread effects of the crisis has been the decline in earnings: "Reports state that over 60 percent of workers are facing cuts in real and nominal wages, including withdrawal of bonuses, wage freezes, and cuts in wages and overtime work" (p. 23).

In South Korea, unemployment increased from its precrisis level of 2.5 percent to 7.7 percent in 1998. In contrast to Thailand, Indonesia, and Malaysia, South Korea does have an unemployment insurance fund. But, it is "limited in both its coverage of workers and its duration" (*Asian Labour Update*, 1998a, p. 3). And, as in the other countries, wages have fallen sharply. According to one employers' association official, the crisis has enabled most companies to secure wage cuts of 40 to 50 percent (Kang, 1998, pp. 28–29). Mass homelessness has also reappeared for the first time since the 1950s, with "thousands of homeless people now dwelling in railway stations in Seoul" (p. 29). One measure of the desperation that now exists: by mid-1998, suicides reached "an alarming average of about 25 per day—up 36% from a year ago" (Bremner and Moon, 1998, p. 52).

The Crisis and Working-Class Resistance to Capitalism

When the mainstream media does choose to acknowledge the hardships facing working people in East Asia, it most often does so to discourage them (or their working-class sisters and brothers in other countries) from organizing and engaging in anti-capitalist activities. Ironically, given its precrisis perspective, the media has pursued this goal by arguing that the past boom brought few benefits to working people, thus they have not lost as much as it might seem; that the crisis was predictable given the corruption and inefficiencies underlying East Asian political economies; and, therefore, that the crisis and resulting IMF-imposed restructuring should really be welcomed by all East Asians. For example, when discussing the economic problems of Thai workers, a *New York Times* article reported that:

> there was always an underside to the boom: fully 60 percent of the country's 60 million people remained poor. Half the nation's wealth was in the hands of its richest 10 percent. The disparity in income between the country's rich and poor became one of the five sharpest in the world, according to World Bank figures. Throughout the region, to varying degrees, economic growth

has brought the greatest benefits to a privileged few. The poor majority often gained better health care and better social services, but they remained poor. (Mydans, 1997)

The article focused on a group of workers who were at one time employed by the PAR Garment Factory, a producer of clothes bearing such brand names as Nike, The Gap, London Fog, and Old Navy. Arriving for work one day in late October 1997, these workers were greeted by a sign that said the company was closed and armed guards who told them to go home. One of the workers, Miss Suthasini, had worked at the factory for ten years. According to the article, she earned the minimum wage on her first day at work and the minimum wage on her last day. "Far from making her wealthy, her salary of $3.50 a day was not even enough to cover her basic needs." When the company closed Miss Suthasini was "left not only jobless but also in debt. She owes $40, or nearly two weeks pay. Beyond this, she has little to show for Thailand's economic boom" (Mydans, 1997).

The mainstream press has often treated the crisis as an unavoidable, although painful, step on the road to the creation of democratic and efficient East Asian economies. In a typical *New York Times* column, Thomas Friedman argued against the

notion floating around out there that countries such as Thailand, South Korea and Indonesia were all doing just fine until the ugly, greedy forces of globalization disrupted them. That is pure nonsense. They were all accidents waiting to happen. .... Thais will freely tell you today that they had a corrupt, crony-capitalist system with no transparency, a plethora of insider dealings, a less than democratic regime and a public often living beyond its means. And what the global economic crisis did was expose the rot and force changes onto Thailand—democratizing changes—that the traditional elite families and power brokers were resisting. (Friedman, 1999)

Such reporting, with its underlying message to keep calm and wait for market forces to produce progress, is clearly motivated more by ideology than by a desire to accurately describe—much less encourage—efforts by East Asian workers to respond to the crisis. This is easily highlighted by revisiting the story of the PAR workers. The *New York Times* story implied that the plant shutdown was the result of the economic crisis and that, sadly, the workers had little choice but to accept their fate. In fact, the workers had already battled the company months earlier over its refusal to pay wages on time: "four hundred women workers occupied the factory and blockaded some of the managers in the office, forcing them to negotiate an agreement" (Ungpakorn, 1999, p. 21). When a new dispute over wages and working conditions broke out in October 1997, the company responded by locking the workers out so they could not again occupy the factory. The workers responded by camping outside the factory gates, next to a ten-lane highway, for six months, whereupon they finally won government support and the company's agreement "not to cut bonuses and the holiday entitlement" and to "take the 449 employees back" as well as "hold a monthly meeting with the union" (*Asian Labour Update*, 1998b, p. 28).

This kind of resistance is far from unusual. Simply put, workers do not have the luxury of patience. With their survival literally on the line, they are often quite willing and able to take direct action in support of their basic needs. At the same time, however, struggles such as the one at PAR are largely defensive and usually carried out in isolation from similar struggles by other workers. As such, they are by themselves unable to produce the kind of structural changes necessary to enable workers to secure meaningful and lasting improvements in their living and working conditions. Clearly, the challenge for those pursuing this goal is to find ways of building upon this resistance in the context of developing a more coordinated and focused effort aimed at broad-based social transformation.

A Marxism that critically engages popular movements can provide the theoretical and strategic orientation necessary to meet this challenge. There is no universal Marxist program of action that activists need only follow to empower working people. But Marxism provides a framework for analysis and criteria for action that can help working people overcome the structural contradictions and limits of capitalism. While always aware of the objective realities of capitalism, Marxism "derives" its socialist visions only from popular struggles in and against capitalist relations of production and competition; hence a critical, forward-looking, and transformative engagement with worker-community movements is built into the Marxist orientation itself. The remainder of this chapter shows how such a popularly-informed Marxism can assist the development of worker-community struggles for a more cooperative-democratic economic system in East Asia and elsewhere. The discussion begins with a critical examination of the region's dominant (non-Marxist) progressive organizing efforts, most of which have been spearheaded by leading non-governmental organizations (NGOs).[3]

Beginning in the mid- to late 1980s, South Korea and the SEA-3 countries experienced a rapid growth in NGOs, which have come to constitute the heart of what many in the progressive movement call (depending on the country) "civil society," "the citizens' movement," or "the peoples' sector." The growth of these NGOs was largely the result of the sizeable expansion of the middle class, which was, in turn, the result of the region's rapid economic growth. Many members of this newly expanded middle class, although pleased with their new economic status, remained determined to promote further political, social, and economic reforms in their respective societies. Among the most important changes sought were a more open and responsive political system, greater guarantees of human and civil rights, a safer environment, and improvements in the status of women. Thus, activists from this social sector began to form organizations which, in contrast to left-oriented, working-class based organizations, were more concerned with achieving issue-focused reforms than advancing "transformative" or "totalizing" projects. As a result, these NGOs, operating individually and collectively, tended to promote a non-class, although activist, movement for social reform.

In response to the crisis, NGOs, motivated by different understandings of the crisis, have tended to follow different organizing strategies, although two main approaches have tended to dominate. Many NGOs, understanding the crisis to be largely the result of a lack of democracy, have focused their efforts on promoting democratic reforms as the best response to the crisis. Another large group of (more radically inclined) NGOs have tended to blame the crisis on unregulated international financial speculation, TNCs, and/or Western imperialism. They have sought to win majority support for broad political and economic changes by presenting them as necessary to defend the national interest. Unfortunately, as is shown next, neither approach has served to advance working-class interests.

The Failure of Non-Class Strategies: Organizing for "Democracy"

As was discussed in Chapter 13, it has become popular to blame the East Asian crisis on "cronyism" or the lack of transparency and accountability in East Asian political and economic institutions. There is no disputing the fact that democracy has been severely limited in East Asia, and many activists from the left, labor, and NGO community have long been struggling to promote it. Thus, the struggle for democracy clearly predated the crisis. This history has predisposed many activists, especially those from the middle-class based NGO community, to embrace the "lack of democracy" explanation for the crisis. No doubt they believe that this explanation adds extra weight and legitimacy to their ongoing efforts to reform their respective national political systems.

The work of one of the more prominent NGO groups in South Korea, the Citizens' Coalition for Economic Justice (CCEJ), offers a good illustration of the strategic implications of this perspective. In the political arena, the CCEJ has focused its efforts on increasing participation, accountability, and transparency. For example, it has begun monitoring the attendance and participation of National Assembly members, actually filing a lawsuit in 1998 against the legislature for "dereliction of duty in the face of the economic crisis" (*Civic Society*, 1998, p. 2). It is also working to establish recall movements against those National Assembly members who do not adequately represent the public interest (Ha, 1998b, p. 1).

In the economic arena, the CCEJ has been focusing on similar objectives, in particular making economic institutions more accountable and transparent. It is promoting efforts to transform the *chaebol* group structure, its goal being the creation of "independent firm-based management in parallel with the separation of ownership from management" (Choi, 1998, p. 4). In addition, the CCEJ's Citizens' Fair Trade Commission is working to oppose *chaebol* dominance of the economy by trying to protect the interests of small- and medium-sized enterprises and consumers (Cho, 1998, p. 5).

This approach is obviously based on a very limited conception of democracy—one that accepts the existing political-institutional framework while seeking to make it more open and transparent (and thus more democratic and responsive to popular interests). In the same way it also hopes to create a more efficient and responsive economic system, thereby solving the economic crisis. As may be apparent, this political perspective shares much in common with neoliberalism, which claims that a free market system is the best way to end the twin plagues of cronyism and monopoly, and achieve democracy and efficiency. Not surprisingly, then, the CCEJ and many other South Korean NGOs have supported South Korean president Kim Dae Jung's efforts to promote a free-market economy through the implementation of IMF structural-adjustment policies.

This approach has led many NGO activists to advocate policies that are both politically divisive and incapable of achieving a progressive resolution of the crisis. For example, when the crisis first exploded, President Kim Dae Jung, like most South Koreans, blamed it on the *chaebol*, highlighting their corrupt and inefficient practices. While the *chaebol* clearly deserved blame, neither Kim nor the majority of the NGO community extended their critique to the broader capitalist system. Rather, they called for a strengthening of market forces, arguing that this would not only weaken *chaebol* monopoly power and state-*chaebol* collaboration, but also help to weed out inefficient *chaebol* business practices from the economy. In short, they hoped to replace their deficient (monopoly) capitalist system with a superior (free market and Western-oriented) capitalist system.

For structural reasons, South Korean government attempts to reform the *chaebol* could only be half-hearted. Given that the country was in desperate need of foreign exchange and the *chaebol* were the country's most important and dynamic exporters, the government could not afford to weaken them. As a result, it was not long before official criticism of the *chaebol* and their policies became muted and a new "villain" was found. More specifically, with the encouragement of the IMF, labor "flexibility" became the linchpin for the successful remaking of South Korea's economy; those workers and their unions that resisted this flexibility quickly became targeted as the main obstacles to the nation's economic recovery.

The major domestic beneficiaries of Kim's policies have been the *chaebol*. The government and the NGO community continue to criticize them for their debts and non-transparent corporate structure. But, despite the fact that "the conglomerates [were] supposed to be so whipped by economic crisis that they would follow quietly along the path of reform . . . it hasn't happened that way. . . . Korea's Big Five conglomerates—Daewoo, Samsung, Hyundai, LG, and SK—have actually strengthened their grip on the economy since the crisis began" (Clifford, 1998, p. 56). Thus, marketization proceeds apace: the *chaebol* (and foreign capital) increase their dominance, and workers suffer from growing unemployment and wage cuts.

While NGO "democracy" advocates truly regret the enormous sacrifices being forced on working people, the logic of their position as described above leaves them with no choice but to encourage the restructuring process. This is made explicit in an article by the Director of CCEJ's Policy Research Department, in which he describes how "The government has committed itself to both structural adjustment of the economy and protection of the fired workers. . . . The dilemma is that structural adjustment will increase the number of unemployed; but if mass firings are not carried out, structural adjustment is impossible" (Ha, 1998a, p. 1). So what is to be done? According to the Director, "CCEJ views structural adjustment as absolutely necessary for the reformation of the social system. . . . [Thus] the most important role of the Kim Dae Jung government is to support civilian movements that are working to enable unemployed persons to regain their ability of self-support" (p. 1). As to the initiatives which the CCEJ supports, they include shelters for the homeless, food banks, and job counseling (Park, 1998). Such a strategy is not only based on a faulty understanding of the causes of the crisis, but also clearly works against the kind of political understandings and alliances necessary to build a meaningful response to it.

Unfortunately, many NGOs have pursued a similar strategy in Thailand, highlighted by their strong and largely uncritical support for their country's new constitution. The *New York Times* describes this constitution, which was approved in September 1997, as

> the most democratic constitution in the country's history—including a freedom of information act, which has set loose the media hounds on every government department—as well as 11 economic reform bills, including this month's [March 1999] new laws for bankruptcy and corporate restructuring. So many of the Asian Tigers never had real bankruptcy laws because everyone was just growing. They were like towns with only maternity wards and no funeral homes. But corporate funeral homes are critical to clear up a rotten economy, and now Thailand has them, as well as a whole new set of laws banning insider dealings and vote buying by officials. (Friedman, 1999)

Kavi Chongkittavron, executive editor of Thailand's *Nation* newspaper, makes explicit the connection between the new constitution (and its provisions to enhance transparency and accountability) and economic renewal as follows: "The economic problem here was political in nature and it could not be solved without changing these bad politicians" (Friedman, 1999).

Many of Thailand's middle-class based NGOs view "the major division [in Thai society] as between 'state' and 'society,' not between various classes" (Ungpakorn, 1999, p. 97). They therefore gave top priority to reforming the political sphere, not only to secure greater political and social rights, but also to end the corruption that they believed was largely responsible for the country's economic instabilities and inequalities. As in South Korea, the crisis only increased their motivation to work for political reform; not surprisingly, passage of the new constitution became their prime focus. As one scholar explained:

> Seeking something like a form of social democracy, the NGO movement had staked a lot on the development of a parliamentary system whereby interests could be articulated and aggregated. Their experience of marginalization in a parliamentary system dominated by money-politics has made them reconsider the political forms worthy of support—and many embraced PR [political reform] as a way of opening new channels for political participation and human rights protection. (Connors, 1999, p. 212)

The NGO community participated as actively as it could in the constitutional drafting process, and remained committed to the process despite
the fact that "politically oriented NGOs, numbering several hundred . . .
contributed many suggestions to the CDA [Constitutional Drafting Assem-
bly] . . . [but their suggestions] were only taken up when they fitted into
the general CDA agenda" (p. 217). The one major victory for NGO forces
was the CDA's agreement to accept the establishment of a Human Rights
Organization. Although the final draft constitution did contain a number
of other positive reforms, including an elected senate and the right for citizens to initiate legislation and impeachment, the class bias of the draft was
obvious.

For example, it allowed only individuals holding a university degree to
run for parliament. In addition, it required citizens to vote in the district
where they were officially registered to live. The problem with this requirement is that many workers, originally registered in their rural homelands,
now live and work in urban areas. Many are reluctant to change their registration for reasons of cost, fear of losing their inheritance rights to land,
and uncertainty over whether their current landlord would support their
re-registration. As a result of this requirement, they have been effectively
disenfranchised (Ungpakorn, 1999, p. 105). Worker groups submitted a
number of proposals, including measures to simplify the voter registration
process, increase public provision of social goods, and protect union rights;
all were rejected by the CDA. As a result, many of the "labor leaders who
were active in democracy organizations were quite critical of the draft"
(Connors, 1999, p. 218).

Despite the generally conservative nature of the draft, the parliament
voted in August 1997 to table it. However, crisis-generated popular disen-
chantment and NGO organizing eventually convinced Thai political leaders to change their decision; they approved the new constitution the
following month. The NGO community generally viewed adoption of this
new constitution as a major victory. Yet, its main significance is that it
promises to "increase government stability by favoring large parties
(through a semi-'party list' voting system) and by making it more difficult
to bring down governments mid term" (Ungpakorn, 1999, p. 102; Connors, 1999, pp. 202-203). It is hard to see how this represents a significant
step forward for Thai workers given the nature of the existing social order.

In sum, the NGO strategy highlighted here does not offer much of a
solution to the problems faced by working people in East Asia. It leads to
a very narrow notion of democracy and encourages a dangerous misunderstanding of capitalist logic and the causes of the crisis. Most importantly,

rather than building support for worker resistance to structural adjustment and encouraging efforts to develop an alternative vision of development, it ends up isolating working people and, in the case of South Korea, actually painting labor activists as opponents of economic renewal.

The Failure of Non-Class Strategies: Defending "The National Interest"

Other, more radical groups within the NGO community, while supporting increased popular participation in the formal political sector, believe that more far-reaching structural changes are needed to overcome the crisis. They have adopted an organizing strategy based not just on promotion of democracy, but even more so on defending "the national interest." There is certainly no direct conflict between the two approaches since, as defined, both are non-class in nature, and even the less radical NGOs that organize on the basis of promoting democracy claim to do so for the benefit of the entire nation. Still, organizing in defense of the national interest has allowed—if not encouraged—the more radical NGOs to directly raise issues dealing with the economy, and thus to directly challenge economic as well as political relationships and structures.

There are, of course, conservative as well as radical NGO approaches to defending the national interest. Those favoring a more conservative approach normally do not place a high priority on determining the causes of the economic crisis. What is critical to them is rallying the population to save the country from the resulting hardships and potential descent back into third world status.

Conservative efforts to defend the national interest are easily hijacked by governments and corporate elites. One example involves citizen donations of gold. In South Korea, "A state-run television network launched a campaign [in January 1998] to collect and export gold to raise hard currency. Nearly two million Koreans accepted weak won for their gold jewelry, with which the government raised $1.3 billion. Egging them on was a government-sponsored TV advertisement featuring Koreans winning a hard-fought tug-of-war. The message: 'Let us overcome the economic crisis'" (Schuman, 1999, p. A6). In Thailand, the government followed a similar strategy, promoting the "Thais help Thais" campaign to encourage people to "donate gold and foreign currency to the government" (Ungpakorn, 1999, p. 40).

Even when such campaigns are not taken seriously by the majority of the population, the general call for national sacrifice in defense of the country can be used against the working class. In South Korea, for example, Kim Dae Jung

> quickly set about getting powerful interest groups—big business and the unions—behind stringent reforms. On Jan. 15, 1998, a month before his inauguration, his party formed a commission of government, business and labor representatives to hammer out a labor agreement. Meeting resistance from union leaders, the government appealed to their nationalism, saying that "unless Korea followed the IMF conditions, then we cannot expect any more financial support," says Labor Minister Lee Ki Ho. The unions accepted changing the law to allow easier layoffs after the government promised to monitor companies for any abuses of the new law. (Schuman, 1999, pp. A1, A6)

In fact, the democratic and independent Korean Confederation of Trade Unions (KCTU) accepted this compromise not so much because it thought it was a good deal, but because it worried about losing broad support if it opposed an agreement allegedly in the national interest. As it turned out, all the compromises were made by the workers, and the KCTU's participation on the commission only served to confuse its members and weaken their struggle to protect their jobs.

Similar pressures have put working people on the defensive in Thailand. As a Thai scholar explained:

> Across-class unity like this in a time of economic recession, inevitably results in workers sympathizing with the bosses and the government and toning down demands for improved wages and conditions. A good example of this was the torrent of abuse from within the labor movement, including from the rank and file Rangsit Area committee, when workers at PAR Garment demanded a better annual contract in 1997. The PAR Garment workers were accused of being unrealistic hot-heads, bent on destroying themselves and the company. Another example was the retreat demonstrated by the President of the Labor Congress of Thailand, Prateung Sangsung, in his acceptance of a proposal by the World Bank, that a proper unemployment benefit scheme was no longer possible in Thailand under present crisis conditions. (Ungpakorn, 1999, p. 40)

The more radical approach to organizing in defense of the national interest differs in a number of important ways from the conservative. First, it gives prominence to the interests of workers and farmers. Second, it gives high priority to promoting popular understanding of the causes of the crisis, which for most supporters of this approach involve either the manic logic of global speculation or the profit-maximizing machinations of Western imperialism, especially the United States and the IMF. Significantly, Japanese imperialism does not receive anything like the same critical attention. Third, it views far-reaching economic restructuring as necessary to defend popular interests and solve the economic crisis.

Despite their intentions, NGO efforts to advance a more radical notion of the national interest can also end up limiting, if not undermining, working-class militancy and alternative visions of development. Left-nationalists are, with good reason, highly critical of TNCs, the IMF, and neoliberalism. Therefore, although generally critical of existing state policies, they also tend to advocate a strong state as a core feature of their recovery programs. The problem with their strategy stems from the way in which their non-class projection of the national interest shapes their defense of state ownership and opposition to privatization.

In Thailand for example, the IMF had pushed for, and the NGO community as well as many workers had opposed, the privatization of the Electricity Generating Authority of Thailand (EGAT). The campaign was organized mainly around opposition to foreign ownership and the danger that privatization might lead to higher electricity prices. As a result, "Workers' leaders often toned down the issue of workers' interests in favor of running a campaign on nationalist and public interest grounds" (Ungpakorn, 1999, p. 46). When the government finally announced it would not sell off the majority of shares to foreigners or increase electricity prices, the movement found itself at a political dead end, with no way to promote a more expansive vision of public ownership. Moreover, workers employed by the EGAT found themselves unable to mount a campaign in support of improved working conditions or better wages. In fact, oftentimes such "victories" against privatization require workers to make sacrifices which, if resisted, cast workers in the position of appearing unconcerned with the general welfare.

The same strategic orientation has also led left-nationalists to ally with any political leader who seemed willing to oppose neoliberalism or the IMF. "The extent of the depths to which the Left Nationalists can sink was indicated by the fact that vile dictators like Mahathir of Malaysia, who make vague anti-Western noises, became the heroes of such people. Even President Habibie of Indonesia came in for some praise for re-negotiating IMF conditions" (Ungpakorn, 1999, p. 44). Such alliances are problematic because they encourage a misunderstanding of the causes of the crisis and undermine the ability of popular movements to develop independent, alternative visions of development.

Many left-oriented NGOs see their support of the existing state (and its leadership) as only a tactical maneuver, one designed to produce political and ideological space for more radical initiatives. As such, they recognize that defense of the national interest also requires challenging existing state policy. Therefore, their main energies are normally directed to the creation and promotion of new economic strategies. Many NGO experts believe that this is an auspicious time for such work, in large part because they believe that the crisis has made state planners more receptive to NGO criticisms of neoliberalism and past government policies.

Unfortunately, in an attempt to demonstrate that there are "workable" and "reasonable" alternatives to established capitalist practices, many NGOs and their experts become trapped in the policy "game." In broad terms, progressive NGO policy formulations are very attractive. Most involve debt cancellation; opposition to the policies of the IMF, World Bank, and World Trade Organization; regulation of international capital mobility; greater democracy; and the establishment of "a job-creating, equitable and environmentally sustainable real economy" (Focus on the Global South, 1999). However, once advocates of such policies seek to covert them into concrete economic initiatives, they often find themselves bogged down in debates over their relative practicality. For example, they are challenged by their opponents in the government, universities, and the media, not only to prove that public ownership can be more efficient than private ownership, but to defend a specific structure of public ownership. Similar challenges are issued regarding capital controls, and so on. Moreover, no matter how well the various policies are researched and defended, most technocrats and media analysts still reject them on the grounds that they can never be implemented because the IMF and Western creditors are unlikely to allow any major deviations from neoliberal orthodoxy. Ironically, then, what begins as an attempt to craft alternatives is likely to end up leaving most people believing that there are no workable alternatives to the status quo.

Even if a mass movement were able to force a government to adopt the basic left-nationalist program, it is likely that the policymaking process would strip it of its progressive aspects. Thus, a government might choose to adopt some of the policies advocated by the progressive NGO community, but implement them in ways that are likely to eventually discredit them. For example, capital controls might well be introduced, as in Malaysia, in a manner that mainly benefits the national elite (by allowing them to cover their foreign debts in a less costly fashion), not the majority of the population. Similarly, one can imagine selective nationalizations taking place (as they have in the financial sector), but again, more often than not they would support elite interests, not a democratic restructuring of class relations.

A related problem with the left-nationalist approach is that it leads naturally to the depoliticization of mass movements and the elevation of progressive technocrats, with an accompanying change in the terrain of struggle from the workplace and community to government bureaus and official negotiating sessions. Operating within the confines of the policy game, many NGO policy advocates and activists come to view policy development not only in isolation from working-class activism, but also as the main source of inspiration for it. More precisely, many come to believe that a "sound" or "sensible" program is necessary if activists are to have a platform from which to organize people, and a set of issues to guide the organizing. Since the policy proposals are often understood as serving the broad national interest, it is not surprising that many policy experts come to see little reason for thinking critically about the relationship between program and movement building. In fact, some NGO experts come to view policy development not only as starting before organizing, but actually as a substitute for organizing, with the main task after the creation of the program being one of publicizing the benefits available to the nation from its adoption. In sum, it is hard to see this process either promoting the kind of broad social transformation NGO policymakers favor or inspiring the population to fight harder to achieve it.

Organizing on the Basis of Class

Even recognizing the diverse views and practices of those that support them, the above non-class approaches are clearly incapable of mobilizing the social forces required to promote significant popular transformations of the East Asian political economies. This is not meant to be dismissive of the efforts of NGO activists; organizing for change is no simple matter and there are no "models" of successful social transformation that activists can study for reference. Moreover, an expansion of democracy, even when limited by capitalist imperatives, is an achievement not to be taken lightly; the same goes for the construction of alternative development strategies that can lead people to think more critically about government policy. Nonetheless, there are, for the reasons highlighted above, serious limits to what these non-Marxist approaches can accomplish.

There are always choices to make about how to advance a movement for change, and Marxism offers a strategic perspective that can assist workers' individual and collective struggles to gain control over their lives. In brief, that perspective places highest priority on the creation of a working-class centered social movement guided by anti-capitalist consciousness. While this priority may seem simplistic, it does suggest organizing criteria and strategies that are different from the ones previously examined. And, such differences are anything but trivial.

Many progressives currently view any strategy based on working-class activism and directed towards replacing capitalism as fanciful. Reasons vary, but most normally involve some belief that globalization has rendered working people relatively powerless and socialism impossible.[4] However, the actions of East Asian working people as well as the nature and severity of the crisis provide strong evidence to the contrary (McNally, 1998).

Developments in Indonesia provide a good example of the potential for dramatic change to take place. In 1996, Indonesia was considered one of capitalism's greatest success stories and its dictator/president, Suharto, a wise leader. But, in 1997, right before the start of the country's parliamentary election campaign,

> there was a wave of protests and strikes involving thousands of workers in a number of industrial areas in Java. . . . These protests came as a considerable surprise given earlier warnings by officials that action would be taken against any possible threat to the smooth running of the 29 May election. . . . [Such protests pointed] to the significant role of workers as a determining factor in assisting the climate of political change in Indonesia. (Simanjuntak, 1997, p. 15)

The growing economic crisis intensified the hardships of working people and their anger against the government. Still, Suharto appeared firmly in control; he was unanimously reelected for a seventh five-year term by his hand-picked People's Consultative Assembly in March 1998. However, popular pressures continued to be exerted through nationwide demonstrations by students, the sacrifices (arrests and deaths) of pro-democracy demonstrators, mass protests, and other actions by the urban poor and workers against IMF-sponsored price hikes in food and fuel, and the ongoing national liberation struggle of the East Timorese people. These pressures—together with the brutality of the military which sought to provoke ethnic violence to deflect anger against the government—all combined to topple the Suharto regime a mere two months later.[5]

One important force behind this victory (which thus far has led to some significant political reforms but not the transformation of the country's political economy), was the work of the People's Democratic Party (PRD) and its affiliated organizations—the Indonesian Center for Workers' Struggle (PPBI), and the Indonesian Students' Solidarity for Democracy (SMID). In 1995, for example, the PPBI and SMID coordinated a strike involving some 12,000 workers from a Central Java textile factory. In July 1996, the PPBI was involved in coordinating a demonstration of tens of thousands of workers in the industrial area of East Java (Simanjuntak, 1997, p. 19). In October 1997, the PPBI helped organize a strike of some 16,000 workers at the state aircraft company in Bandung. The PPBI was unique among labor groups in Indonesia in that it always combined both political and economic demands in its demonstrations, thereby raising the political vision of those involved. The PRD and its affiliates were also among the few mass organizations to intensively work among the urban poor, who became a driving force in the political protests against the government and its policies.

It was this kind of grassroots work with students, workers, and the urban poor, in which activism was encouraged and issues were joined, that helped to make the country ungovernable and encouraged the Indonesian military and U.S. government to abandon its support of Suharto. Moreover, the PRD's program has not been exhausted by this success. It has always made clear that what was needed to truly meet people's needs was something more than reform of the existing system:

> We are in favor of an uninterrupted movement, an uninterrupted revolution. The struggle for democracy means a freeway to socialism. A strategic demand for the actual situation is the building of people's councils at every level. The nationalization of crony capitalism will have to develop into the nationalization of the whole economy. Of course, the objective conditions for socialism are difficult. The workers movement is not well organized and the workers' consciousness is still low. But we need to develop anti-capitalist consciousness. In our program we are preparing for socialism. (*Links*, 1999b, p. 93)

Activists inside and outside of East Asia have tended to look to South Korea, even more than to Indonesia, for inspiration about the potential of working people to overcome the current crisis. A Thai scholar writes:

> Because the situation [in Thailand] is contradictory, it is not possible to predict the future direction of workers' struggles. In the early period of the crisis, anger and fear were finely balanced. If tipped either way, the situation might change. Television and newspaper pictures of struggles in Indonesia, and even more importantly, militant workers' struggles in South Korea have been seen and remembered by Thai workers. (Ungpakorn, 1999, p. 54)

A U.S. socialist publication makes the same point: "While there have been important organizing efforts and militant stirring within the emerging Indonesian working class, its development is nothing like that achieved by industrial workers in South Korea—where unions are carrying out massive strikes against factory layoffs caused by 'reforms' demanded by the new Kim Dae Jung government" (Editors, 1998, p. 45).

South Korean workers, in particular those associated with the KCTU, have certainly demonstrated a great class consciousness and fighting spirit both before and after the start of the East Asian crisis (Hart-Landsberg, 1993 and 1998b). The KCTU was declared illegal by the South Korean government even before its formation in November 1995. Yet, in December 1996 and January 1997, it launched a series of strikes involving over 600,000 workers which forced the government to withdraw new labor laws designed to facilitate mass layoffs. Emboldened by IMF encouragement, the South Korean government eventually succeeded in passing similar legislation in early 1998. But, the KCTU has waged a series of struggles to prevent the government and *chaebol* from taking advantage of it. These include a wave of coordinated strikes involving approximately 120,000 workers in May 1998, and a series of rolling strikes and public demonstrations, each involving tens of thousands of workers, in late 1998 and throughout the first half of 1999.

These developments in Indonesia and South Korea demonstrate that struggle can produce significant political changes and that East Asian workers are capable of disciplined, militant, and independent action. At the same time, a brief account of struggles is not the same as a critical discussion of strategy. Moreover, there is a big difference between trade union organizing and militancy, such as exists in South Korea, and social movement building and anti-capitalist consciousness. In fact, for all their valiant efforts, the KCTU and its allies remain on the defensive. For example, the KCTU has not yet succeeded in winning majority support for its efforts to oppose "labor flexibility" and, as a result, it is finding it increasingly difficult to sustain its strikes much less win significant concessions from the government or the *chaebol*.

Having demonstrated the value of a Marxist perspective in building effective grassroots resistance to capitalist crisis and elite restructuring efforts, it is still necessary to show how a Marxist focus on class and social transformation promotes a very different set of strategic priorities than the non-Marxist approaches highlighted above. The next section does this by offering a Marxist assessment of the primary organizational challenges facing labor and community activists in South Korea. Differences among the various countries in East Asia are great enough that no single organizing strategy could possibly be adopted for all of them. Nonetheless, the focus on one country does help illustrate the general approach to organizing, not just a specific set of policies. South Korea seems an appropriate focus given this chapter's prior coverage of that country's NGO movements. Besides, as noted above, the South Korean labor movement is both highly dynamic and widely studied by labor activists throughout the region.

Challenges to Worker-Community Movements: The Case of South Korea

Five key challenges must be addressed if South Korean workers are to succeed in restructuring their country's political economy. These are: rebuilding a broad-based left movement; strengthening the political unity of the South Korean working class; building a left-oriented, labor-NGO bloc; promoting greater regional and international labor solidarity; and strengthening rank-and-file democracy and political education within the KCTU.[6] What follows is an explanation of, and critical commentary on, each of these challenges.

Challenge 1

The need to rebuild a broad-based left movement is an obvious strategic starting point. Celebrations of the success of one sector of the South Korean labor movement in building the KCTU have often overshadowed the failure of recent attempts to build a structured, left-led, working-class centered, social movement. In 1984, activists from a number of different social movement and NGO groups formed the United Minjung Movement for Democracy and Unification (UMMDU) in an attempt to unite the various organizations into a coherent organizational form so as to promote a broader and more coherent vision of change. These activists also recognized the importance of the working class in anchoring this process and so gave priority to, and indeed succeeded in, promoting worker organizing.

Building on this success, the UMMDU dissolved itself in 1991 in favor of a new organization, the National Alliance for Democracy and National Reunification (NADNR). Activists associated with the new militant labor movement played a central role in building this new organization, which was based on structured participation by activist representatives from a number of movements, most importantly the labor, urban poor peoples', and farmers' movements. In the early 1990s, NADNR played a significant role in promoting alternative political activities and visions. However, before it was able to consolidate its internal structure and organizational ties with its various member organizations, the entire progressive movement was hit hard by government repression. Gradually NADNR lost popular support as well as the support of activists from the various individual organizations.

As a result, the KCTU now exists largely outside of any structured, left-oriented movement for social change. And, with no larger movement to project alternative social visions and mobilize support for them, the KCTU has tended to concentrate its efforts on supporting the enterprise struggles of its members. Labor activists who were central in past efforts at social movement building have generally either been replaced by activists that are more focused on developing the trade union movement or have lost energy for their earlier work. This development has, among other things, made it more difficult for the KCTU to protect workers from the crisis. With no counter-vision supported by a majority of working people, the KCTU is forced to fight a largely defensive battle against government and IMF initiatives, a battle it is not likely to win.

As argued in Chapter 11, the crisis in South Korea is very much a crisis of capitalism compounded by contradictions inherent in the country's previous growth strategy. Thus, only a movement of socialism from below offers workers a foundation upon which to build a secure, sustainable, and democratic future. From this perspective, labor activists, especially those in the KCTU, should give a high priority to rebuilding a socialist-oriented alliance anchored in the working class. This does not mean pursuit of a socialist project *at the expense of* the "bread and butter" labor movement. Rather, without a broader social vision and organization, even the most militant trade union will find itself facing a series of ever less attractive trade-offs. As a first step in this socialist direction, left-oriented activists from the labor, urban poor peoples', farmers', and NGO movements should get together and hammer out a shared understanding of capitalist crisis and restructuring.

The development of a broad progressive program of action could help cement the alliance and provide a vehicle for popular organizing. Goals of such a program would likely include strengthening popular resistance to structural adjustment and building new organizational mechanisms to promote greater popular education, mobilization, and participation in political and economic decision making; a reorientation of economic activity away from exporting toward meeting domestic needs in an ecologically sensitive and technologically sustainable manner; and a complimentary, regionally-negotiated foreign debt, investment, and trade strategy. Another priority would be abolishing the National Security Law, which successive governments have used to crush organizing efforts by both labor and the left.

Challenge 2

The South Korean working class must strengthen itself organizationally and unify itself politically. The overall rate of unionization fell from a high of 21 percent in 1989 to just 13 percent before the crisis. Since then, both the KCTU and its conservative rival, the Korean Federation of Trade Unions (KFTU), have each lost about 10 percent of their respective membership. Unionization is also highly concentrated in large enterprises. Indeed, "the organizational rate of workers in mainly large companies, over 500, is as high as 85% while that in small-sized, less than 300, is as low as below 3%" (Lim, 1998, p 8). KCTU representation is also heavily concentrated among workers at large enterprises.

This stratification of the labor force has become an even more serious problem since the start of the crisis. The reason is that the great majority of those who have lost their jobs "are from these small sized companies with no or very weak unions" (Lim, 1998, p. 8). This partly explains why KCTU struggles have not had much success in halting the rise in unemployment. However, it also means that its militant struggles to defend the jobs of its member-workers at the large enterprises are not of immediate relevance to large numbers of the most vulnerable workers.

Successful resistance to neoliberalism will require a united working class. The KCTU must broaden its program to speak for and defend the interests of workers more generally, with special emphasis on the situations of women and migrants. Its attempt, so far deemed illegal by the South Korean government, to unionize the unemployed is a positive step in this direction. A broad-based socialist action program would provide a framework within which the KCTU and its member unions could touch base with the unorganized and unemployed.

Challenge 3

The divide between the KCTU and the progressive NGO community must be overcome. A number, perhaps a majority, of NGOs now recognize that IMF-inspired or mandated policies are counterproductive in terms of NGO goals of a more democratic, egalitarian, and environmentally sustainable economic system. In fact, some NGOs are beginning to think in terms of the formation of a new left-oriented bloc featuring closer coordination of NGO and KCTU actions. This movement deserves strong support, and it will surely grow if labor and NGO activists can find opportunities to jointly examine the causes of the crisis and the structural limits inherent in capitalist "adjustment."

NGO activists have much to contribute to a movement of socialism from below. They have educational and technical skills that can help secure and concretize victories. They also have crucial connections to social sectors not easily reached by labor activists. Moreover, their activities, especially those on behalf of women, the environment, and civil liberties, have been extremely important in protecting the rights of individuals and promoting new visions of living and working. Socialism from below must emerge out of the creative interaction of struggles to transform work and community life, and a strong representation of these rights and visions is essential to the successful advancement of the project.

However, these contributions can be fully realized only to the extent that NGO actions take place within a class framework. And, such a framework requires that the NGO-labor alliance develop within an emerging left presence. Only then will worker-community campaigns develop the kind of grassroots solidarity needed to envision and implement more democratic structures of political power and economy.

The South Korean NGO, People's Solidarity for Participatory Democracy (PSPD), is involved in several initiatives that highlight the possibilities. One is a campaign to promote "citizen rights." While this campaign does include the provision of legal aid type services to individuals, it is primarily focused on "structural problems . . . which harm the public interests as well as individual's rights" (Park, 1999, p. 13). One of its projects involves organizing a class-action suit on behalf of mostly working-class families that live near Kimpo International Airport and suffer from extreme noise pollution (Park, 1999, p. 13). Such efforts, which also include support for community self-organization and demonstrations, can help mobilize and empower working people. Citizen rights campaigns, when directed at class-based concerns such as the public's "right to know" about the environmental effects of corporate and government actions, also have the potential to unify, and thereby strengthen, community and workplace connections and struggles.

The importance of a class perspective becomes clear when examining another PSPD initiative: the minority shareholder campaign. This action involves organizing minority stockholders to demand accountability from the large *chaebol*. Investigations have been launched into back room dealings such as secret loans, foreign currency manipulations, and stock conversions (Participatory Economic Committee, 1999, pp. 8-11). While these efforts have forced the *chaebol* to reform some of their business practices, they generally work to strengthen popular perceptions of the reformability of capitalism. Far less effort has gone into pressing the *chaebol* to "open their books" more generally or to change their labor practices (especially their anti-union activities) as part of a broad effort to contest capitalist rationality.

Challenge 4

The KCTU should continue its efforts to build solidarity with workers in other countries, inside and outside East Asia. Given the regional nature of the accumulation process in East Asia, coordinated struggles are bound to become more central to national organizing efforts. National attempts at radical transformation gain credibility when supported by complementary efforts in other countries, especially those in the region. The objective conditions for regional solidarity have certainly been enhanced by the crisis, as workers in Japan, South Korea, Thailand, Malaysia, and Indonesia face growing hardships as a result of similar (and in many cases the same) dynamics of competition and accumulation.

Challenge 5

The KCTU and its member unions must redouble their internal organizing efforts, including political education. Union efforts to support a socialist project and defend broad working-class interests must be modeled through internal organizations that maximize democracy. A critical component of this practice is a political education program that equips workers to control union decision making and to understand the structural causes of the South Korean crisis and the "recovery" logic of capitalism.

In sum, to the extent that progress in meeting these five challenges remains limited, neoliberalism will retain the offensive to the detriment of the great majority of South Koreans. Obviously, responding successfully to these five challenges is no simple task. In fact, each challenge contains its own particular set of sub-challenges. The process implicit in what we are advocating is not designed to produce a quick fix. Its strength is that while building unity for resistance to capitalist restructuring and competitive pressures, it also lays necessary groundwork for the long-term struggle for socialism.

Long-Term Perspective

At present, the media and some economists, including those employed by the IMF and World Bank, are signaling that the crisis in East Asia is over. There are indeed signs of recovery from the depths of the recession. However, what is happening is more a short-term recovery of profits and production than a meaningful improvement in people's lives. As *Business Week* noted when talking about South Korea, "Korea is indeed recovering. Yet it's a pitiless recovery that will not swiftly reduce joblessness—it may even increase it. Like the former communist countries of Eastern Europe, which now produce high growth rates but still suffer from high unemployment, Korea is embarking on a difficult transition that will produce plenty of fresh growth, but also pain and turmoil for the working class" (Veale, 1999, p. 54).

In fact, it is doubtful that the recovery of production will be as vibrant as *Business Week* suggests. Production in East Asia is rising but largely as a result of IMF fears of worker unrest. Hoping to head off any kind of serious challenge to existing capitalist relations, the IMF has backed off from some of its most stringent austerity conditions. For example, shortly after Suharto resigned in Indonesia, "the International Monetary Fund agreed to soften implementation of its economic austerity package to give Habibie and the military more time to hopefully bring political stability. In addition, the big Western banks, led by Chase Manhattan, have agreed to reschedule repayment of nearly $80 billion in private debt" (Miah, 1998b, p. 6). In South Korea, the IMF has given the South Korean government permission to let the budget deficit rise as high as 5.5 percent of GDP in 1999 (Burton, 1999, p. 6). In other words, East Asia is experiencing short-term improvements in response to short-term policy adjustments.

More fundamentally, there is little reason to believe that there will be any kind of real recovery in the foreseeable future. As the *Far Eastern Economic Review* pointed out:

> Fast moving technology is shrinking product cycles, while oversupply pushes down prices and profits worldwide. Both trends challenge Asia, which prospered by marrying imported technology with cheap labor. But the biggest challenge is new and vigorous competition from the emerging markets. Mexico's exports have tripled in the last 10 years. Brazil is tied with China as the second-favorite investment destination for multinationals, trailing the United States. Gone are the days when a handful of Asian nations competed mainly with each other for export orders and foreign investment. (Goad, 1999, p. 10)

Even more importantly, much of the limited recovery in East Asia has been based on exports to the U.S. market. However, there is every reason to believe that the U.S. "boom," built on ever-increasing consumer debt and stock market expansion supported by massive inflows of foreign capital, will soon come to an end (Moseley, 1999). Whether what follows will be stagnation or outright recession is difficult to predict. Regardless, it seems certain that there are limits to the ability of the US economy to support East Asian recovery.

As always under capitalism, new crises lie ahead—and not just for East Asia. There are, as noted above, political choices to be made. In East Asia these choices are being made under economic conditions that threaten the immediate survival of broad sections of the working class. Such pressures should, if anything, add urgency to the building of movements guided by both an accurate understanding of capitalism and worker-community centered visions of development. Now is the time to move beyond TINA, and toward socialism.

Notes

Introduction

1. Here, "East Asia" connotes countries in both Northeast and Southeast Asia. The focus of this book is on Japan and South Korea (in Northeast Asia) and Thailand, Malaysia, and Indonesia (in Southeast Asia). Present references to "the East Asian experience" are not meant to imply, as do many analysts, that all of these countries share either a similar political and social history or identical growth processes. Rejecting oversimplified "East Asian model" perspectives, the focus here is on the class and competitive dynamics of uneven development. This focus allows for differences in national structures as well as the contradictory unity of regional developments (Bernard, 1999, pp. 183-184).

2. For example, Alice Amsden, when discussing political liberalization in South Korea—in particular the popular victory in 1987 that allowed the direct election of the president—commented that. "Economic success on the basis of strong government intervention, heavy industry, and big business is evidently compatible with political democracy. Indeed, one can make the case that the concentration of large groups of workers under one roof, and the priming of large numbers of students-cum-salaried managers, furthered political mobilization" (Amsden, 1989, p. 327).

3. Among the important Marxist works that have been ignored or forgotten, one must include the writings of Jon Halliday (1978), Halliday and Gavan McCormack (1973), Joe Moore (1983), and Rob Steven (1983, 1990, 1996). For further critical discussion of the disappearance of "imperialism" and "dependency" from development thinking, see Patnaik (1990), Magdoff (1993), and James (1997).

4. DeMartino (1996) provides an incisive survey and critique of such "progressive competitiveness" thinking.

5. Robert Wade offers a case study of one of "Japan's attempts over the 1980s and 1990s to assert itself on the world stage, to move beyond the constraints of dependency in a US-centered world economic system" (Wade, 1996, p. 4). He describes how, determined to promote its own state-guided version of capitalism, the Japanese government challenged the World Bank to study the East Asian experience and even agreed to fund the research. The outcome was the World Bank's 1993 report, *The East Asian Miracle: Economic Growth and Public Policy.*

Chapter 1

1. World Bank (1993) illustrates the standard neoliberal interpretation of the East Asian experience. For other neoliberal studies of East Asia, see Hughes (1988), Yue (1993), Kim (1994), Blomqvist (1995), Teranishi (1996), and Van Der Meulen Rodgers (1996).
2. See Wade's (1996) account of the debate over the World Bank's (1993) report *The East Asian Miracle*. For structural-institutionalist analyses of the NIEs, see Amsden (1989), Wade (1990), Rodrik (1994), Huff (1995), Cassen and Lall (1996), and Brohman (1996). Some extensions to the SEA-3 experience are given by Bello (1996a) and Amsden (1991, 1996).
3. For example, Engardio (1996, p. 44) observes that a serious "problem" in East Asia "is the overcapacity in next-generation industries. Much of the region is counting on petrochemicals, autos, consumer electronics, and semiconductors to move up the value-added ladder as they lose their cheap-labor advantage. . . . Says Standard Chartered Bank's economist Kwok Kwok-chuen: 'Overcapacity is becoming conspicuous. Ultimately there will be a shakeout.'"
4. Some neoliberals, like Jeffrey Sachs, Paul Krugman, and Joseph Stiglitz, joined the structural-institutionalists in treating the crisis as mainly a speculative bubble traceable to inadequate regulation of domestic and external finance. See Chapter 13 for a fuller survey and critique of neoliberal and structural-institutionalist responses to the crisis.
5. See Chapters 9 through 12 for a discussion of this critical dynamic.
6. The transnationalization of NIE-based firms remains different from that of core-based firms insofar as the former are still heavily dependent on inputs and technologies purchased from the core in such fashion as to slant the distribution of value added in favor of core enterprises (see the discussion of dependency approaches in Chapter 3).
7. See Burkett (1997) for a general discussion of neoliberalism, democracy, and development.
8. For example, Chang's (1997) structural-institutional account of the South Korean crisis emphasized the need to manage the "massive political resistance" to the "sharp rise in unemployment" and "fiscal retrenchment" under

IMF stabilization policies. Chang suggested that "the new government of Kim Dae Jung, with its more consensual approach to politics and stronger ties to the small firms and trade unions that are going to be hurt most in the process, may be in a better position to pull the country through a period of deflation and job losses and toward robust growth." This suggestion paralleled the neoliberal argument that democratically elected governments—properly disciplined by international financial markets—could legitimize IMF-type austerity more effectively than could unpopular authoritarian regimes (Kristof, 1997c).

9. More basically, uneven development is rooted in the contradiction between capital as quantitative value expansion (money begetting more money) and the qualities of production as a material and social process. Uneven development is thus a necessary form of the use value versus exchange value contradiction underlying the various crisis tendencies (economic, political, cultural, and ecological) of capitalism (Smith, 1984).

10. As part of their ad hoc responses to the East Asian crisis, neoliberals began referring to the special Cold War circumstances of the East Asian growth miracles. But they failed to reconcile such references with their previous free-market explanations of the miracles themselves; nor did they pursue the implications for the replicability of East Asian successes. See Chapter 13 for a discussion of this point.

Chapter 2

1. See Akamatsu (1961; 1962) for English-language outlines of the original flying geese framework. Korhonen (1994) offers a survey and assessment of Akamatsu's lifelong work on the flying geese approach, including its philosophical foundations. Many contemporary analyses of East Asian economic dynamics utilize flying geese themes, but in less nuanced fashion than Akamatsu. See, for example, Doner (1993), Ozawa (1993), Seki (1995), and UNCTAD (1995, pp. 258–260; 1996a, pp. 75–105).

2. See also Seki (1995, pp. 13–14). UNCTAD (1995, pp. 250–256) provides an interesting case study of the sequential upgrading of the South Korean and Taiwanese electronics industries, in which Japanese (and United States) transnationals played crucial roles in terms of "technology transfer, learning and access to export markets" (p. 250).

3. The greater reliance of contemporary flying geese formulations on the standard theory of comparative advantage helps explain their greater neoliberal emphasis relative to Akamatsu.

4. As early as 1988, the total stock of Japanese manufacturing FDI in the NIEs, SEA-3, the Philippines, and the PRC "had become twice the size of comparable U.S. investments and constituted a larger share of total Japanese FDI in the region" (Doner, 1993, p. 165).

5. See Chapter 3 for elaboration of this point.

6. This pattern is more fully discussed in Chapter 9.

7. The Japanese experience supports Ietto-Gillies's (1988) argument that transnationalization of industrial capital may be driven by firms' attempts to profitably internalize competitive advantages by avoiding the generation of the "stronger and more militant labour" resulting from purely national operations. Here, "multi-nationalization of production generates a situation in which labour—though working under the same ownership umbrella—is more dispersed and fragmented and thus finds it more difficult to organize itself compared to a situation in which internalization takes place in the domestic environment, whether within the same plant or on a multi-plants basis" (pp. 29-30).

8. Domestic profitability problems were accentuated by U.S. pressures on both South Korea and Taiwan to revalue their currencies and open their markets to U.S. imports. A contributing factor was dependence on Japanese corporations who began to withhold key technologies to protect their own competitive positions in the wake of the increasing value of the yen after the 1985 Plaza Accord. See Chapter 11 for details.

9. Shu-Ki (1996, p. 28), for example, observes how "the China link" through outward direct investment "offered an 'easy' way out, 'short-circuiting' the rapidly approaching difficulties" of Taiwan and Hong Kong enterprises—especially "domestic constraints in the form of rising costs as well as external market restrictions." For further discussion of the forces driving foreign investment by NIE-based firms, see Doner (1993, pp. 161-164), Schive (1993), Shin and Lee (1995), and Chapters 11 to 12 of the present work.

10. See Seki (1995) and Terry (1996) for examples of flying geese propaganda.

11. Shu-Ki (1996), Rowley and Lewis (1996), Selden (1997), and Kwang-yong (1999) give sympathetic overviews of Greater China constructs and their empirical foundations. For applications, see Hsing (1996), Lever-Tracy, et al. (1996), Hamashita (1997), Yeung (1997), and Zhao (1997).

12. Cumings (1997b) even asserts that the real "lead goose" in East Asia is still the United States with its unrivaled combination of military, political, and economic strength. However, most Greater China theorists addressing this issue see a more coequal, "multi-polar" regional power structure developing among the United States, Japan, and the reemergent PRC; see especially Selden (1997), Zhao (1997), and Kwang-yong (1999).

13. The reality of this hierarchy becomes more difficult to deny when one considers that while "Japan was home to 149 companies ranking among the Fortune 500 largest companies in the world in 1995, not far behind the United States, which led with 151, . . . South Korea could boast of only 8 such companies, while Taiwan has 2 [and] no other East or Southeast Asian country even makes the list" (Pempel, 1996/97, p. 21).

14. Beach (1999, pp. 22-23) observes that even though the official trade union

federation "promotes government policy more than it protects workers' interests . . . sporadic worker protests, mostly concerning unpaid wages or pensions, have broken out with increasing frequency around the country." For additional reports on worker unrest in the PRC, see Eckholm (1997, 1998), and Associated Press (1997, 1998).

Chapter 3

1. Our summary is based on the following works on East Asia that utilize dependency constructs (often combined with other methodologies): Bello and Rosenfeld (1990), Bello (1992), Fallows (1994), Tabb (1994; 1996), Bernard and Ravenhill (1995), and Bello (1996a).
2. For details, see Fallows (1994), Bernard and Ravenhill (1995), Hatch and Yamamura (1996), Athukorala and Menon (1997), and Steven (1997).
3. In electronics, Matsushita makes electron guns for TVs in its Malaysian factory, which are then exported to Singapore where they are assembled into picture tubes at a Hitachi plant. The tubes are then sent back to Matsushita's factories in Malaysia and Thailand for assembly into finished TVs for export (Fallows, 1994, p. 271). "Each country has a definite function for the electronics giant: Malaysia focuses on color TVs and electric irons (half for export), Singapore on semi-conductors (90 per cent for export), the Philippines on dry-cell batteries as well as floppy-disk drives and electrolytic capacitors" (Steven, 1990, p. 116).
4. Beginning in the late 1980s, the South Korean trade deficit problem was accentuated by the outward migration of many small- and medium-sized export businesses in search of lower wage costs (Shin and Lee, 1995), followed by a growing substitution of foreign for domestic investment by the larger *chaebol* enterprises (Hart-Landsberg and Burkett, 1998, pp. 97–99). See Chapter 11 for a fuller discussion.
5. Yam (1995) details the growing competition between China and the SEA-3 for direct investment inflows. He suggests that the "competitive pressure" to sustain these inflows was "a key factor driving the process of unilateral liberalization in trading and investment regimes in the region" (ibid., p. 64).
6. The criticisms in the present paragraph apply in particular to Tabb (1992; 1994) and Bello (1996a; 1996b; 1996c).

Chapter 4

1. Nancy Folbre thus suggested "that the Japanese are successfully competitive in world markets primarily because they are so cooperative at home" (1994, p. 27). J. R. Stanfield argued the same point even more strongly: "Japan . . . must be interpreted in light of the population's nationalist commitment and respect for hierarchical authority. Beyond one's firm, there is one's *keiretsu*,

beyond one's *keiretsu,* there is one's country. Such rank ordered commitments are less evident in an individualistic economic setting . . . *solidaristic sentiment plays a more pervasive role in Japanese economic relationships and calculations than in the American instance"* (1994, p. 11; emphases in original).

2. Walden Bello also offered high praise for the Japanese work model: "The much-vaunted Japanese teamwork, the initiative of workers in the production process, the constant efforts collectively to upgrade and diversify the work team's skills—all this stems from a system of production where much of the conflict between labor and management has been reduced or softened. . . . Most Japanese 'core workers'—the dynamo of the firm—are far less alienated from management than American workers are. Moreover, management knows that non-alienated workers are the key to competitiveness. . . . Whereas automation has been used to enhance worker skills in Japan, it has been utilized by American managers to deskill and reduce their workforces" (1994, pp. 100-102).

3. An important element of this situation is that "even though the age of formal retirement is relatively early in Japan, workers typically continue working until very late in life. In fact, the labor force participation rate of the aged in Japan is one of the highest among the developed countries. However, since workers typically experience a substantial reduction in wages after formal retirement, saving in preparation for life after formal retirement will be necessary even if the individual continues working if he or she wishes to maintain the same standard of living he or she enjoyed prior to formal retirement" (Horioka, 1990, pp. 70-71). In other words, post-"retirement" wage reductions (on which there is more below) provide an additional impetus to the high overall savings rates of Japanese working-class households.

4. By October 1995, in the wake of the Daiwa Bank scandal and other related problems, U.S. authorities were indicating that they were standing by to help troubled Japanese banks (Gonzalez, 1995). Japanese banks were already paying a premium between 0.30 and 0.41 percent in global interbank markets, having received new, lower credit ratings from Moody's in August (Sapsford, 1995b; Steiner, 1995). The role of the real estate bubble in the emergent crisis is emphasized in Williams and Sapsford (1995), Jenkins (1995), Sapsford (1995d) and Pacelle (1995). For the similarity between Japanese and earlier U.S. financial cleanup plans, and the connection of Japanese regulatory reforms with Japan's surprisingly weak and understaffed bank inspection system, see Williams and Steiner (1995), Sapsford (1995c, 1995e, 1995f), and Williams (1995).

5. In 1993, part-time and temporary workers together made up roughly 15 percent of employment in firms with 1000 or more workers. In wholesale and retail trade, the proportion exceeded 44 percent (Houseman and Osawa, 1995, p. 15). Over 20 percent of "part-time" employees "worked as

many hours as did regular, full-time workers" in 1990—and this fraction appears to be on the rise (ibid., p. 10).

6. "The overall pay gap between Japanese men and women remains dramatic. In 1988, the average female employee in Japan earned 57 per cent of the average male employee's earnings" (Hill, 1996, pp. 145-147). A study by the International Labor Organization found that Japan was the only developed country "where the difference between the salaries of men and women had increased from 1975 to 1984" (Ogawa and Clark, 1995, p. 296).

7. Meanwhile, "the state, by keeping down spending on social services, has actively fostered the conditions under which business has been able to seize and hold labor" (Halliday, 1978, p. 231).

8. By June 1999, even the official Japanese unemployment rate had risen to 4.9 percent, with true unemployment easily at double-digit levels (see Chapter 5).

9. For further discussion of the sources of inaccuracy in Japan's official unemployment rate, see Steven (1990, pp. 49-50), Elder and Sorrentino (1993), Chriszt (1993), Sapsford (1995a), and *Economist* (1995).

10. See, for example, Halliday and McCormack (1973), Steven (1990, 1996, and 1997), Howard (1993), Ofreneo (1993), McCormack (1996, Chapter 3), and Dauvergne (1997).

Chapter 5

1. As Ronald Bevacqua, an economist at Merrill Lynch in Tokyo, put it, "people on the margins— women, older men, younger men— are taking the brunt of the adjustment to keep the men of prime working age at work" (Strom, 1998b, p. C3). Indeed, the 4.1 percent official unemployment rate in June 1998 "translate[d] into virtually no jobs for unemployed people aged 50 or over" (Shimbun, 1998).

2. "On average, companies reduced overtime pay by almost 1 percent in August and severely cut other allowances, such as transportation expenses, by almost 40 percent" (Strom, 1998d, p. C4).

3. Although the Nikkei rebounded to over 18,000 by July 1999, the significance of the new stock-market rally was unclear given continued recession and rising unemployment in the real economy. See Chapter 10 for further discussion.

4. "Debt left behind by collapsed companies rose 2.6 percent to $126 billion, the highest since 1945, said the Teikoky Databank Ltd. The previous record of $125 billion was set in 1997" (Associated Press, 1999a, p. A5).

5. The *New York Times* added that "market liberalization in Japan had helped encourage investment overseas. . . . The government has begun loosening foreign exchange regulations and so now it is easier for Japanese savers to turn their savings into dollars or marks and invest in the United States and

Europe to get the higher returns" (WuDunn, 1998b, p. C8). "The biggest worry among currency traders is that the yen is reaching a level where Japanese housewives, who control the family purse strings and thus a vast pool of savings, are swapping their yen for dollars, German marks and pounds sterling. . . . 'Of particular concern is the potential for volatile portfolio shifts into foreign currency assets by Japanese residents in the post-Big Bang environment,' Moody's said in its news release, referring to sweeping financial reform measures that went into effect on April 1" (Strom, 1998c, p. C5).

6. "The yen's 15 percent year-over-year decline gave Sony a big boost; the company obtains about 70 percent of its revenue outside Japan. Had currency rates not changed, the company said, its revenue would have been the yen equivalent of $4.2 billion lower than reported, and its operating income would have dropped 6.9 percent rather than risen 57.4 percent" (Pollack, 1997, p. C2).

7. "'At 110 [yen to the dollar], most of the big [Japanese] companies can still export, but their profit margins are shaved quite closely; most smaller firms are being squeezed,' said Ron Bevacqua, an economist with Merrill Lynch & Co. in Tokyo. 'At 100, even some of the large firms start hurting'" (Sesit and Spindle, 1999, p. A2). In mid-1999, the Bank of Japan once again "had to intervene massively in the foreign-exchange markets," as a new appreciation of the yen "threaten[ed] to nip Japan's nascent recovery in the bud" (*Economist,* 1999f, p. 65).

8. "The single biggest reason for lack of change, argues Kathy Matsui, of Goldman Sachs, is that . . . managers whose firms fail to produce decent profits risk neither losing their jobs nor being taken over" (*Economist,* 1998e, p. 56).

9. Indeed, "as pressure has grown for the government to spend more, the quality of *zaito*-financed projects has dropped sharply. . . . There is no procedure for writing down the value of such loans, no matter how questionable their worth. . . . The danger is that more and more of *zaito*'s clients are being kept alive only through periodic infusions of cheap debt" (*Economist,* 1998g, pp. 71-72).

10. "Like a recalcitrant heart patient, Japan resists the doctor's orders. Forthrightly addressing its problems may be a difficult regimen. But the longer Japan waits, the more drastic the surgery will be" (Katz, 1998, p. A21).

11. This argument is especially common among "flying geese" theorists (see Chapter 2), but its broader influence is clear from the *New York Times'* glib suggestion that one "reason for the relative calm" in Japan during the early phases of the 1997-98 East Asian financial crisis was "that an ever-increasing amount of Japanese production is based outside Japan, which lessens the impact of sudden swings in currencies" (Strom, 1997, p. B1). Here, the identity of interests between Japanese capital and Japanese workers and communities is taken as a natural "given."

Chapter 6

1. As Perry Anderson puts it, in Japan the "intra-feudal relationship proper was
. . . more unilaterally hierarchical; its terminology was borrowed from that
of paternal authority and the kinship system. European feudalism was always
rife with inter-familial quarrels, and was characterized by an extreme liti-
giousness; Japanese feudalism, however, not only lacked any legalistic bent,
but its quasi-patriarchal cast was rendered the more authoritarian by extensive paternal rights of adoption and disinheritance which effectively
deterred filial insubordination of the type common in Europe" (1974, pp.
439-440). The intensive exploitation of labor under this system is shown by
the repeated instances in which "peasants rose in revolt against their feudal
lords and against the appropriation of their hard-earned 'surplus.' These
revolts occurred in spite of very harsh laws introduced in 1741 . . . an
attempt at 'tranquilization by intimidation' which included an almost certain death penalty, usually by crucifixion, for the leaders of the revolt irre-
spective of whether or not the peasants' complaints were acknowledged to
be 'justified' . . The shogunate was organized on a national level against
peasant revolts, and daimyo [great lords] were enjoined to assist one another
where necessary" (Halliday, 1978, pp. 12-13).

2. See Anderson (1974, pp. 450-452) and Halliday (1978, pp. 8-10) on the
development of urban capitalist activity (mainly trade and finance) within
Tokugawa feudalism. Overall, "if the nature of Tokugawa government
bequeathed to modern Japan the makings of a bureaucracy, social change in
the village provided both the elements of a non-agricultural work-force and
the nucleus of an elite concerned with commerce and industry. . . . Farming and commerce in the Tokugawa period had led to an accumulation of
capital in private hands which proved sufficient to fund the first stages of
growth, once government had provided an infrastructure and established
the machinery by which to channel investment in appropriate directions"
(Beasley, 1995, pp. 14, 114-115). Regarding the Tokugawa bureaucracy, Halliday emphasizes how "the system of feudal political control directly affected
the long-term development of the economy in every respect"; it not only
"strengthened state-industry ties along monopoly lines" but also "reinforced
the ruling bloc in consolidating a system of capital accumulation based on
a very high level of exploitation of labor" (1978, p. 11).

3. After 1800, the combination of growing "exploitation of poor peasants by
rich peasants" and "the entry of feudal authority into the business of
monopolies" (depressing marketed crop prices) caused peasant revolts to
"grow rapidly in scale and frequency" (Beasley, 1995, p. 15). Indeed, "the
evidence that exists, allowing for ups and downs within the general trend,
shows a steady trend upwards in peasant uprisings throughout the Tokugawa
period. The curve continues upwards through the restoration and peaks in

1873" (Halliday, 1978, p. 12). These uprisings "made it impossible for the feudal administration, depending as it ultimately did on the dominance of the feudal mode of production, to continue" (ibid., p. 13).

4. The design of the Bank of Japan, for example, was based on a detailed study of other advanced capitalist central banks—the explicit intent being the combination of institutional features that would most effectively insulate monetary and financial policies from popular pressures (Yoshino, 1977).

5. See Baran (1957, pp. 151–161) for an overview of the activist policies by which "the regime emerging from the Restoration drastically shifted the country's economic gears and provided a tremendous impetus both to the still incomplete primary accumulation of capital and to its transfer from purely mercantile to industrial pursuits" (ibid., p. 154). The Meiji government played an especially important leading role in the organization of new financial institutions (banks, insurance companies, and a postal savings system) for mobilizing economic surpluses and allocating them to productive public- and private-sector investments; for details see Ott (1961), Yamamura (1972), and Goldsmith (1983).

6. The generally increasing gap between productivity and real wages helps explain the "long-run deteriorating trend in income distribution in Japan during the period from the 1890s to the 1930s" (Minami, 1998, p. 54). Minami's careful study finds "a declining trend in labour's share in the non-primary sector" during this period (ibid.). Ohkawa and Rosovsky (1973, pp. 118–119) document the fact that "productivity rose much more rapidly than wages" during all the upswings of the Japanese economy between 1900 and the Second World War.

7. The bottom-line importance of labor's challenge is indicated by the temporary growth of non-agricultural wages relative to productivity in the years 1917 to 1925 (Ohkawa and Rosovsky, 1973, p. 119). Estimates by Minami (1998, p. 49) also show a definite upswing in labor's share of industrial value added during this period.

8. Indeed, by the early 1930s—that is, just as the temporary worker system was being consolidated—wage differentials by size of industrial establishment had already increased to post–World War II levels, whether establishment-size is measured by number of workers or by capital stock (Yasuba, 1976, p. 257).

9. Beasley notes that the official index of total manufacturing production "almost doubled between 1925-9 and 1935-9," with military-related sectors such as metals and machinery, chemicals, and shipbuilding exhibiting even higher rates of growth (1995, p. 188). This "rapid growth of heavy industry," which greatly strengthened *zaibatsu*-dominated manufacturing, included not only "significant development in the electrical and machinery industries," but also "the growth of new enterprises in fields like aircraft and automobiles" that "were to benefit from the expansion of military industry after 1936" (ibid., p. 189).

Chapter 7

1. As Joyce Kolko and Gabriel Kolko observe: "The question of retaining the Emperor was a critical index to the future of Japan's ruling class. And Washington formally resolved this issue in the affirmative no later than May 1945" (1972, p. 300). Even in "the spring of 1944," when "the state department pushed ahead on planning for the postwar role of Japan in the Far East," U.S. policymakers were already projecting that "they would reduce the power of the Emperor, but would maintain the institution unless the Japanese themselves chose to abolish it" (Kolko, 1968, p. 544). For the impact of the "vast upsurge of nationalist and revolutionary independence movements" on U.S. policy thinking toward Japan, see ibid., Chapter 24 (quote from p. 594).

2. However, even during and immediately after the war, other U.S. officials—including the former U.S. Ambassador to Japan, Joseph Grew—saw the *zaibatsu* "as the element most likely to cooperate with the United States . . . in an anti-left alliance" (Kolko and Kolko, 1972, p. 319). In opposing anything beyond "symbolic gesture[s] of reform" toward the *zaibatsu* system, this U.S. policy faction was supported by "United States investors in Japan, such as GE, Westinghouse, and a number of oil companies and banking firms" (ibid.).

3. Bisson (1947, p. 242) described immediate post-surrender developments in Japan as follows: "Commodity stocks moved largely into private hoards through Army-Navy collusion with Zaibatsu firms or individuals; public funds were lavishly expended to bail out the bankrupt wartime munitions producers; allocations of industrial materials and price controls were feebly handled or deliberately manipulated to the advantage of the big private concerns. These characteristic features of Japan's postwar economic management were all conspicuously in evidence when the occupation forces arrived. By one device or another, the Japanese officials and businessmen thereafter continued to pursue the same ends. . . . The program successfully carried through by Japan's business-bureaucrat group has undermined all aspects of the national economy."

4. Another elite faction that profited from post-surrender shortages was "the landlords and merchants who controlled the Agricultural Association" (Bisson, 1947, p. 242). Assisted by the loose requisitioning policies of Japanese government authorities (which resulted in a 20 percent reduction in rice requisitions compared to the war years despite a bumper rice crop in 1946), this "small landlord-merchant group engaged in black-market activities on a large scale to amass big profits" (ibid., p. 243). By mid-1947, for example, "black-market rice was selling at nearly twenty times the official price" (ibid.).

5. For example, as of "June 1946 money wages were nine times those of 1937, while real wages were only 24 percent of that year" (Kolko and Kolko, 1972, p. 313).

6. When not channeled directly into the black market, the emergency food shipments often displaced domestically-produced food from the official rationing centers—with the domestic supplies then being sold on the black market (Bisson, 1947, pp. 242-243).

7. "War destruction of physical plant as a decisive limiting factor can be dismissed at the outset. Productive capacity in key industries like steel, aluminum, coal, power, chemicals, and machine tools remaining after the end of the war was actually greater than 1935-37 levels, more than adequate for supplying the minimum needs of the postwar civilian economy" (Moore, 1983, p. 78). Tsuru (1993, p. 8) similarly estimates that total tangible wealth remaining in Japan at war's end was roughly "equivalent to the amount existing in 1935." Bisson's first-hand observations also strongly support the conclusion that "with proper management, Japan could have made the transition to a peacetime economy, if not without a severe wrench, at least without experiencing the economic catastrophe that has overtaken it" (1947, pp. 241-242).

8. The basic motivation for workers to take control of production has been clearly explained by Jon Halliday: "Business's straight refusal to invest, or often even to keep production going, was accompanied by massive government protection for looting and stockpiling, a form of long-term retrenchment in favor of private interests which was particularly deleterious to the working population. . . . Under these circumstances of capitalist sabotage and extreme scarcity, the Japanese workers perceived the top priorities to be both employment and production" (1978, p. 208).

9. As Joe Moore observes, "the widespread social influence of production control was extraordinary" (1997, p. 19). When workers took over the *Yomiuri* newspaper, for example, other "workers and organizers streamed to Tokyo *Yomiuri* headquarters from all parts of Japan to learn at first hand how to organize themselves and take action. And of course the *Yomiuri* newspaper, with its wide national circulation, carried the message to uncounted others unable to make the pilgrimage to Tokyo" (ibid.).

10. "By October [1946] the police and the American Counter Intelligence Corps were violently breaking up labor demonstrations, and within SCAP this policy was known as 'housebreaking the labor movement'" (Kolko and Kolko, 1972, p. 314).

11. "Living conditions were especially serious for the government workers in the railroads, postal, salt, and tobacco monopolies. These workers were well organized and militant, and they comprised over one-quarter of Japan's organized work force" (Kolko and Kolko, 1972, p. 512).

Chapter 8

1. The "American business interests" strongly favoring the recovery of the Japanese system "were almost exclusively in world market-competitive industries with nothing to fear from Japanese revival, such as General Electric, Westinghouse, Reynolds Aluminum, Standard Oil, Socony-Vacuum, and various Wall Street banking and investment interests, including the Chase, First National City, and Chemical Banks" (Cumings, 1990, p. 175). Unlike "declining American industries like textiles," these more advanced factions of U.S. capital were "anxious for trade with or investment in Japan" (ibid.). They were prominently represented in the influential American Council on Japan, whose members "functioned both outside and inside the American state" (ibid.).

2. In the United States, the powerful "Japan Lobby," led by the American Council on Japan, "oppose[d] the purge of wartime business leaders linked to Japanese militarism." The lobby's immediate goal was "to bring to an end the 'democratization and demilitarization' emphasis of the early occupation, and instead revive the Japanese industrial economy" (Cumings, 1990, p. 176).

3. "Perhaps least affected by the years of stress and upheaval was the Japanese bureaucracy. It was like an iceberg buffeted by a storm. Some of the pinnacles were cracked or chipped, some even broke off and disappeared, but the vast submerged section drifted on unaffected and unscarred" (Cohen, 1958, p. 192). "With the vital exception of the military and their allies in the bureaucracy, whose demise was sought by their industrial opponents, the other purges of the elite were a facade and quite ineffectual. . . . By and large only the unimportant disappeared" (Kolko and Kolko, 1972, p. 317).

4. No wonder that "Yamaguchi Takehide, leader of the farmers union, responded to the land reform with hostility. 'When I heard the news I thought "damn," if they had not done that we should have had a revolutionary government in Tokyo in a couple of years'" (Kolko and Kolko, 1972, p. 318). Indeed, the land reform began yielding dividends to the Japanese ruling class immediately after its passage by the Diet in October 1946. It not only took "much of the initiative from the radical farmers' organizations," but also—in conjunction with stepped-up emergency food imports by the SCAP—partially defused the politically charged issue of food distribution "well before the next upsurge in the workers' movement in the winter of 1946-47" (Moore, 1983, p. 240; 1997, p. 37). As a result, "the links with farmers' organizations and city groups of spring 1946 had no real counterpart in the winter of 1947" (Moore, 1983, p. 240).

5. In the FEC proceedings, "generous changes were made in virtually all aspects of the interim reparations removal program as originally contemplated. Annual ingot steel capacity has been raised to 3,500,000 metric tons,

compared to the original 2,500,000 tons. A pig iron ceiling of 2,000,000 metric tons is now contemplated, instead of the Pauley figure of 500,000 tons. . . . The ceiling for shipbuilding and repair facilities is set at a level needed to build 150,000 gross tons annually and to service a merchant fleet of 3,000,000 gross tons. The Pauley Report had recommended 1,500,000 gross tons for Japan's postwar merchant marine. Annual ceilings are also fixed for nitric acid (30,000 metric tons), aluminum and magnesium (25,000 metric tons), and ball and roller bearings ($32,000,000 worth). The Pauley Report would have permitted 12,500 tons of nitric acid, but no aluminum, magnesium, or bearings" (Bisson, 1947, pp. 244-245).

6. The loans for the previously mentioned triangular trade program thus "came both directly from the United States and through the various 'international' bodies dominated by it, such as the World Bank, which was tightly controlled by the same group of oil company lawyers and bankers who were connected to the biggest U.S. economic interests in and around Japan and who also managed most of American foreign policy towards the Far East" (Halliday, 1978, pp. 186-187).

7. As Cohen observed: "The regrouping of the Zaibatsu enterprises is not being undertaken through family auspices or holding companies, as before the war, but rather by three means: (a) purchase of stock by one company in another, (b) interlocking directorates for veteran Zaibatsu managers, and especially (c) Zaibatsu bank leadership in pulling together, financing, and organizing the scattered companies" (1958, p. 200). The first two devices were not openly employed until Japan regained its independence in 1952; early on the banks were the crucial factor (Halliday and McCormack, 1973, p. 166).

8. "The assault on the militant working class on the shop floor was accompanied by action at other levels: in education, where a major purge had been launched by SCAP and the Yoshida regime from the beginning of 1949, in the media, and at the party political level. . . . This purge of political leaders on the left started well before the outbreak of the Korean War, and it was a direct continuation of the dismissals of militant workers which had marked the overall drive to cripple the left" (Halliday, 1978, p. 219).

9. As discussed earlier, the United States "had shown marked reluctance to proceed with designated confiscations" of industrial equipment as reparations, "particularly in the armaments industry." Hence, "most of the productive capacity in this sector was still intact at the beginning of 1951 and was switched into full production to meet U.S. orders for the war against the Korean people" (Halliday and McCormack, 1973, p. 79).

10. Cohen (1958) clarifies the crucial role of U.S. aid and Korean War procurements in the recovery of Japanese capitalism: "In every year from 1945 through 1956 Japan had an unfavorable balance of trade. Its exports increased but its imports rose faster. The total trade gap over the 11-year period amounted to $6,016 million, a deficit which Japan would have been

unable to incur had it not been for U.S. aid and 'special procurement.' Over the same period these amounted to $6,233 million, just covering the trade gap" (pp. 109-111). Korean War procurements fully account for the doubling of total official U.S. transfers to Japan in the second half of the post–1945 decade as compared to the first half (ibid., p. 111).

11. Halliday and McCormack (1973) argue that the *zaibatsu* "not only recovered their prewar position, but actually improved it. In particular, they streamlined their co-ordination so that now erstwhile rivals, such as Mitsubishi, Mitsui and Sumitomo [could] collaborate together in joint ventures" (p. 166).

12. "During the high-growth period of 1950-1973, nearly one-third of total private savings was captured by the government in the form of postal savings accounts" (Ozawa, 1999, p. 353).

13. "In 1972 the top ten handled half [of Japan's] exports, 62 per cent of its imports and 20 per cent of domestic wholesale transactions" (Halliday, 1978, p. 276). The shares "held by each of these 'Big Ten' ranged between 1.8 and 9.9 percent of Japan's total exports and between 2.5 and 16.5 percent of total imports" (Yamamura, 1976, p. 161). Dahlby (1980) observed that each of the nine largest GTCs was "closely tied into one of the seven giant industrial conglomerates (Mitsubishi, Mitsui, Sumitomo, Fuyo, Daiichi Kangyo, Sanwa and Tokai) which, in turn, have at their nucleus a major city bank. In addition to these firmly cemented commercial credit lines, the sogo shosha [could] count on the Export and Import Bank of Japan as a major source of long-term credit" (p. 40).

14. The 30 percent figure is based on the combined exports of Hong Kong, Taiwan, South Korea, the Philippines, Malaysia, and Singapore. Hone (1974) also notes that the big Japanese GTCs "are often able to book 60-100 percent of a unit's capacity for one or two years. In such a situation the loss of an order is much more serious than accepting a low price. . . . The costs in terms of low unit prices are considerable, and the power of oligopolistic buying groups is on the increase" (p. 149).

15. The integration of enterprise unions into capitalist control structures was a crucial precondition for the introduction of corporate welfare schemes (housing, transportation, education, and credit subsidies; recreational and dining facilities; and so on). To be consistent with corporate profitability and competitiveness, such welfare schemes had to be limited to "permanent" workers, and this presumed a parallel exclusion of "part-time" and "temporary" workers from union membership (Cho, 1996).

Chapter 9

1. By the late 1970s, Japan's outputs of electricity, crude steel, aluminum, and cement all easily exceeded those of any other capitalist country except the

United States—and in shipbuilding Japan more than doubled the combined production of the United States, West Germany, France, and Great Britain (Sweezy, 1980, p. 4).

2. Exports of iron and steel products accounted for 12.4 percent of total Japanese exports in 1965 (up from 11.5 percent a decade earlier), while chemicals and synthetic rubber made up 6.5 percent (up from 4.5 percent in 1955) (Krause and Sekiguchi, 1976, p. 409).

3. Tensions over Japanese textile exports to the United States seem to have reached a final peak near the end of the first Nixon Administration, when, partly "in order to repay his political debt to Strom Thurmond, Nixon went down the line to impose a particularly harsh and stupid programme restricting textile imports" (Halliday and McCormack, 1973, pp. 211-212). This particular set of restrictions also applied to exports from Hong Kong, Taiwan, and South Korea (countries to which many Japanese textile firms had moved production in the 1960s); nonetheless it still included "a three-year agreement on Japan, pegging increases in detail, by type of product, to tiny amounts per annum" (ibid., p. 212).

4. "In recent years the Japanese labor market has been tightening and wages have been rising rapidly. Whether or not this situation should be described as a labor shortage, it is clear that Japanese producers of labor-intensive products such as textiles and consumer electronics have been losing their competitiveness in domestic plants . . . " (Krause and Sekiguchi, 1976, p. 449). Japan's overall labor-market situation actually reached the point where nonagricultural real wage growth exceeded nonagricultural labor productivity growth for several years beginning in 1962 (Ohkawa and Rosovsky, 1973, p. 119).

5. As Rob Steven relates the process, not only light industry but also coal mining and "much of agriculture (in spite of the latter's subsidisation)" were run down and "scrapped" in order to "generate the surplus for the state to build infrastructure and subsidise heavy industry" (1988b, pp. 77-78). The choice of coal as an industry to be run down is not surprising insofar as it was a traditional center of labor militancy. Meanwhile, the running down of agriculture "meshed well with the political alliance which had been sealed between the ruling classes of Japan and the United States in the Security Treaty of 1952. The United States would find in Japan a market for its agricultural surplus and other raw materials, and simultaneously gain an extra lever with which to keep the Japanese ruling class in line with its military strategy in the Far East" (ibid, p. 78). This is not to deny that the running down of Japanese agriculture produced its own contradictions (see Chapter 10).

6. These figures probably understate the sectoral shift of Japan's exporting core, the reason being that Krause and Sekiguchi (1976) employ a strange definition of "labor-intensive" exports including the category "motorcycles,

ships, and others" (p. 409). Shipbuilding is clearly a "heavy" industry. Using a somewhat different classification, Steven estimates that the share of light industry in total Japanese exports declined from 20.6 percent in 1971 to just 13.4 percent in 1974, and that heavy industry increased its export share from 74.6 percent to a whopping 82.2 percent during the same period (1983, p. 212).

7. As noted by Halliday and McCormack (1973), the response of Japan's capitalist planners to industrial pollution problems was "not to rethink the concepts of growth and GNP, and, more importantly, profit, but rather to set about shifting their difficult and dirty enterprises to areas where opposition to them will certainly be quickly put down. . . . As part of foreign 'aid' programmes they will be exported to places like Korea, Taiwan, Thailand, and so on" (pp. 194–195).

8. Recounting the mid-1970s "deceleration" of unit labor costs in Japanese industry, Tsuyoshi Tsuru (1994) points to management efforts "to alter pattern bargaining . . . by strictly linking workers' wages with the firm's performance rather than going wages" (p 286). Moreover, "in the production process, employers have made substantial efforts in rationalizing the workplace: technologically, they have concentrated new investment on a system using microelectronics equipment; and organizationally they have developed small, informal work-group activities, such as total quality control, and the joint consultation system for information sharing between management and labor. This effort resulted in higher levels of productivity growth. . . . Japanese unions usually cooperated in these actions" (ibid., pp. 286–287). On the intensification of labor and further erosion of union power associated with these management systems, see Dassbach (1993) and Tsuru and Rebitzer (1995).

9. This industrial restructuring—the third major one since the Korean War— is especially important insofar as it largely explains the export-led growth of Indonesia, Thailand, and Malaysia beginning in the mid-1980s. See Chapters 2 and 12 for related discussions.

10. By 1989, "Japan was the world's single largest source of FDI, with an annual outflow of $48 billion (up from $6.5 billion in 1985)" (Bernard and Ravenhill, 1995, p 181).

11. This is calculated from data presented by Steven (1996, p. 170). Here, "East Asia" includes the main ASEAN countries (Indonesia, Malaysia, Thailand, the Philippines, and Singapore) plus Taiwan, Hong Kong, and the Republic of Korea.

12. In addition, the entire postwar process of export-oriented scrap-and-build may have led to a narrowing in the *range of products* produced by the advanced technological edge of Japan's manufacturing base—thereby eroding the overall sales buoyancy of domestic industry. Reduced diversification within leading sectors (the increasing focus on the very most advanced

products and components) may have made the Japanese economy more vulnerable to global ups and downs and competitive pressures. For example, many market analysts felt that the mid-1990s Japanese electronics industry suffered from "overdependence on a single product, the humble memory chip. . . . Japan's Big Five—NEC, Toshiba Corp., Hitachi Ltd., Fujitsu, and Mitsubishi Electrical Corp.—still rely on memory products for roughly a third of their semiconductor revenue. What's more, analysts estimate that the lucrative chips account for one-third to three-quarters of the companies' entire profits, some of which are approaching record levels. . . . The problem is that if memory-chip prices take a serious dive, the Big Five don't have any other products sufficiently strong to pick up the slack in profits" (Hamilton, 1996a, p. B4). By mid-1996, "chip-makers, not long ago among Japan's most profitable companies," were being "battered by the collapse of memory-chip prices since the beginning of the year" (Hamilton, et al., 1996, p. A15).

Chapter 10

1. For this reason, Marx and many subsequent Marxists have treated the contradiction between private appropriation and social production as virtually synonymous with the contradiction between production for profit and production for human needs.
2. Part III analyzes the implications of this broader dynamic for East Asian workers and communities outside Japan.
3. To these corporate investment-seeking surpluses must be added Japan's internationally high rate of household savings (see Chapter 4). Overall, Japan's rate of gross domestic saving (as a share of GNP) reached an astounding average of 39.5 percent over the 1969-73 period—over two-and-a-half times the U.S. rate and nearly one-and-a-half times the respective rates of West Germany and France (Tsuru, 1993, p. 71).
4. Sweezy adds that "the visitor to Japan, and in particular to the capital city of Tokyo, is likely to find the visible signs of the burgeoning unproductive sector at least as striking as in any other country in the world. This holds most of all with respect to the entertainment 'industry' (restaurants, theaters, coffee shops, geisha rendezvous houses, teashops, bars, cabarets, massage bathhouses, and dubious hotels) which are said to employ in Tokyo alone half a million women. . . . A large part of this enormous 'after-working hours' establishment is financed through corporate expense accounts, which could well be called the hallmark of Japanese monopoly capitalism" (1980, p. 13).
5. For example, after observing that "in March 1991, Japanese corporations abroad employed 452,000 local workers in North America, 211,000 in Europe, 666,000 in Asia, and 1,514,000 in the whole world," Makoto Itoh asserted that "Japanese direct investment abroad has not yet brought about

industrial hollowing, unlike the cases of the UK and the USA" (1994, p. 46). This was written at a time when manufacturing employment in Japan was already in sharp decline (see below, in text).

6. Itoh (1994) similarly notes that "it is curious to see how Japanese wages have become internationally so expensive in dollar terms, thus further promoting Japanese foreign investment, despite stagnancy of Japanese real wages in terms of the yen" (p. 17).

7. This problem was eventually worsened by the excess productive capacity built up during the mid- to late 1980s, when Japanese capital had conducted a large-scale upgrading of its domestic facilities to cope with the 1985 revaluation of the yen and to accommodate the growing consumption demands associated with the bubble economy. By the mid-1990s, this excess capacity was acting as a disincentive to new cost-cutting investments; as a result, "Japan's unit labor costs, for the first time in many years, [rose] above those of the United States in some of the key industries in which the two sides compete" (Steven, 1997, p. 205). For further details, see Brenner (1998, pp. 221-222).

8. "Agriculture's roles [before World War II] were seen as producing as much food as possible for local consumption, absorbing rural labor, and providing capital for domestic industrial growth" (Jussaume, 1998, p. 404).

9. "The anomalies of the electoral representation system are such that, for example, the maximum differential in the weight of urban/rural votes is 5:1—i.e. that a Dietman can be elected from a rural constituency with as few as one fifth the votes it might take from an urban one" (Halliday and McCormack, 1973, p. 171).

10. See McCormack (1996, pp. 132-139) for an overview of the regional ecological plunder associated with Japan's agricultural imports.

11. "The official discount rate was lowered five times, from 5.0% in 1985 to 2.5% (an unprecedented low level) in February 1987. Accordingly, market interest rates, both long-term and short-term, had reached unprecedented low levels by May 1987. From May 1987 to February 1988, [the] money supply increased by 10% more than it had done in the same months in the previous year. This remarkably easy access to funds accelerated the money game. . . . Supported by financial institutions, many enterprises and individuals expanded their land acquisitions and sales" (Oizumi, 1994, pp. 202-203).

12. Employment in the Japanese construction industry grew from 2.5 million in 1960 to more than six million in the early 1990s. By comparison, 4.8 million Japanese workers were employed in manufacturing as of 1991 (McCormack, 1996, p. 32). In 1993, construction absorbed 43 percent of the national government budget and 19.1 percent of GDP. "Japan outspends the United States on construction by a ratio of 2.6:1, or in proportion to relative land area, 32:1. Incredibly, Japan spends more on public works than

the United States does on defense, and was doing so even at the height of the Cold War" (ibid., p. 33).

13. As Oizumi (1994) puts it: "The redevelopment of big cities in the 1980s was aimed at 'remaking' urban space, to make it adaptable to a new stage of capital accumulation" based on an "expansion of property finance, which is a part of the accumulation of surplus funds and financial innovation . . . a driving force for the emergence of the 'bubble economy' [and] the growth of the Japanese economy as a global financial power" (p. 199).

14. The typical golf course involves "the application of three to four tons per year of herbicides, germicides, pesticides, coloring agents, organic chlorine, and other fertilizers, including chemicals that are carcinogenic or cause various health abnormalities. This rich brew, three times the intensity of what the most chemically minded farmer would apply to vegetables, ultimately drains off into rivers, ponds, swamps, lakes, or the sea. . . . At the end of the 1980s, the Ministry of Health found 950 places where the quality or quantity of water had been adversely affected by golf-course development" (McCormack, 1996, p. 96).

15. "Japan's construction industry, in particular, is closely tied to Japanese politicians and foreign aid" (Forrest, 1991, p. 27). Forrest's article is a useful overview of environmental malfeasance in Japanese foreign aid programs and the tendency of Japanese aid institutions to see the environment itself as a "growth sector."

16. In May of 1999 the Japanese Diet passed a new law against child pornography and child prostitution. The law's passage "was a victory for international law enforcement officials, who have long been critical of Japan's lax laws against sex with children and child pornography, and for a band of women legislators . . . who have fought for two years to overcome strong opposition to the law on the ground that it would inhibit free speech" (Strom, 1999a, p. A6). However, the legislation's actual effect "will depend on how seriously the police choose to enforce the new law" (*Economist*, 1999c, p. 32).

17. Consider the highly successful Japanese PC-software series entitled "Princess Maker," which "gives the player control over the activities, hobbies and clothing of a girl character he 'raises' from childhood" (Associated Press, 1996, p. A4). In this essentially child-porn game, "the girl character is depicted in sexy, wide-eyed comic-book style, and can be programmed to dress in lingerie or sunbathe naked." According to its creator, Takami Akai, the game also gives "Japanese males a chance to fantasize about conquering the one place where they don't call the shots—the home." Indeed, the player "is presented with an adoptive 'daughter,' aged 10. He names her, picks her birthday, even chooses her blood type, which some in Japan believe determines character traits." The player can then monitor the girl ("who blossoms physically as the years pass") in "two dozen categories,

including sexiness, strength and smarts, which help determine the game's outcome." Despite its hefty price tag of $140 per release, "the series has sold a combined 200,000 copies" and "is exported to South Korea and Taiwan"—with an English-language version in the works (p. A4). Perhaps this is the kind of industrial leadership we should learn to expect from the mature capitalist "lead goose."

18. After 1969 the Japanese quickly "established themselves as the country with the greatest economic stake in Vietnam"—so much so that by "early 1971 Japan was accounting for 48.7 per cent of all non-tied South Vietnamese imports" (Halliday and McCormack, 1973, pp. 47, 56-58).

19. Eventually, dictatorial methods had to be employed to reimpose the treaty on the Japanese people. With the Japanese Socialist Party controlling enough opposing votes to block the revision's passage through the Diet, "the government called in the police to remove all the JSP Dietmen from the Chamber *by force.* The vote ratifying the treaty was then put through with less than half the members of the House present" (Halliday, 1978, p. 264; emphasis in original).

20. Although Japan evidently does not possess any nuclear weapons, it does have the requisite plutonium-generating capacity and trained scientific and engineering personnel (Leventhal, 1994; Nadler, 1994). In short, it has "the capacity to become a nuclear weapons power within a matter of months—if not weeks" (Gerson, 1996, p. 42).

21. "In the period 1991-94," for example, "the U.S. accounted for 43% of the value of all arms transfer agreements with the developing countries of the Asia-Pacific region, far outstripping Western Europe's 26% share and Russia's 23%" (Bello, 1996d).

22. Despite its ascension to the number-one rank among nations in average life expectancy, Japan experienced "a four-fold increase in the general rate of ill health in the community between 1955 and 1985, with high blood pressure and nervous disorders marked by much greater increases. . . . Hypertension as a medical phenomenon increased by more than four times in the three high-growth decades from 1960" (McCormack, 1996, p. 85). The worsening stress and insecurity among Japanese workers help explain the country's high incidence of suicide. At 26 per 100,000 people, the Japanese suicide rate is now second in the world (just below Finland's 27 per 100,000). There were 32,863 suicides in Japan during 1998, a 35 percent increase over the previous year (Coleman, 1999, p. A5). In terms of workplace stress, the *Wall Street Journal* reported that: "About 70% of workers surveyed say bosses are the cause of stress, says Tiger Vacuum Bottle Co. The most common way for Japanese workers to relieve stress is to drink liquor, says another survey, by Chiyoda Mutual Life Insurance Co." (Kanabayashi, 1996b, p. A1).

23. Similarly, Morioka (1991) cites a Japanese government survey indicating that with "voluntary overtime" included, Japanese workers "worked on the

average about 2,400 hours per year" in the late 1980s, with the figure for male workers alone standing at "about 2,600 hours" (p. 23).

24. See also Ozawa (1985-86) for a detailed analysis of wage differentials in Japan during the years 1965 through 1982. He found that such "differentials have been widening among workers by industry, by firm size, by sex and by type of work" (p. 77).

25. Despite this decline, only six out of 48 industry federations of enterprise unions had even one full-time recruiter as of 1989, according to a survey conducted by the Japan Private Sector Union Confederation (Tsuru and Rebitzer, 1995, p. 490, fn. 35).

26. Rengo was established as a result of the 1989 merger of the two main union federations, Domei and Sohyo (Hoogvelt, 1995, p. 725). "Two other national union centres, Zenrokyo and Zenroren, are deeply critical of Japan's TNCs and the spread of its industrial relations. They fight a rearguard action in favour of active international workers solidarity" (ibid.). Unfortunately, Zenrokyo and Zenroren have a combined membership of only 500,000 workers compared to Rengo's eight million, with an even bigger disadvantage in terms of funding (ibid.).

27. Fingleton even asserted that Japan's apparent economic stagnation was a figment of the widespread practice of converting Japanese GDP data into U.S. dollar terms using outdated exchange-rate figures not reflecting the increased U.S. dollar value of the yen (1995, p. 81). This assertion was rendered untenable by Japan's continued stagnation despite the yen's large depreciation between 1995 and 1998.

Chapter 11

1. Both military governments were established in reaction to mass democratic and socialist-oriented upsurges following the Second World War. The South Korean dictatorship was built on the suppression of the popular Korean People's Republic (and its base in industrial unions, peasant unions, and people's committees) by occupying U.S. forces assisted by local military police, and it was reinforced by the Cold War division of Korea. Taiwan's military dictatorship was a by-product of the more successful revolutionary movement in Mainland China, which forced Chiang Kai-Shek's anti-communist Kuomintang regime to relocate offshore and establish a new base built on the violent subjugation of the island's indigenous population. The power of both regimes was solidified through anti-communist land reforms and tight state control over agrarian institutions. For detailed discussions, see Bello and Rosenfeld (1990), Cumings (1981, 1990), and Hart-Landsberg (1998b).

2. See Hart-Landsberg (1993) for a thorough examination of the South Korean growth strategy and its contradictions.

3. The South Korean trade balance with the U.S. rose from a surplus of $3.6 billion in 1984 to a record $9.6 billion surplus in 1987, before falling into deficit in 1991 (Hart-Landsberg, 1993, p. 242).

4. In 1989, for example, average wage costs per hour of a textile operator were $3.56 in Taiwan, $2.87 in South Korea, $0.68 in Thailand, and $0.23 in Indonesia (Bello, 1992, p. 89).

5. These ambitious plans were later put on hold, however. "The plunge in manufacturers' overseas investment [in 1998] was mainly attributable to the worsened business climates in Southeast Asian countries, which stemmed from the Asian financial crisis" (Kwak, 1999).

6. Hatch and Yamamura (1996, Chapter 6) survey a number of studies, all of which conclude that there is a large and growing technology gap between South Korea and Japan.

7. The competitiveness of export prices can also be enhanced by an under-valued exchange rate. In this case, the losses that would otherwise appear directly as low or negative profit margins (in terms of domestic currency) now appear indirectly as a reduction in the real terms of trade.

Chapter 12

1. In each of the SEA-3, cumulative FDI inflows over the years 1990-91 easily exceeded total inflows over the 1985-89 period (Hill and Athukorala, 1998, p. 25).

2. Relationships between Japanese and SEA-3 elites vary by country, thereby imparting a nationally differentiated dynamic to the regional integration process. Steven (1990) provides a useful summary of the formation of elite alliances with Japanese capital in Thailand and Malaysia (Chapter 6) and Indonesia (Chapter 7). Bernard (1999) discusses the development of Thai capital and the social and economic conditions which encouraged its openness to an alliance with Japanese capital.

3. The sharp increase in SEA-3 trade deficits was not caused only by dependence on Japanese components, machinery, and technology. Also important were deteriorating terms of trade, spending for infrastructure construction (undertaken largely by Japanese companies) to attract Japanese foreign direct investment; and a rapid rise in imports of consumer luxuries. In terms of the latter, the *Far Eastern Economic Review* reported that in Malaysia, "calls for the authorities to mount an intensified campaign to combat the more unrestrained forms of consumer spending have left some observers skeptical. 'That doesn't jibe with what [Prime Minister] Mahathir is trying to do. Ostentatious spending is very much part of the milieu,' says a popular Malaysian artist and social critic" (Tsuruoka, 1992, p. 58).

4. See Limqueco, et al. (1989) for an historical overview of state efforts to repress and control organized labor in Thailand (pp. 31-35, 111-113, 154-

155) and Malaysia (pp. 60-63, 68, 108, 158-160). The repression of labor in Indonesia is discussed in Budiardjo (1993), Goodman (1993), and Budiman (1994). SEA-3 electronics operations are especially notorious for their superexploitation of young women workers and for their intense antagonism toward unions; see Lim (1978), Rasiah (1988), Brecher and Costello (1994, pp. 133-134), and Abdullah and Keenoy (1995) for analysis of the Malaysian case. On the use and abuse of migrant labor in the SEA-3, see Martin, et al. (1995), Lee and Sivananthiran (1996), Martin (1996), and Netto (1996). The plunder and despoliation of the natural environment under SEA-3 export-led growth is detailed in Howard (1993), Komin (1993), Baker (1994), Broad (1995), Corben (1995), Press (1996), Thompson and Duggie (1996), Dauvergne (1997), and Paterniti (1998).

5. It was the fastest growing of the SEA-3, with annual rates of GDP growth of eight percent or higher between 1988 and 1995. Thailand also seemed like an unambiguous success for the flying geese approach in that it approved the most FDI inflows over the years 1986-92 and had the greatest share of manufactures in total exports among the SEA-3 (Steven, 1996, p. 93).

6. Despite Thai government efforts to attract additional direct investment from non-Japanese sources, total annual FDI inflows into Thailand suffered a 25 percent decrease over the years 1990-93. By 1996, total FDI inflows still had not recovered to the level achieved in 1990 (Hill and Athukorala, 1998, p. 25).

7. SEA-3 elites also attempted to reverse the shift in Japanese direct investment priorities. One major initiative was the effort to enhance regional trade integration by forming an ASEAN Free Trade Area [AFTA] (Ravenhill, 1995). Although AFTA would purportedly create new trade and investment opportunities for local capital, it was mainly motivated by "the fear of investment diversion and the desire to continue to attract FDI as part of ASEAN members' development strategies. . . . The important changes which led to the fear of investment diversion were the increasing mobility of capital and the increasing competition from other countries as investment sites" (Bowles, 1997, p. 233). Unfortunately, while further weakening the ability of individual countries to establish any kind of autonomous industrial base, AFTA is unlikely to promote any alternative *regionally* autonomous or self-propelled development process, because it does not question the basic logic of dependent growth through competitiveness. As long as this logic remains unchallenged, improvements in wages and other conditions of working people will still appear as simply a cost of development rather than its basic purpose.

8. Bello (1997) offers a very useful and complete analysis of developments in Thailand. All data reported in this paragraph are drawn from this source.

9. The Malaysian government modified the IMF policy line by, among other things, creating special funds to prop up the stock market and businesses owned by elites. It also refused to reduce spending or boost interest rates as

much as the IMF recommended. It deviated still further from IMF orthodoxy when, in September 1998, it decided to boost spending and, to guard against capital flight, make it illegal for investors to take their money out of the economy for one year or engage in trading of the currency outside the country.

10. Mexico's experience is important in this regard since it has now replaced the SEA-3 as the IMF poster country. Mexico suffered a major currency collapse in late 1994. Since then it has closely followed IMF policy advice and, beginning in 1996, recorded three consecutive years of positive GDP growth. Yet, as the *Wall Street Journal* points out, although "Mexico's economy enjoys a stellar reputation," since its "big 1994 currency devaluation, consumers here have suffered a staggering 39% drop in their purchasing power. Just since 1997, the number of people living in extreme poverty—defined as workers earning less than $2 a day—has grown by four million, or twice the growth of the population" (Millman, 1999, p. A1).

Chapter 13

1. Additional references and support for arguments made in this chapter can be found in Burkett and Hart-Landsberg (1998).
2. Leading structuralists Robert Wade and Frank Veneroso broadened this perspective to include all East Asian countries affected by the crisis, arguing that "the calamity unleashed on the region is hugely disproportional to the severity of the problems in the real economy. . . . The great lesson of the Asian crisis is that the desirability of free movements of short-term capital has to be put into question" (1998, pp. 9, 21).

Chapter 14

1. Our focus on working people in this statement is not accidental. In most countries, the wealthy have found ways to avoid the costs of the crisis (Graham, 1999). In South Korea, for example, "wealthy Koreans are earning bundles as banks, desperate to attract deposits and bolster the Korean currency, offer 20 percent interest rates" (Jordan, 1998).
2. In general, female and migrant workers have been among the first and hardest hit by the crisis. "For example, in Thailand, an estimated 80 percent of the one million workers dismissed from August 1997 to April 1998 were women" (*Asian Labour Update*, 1998a, p. 3) Women workers have been the worst affected in South Korea as well. In 1997, women working in companies with less than five workers accounted for approximately 63 percent of all women in the labor force. On average, these enterprises were the first to close (Lee, 1998, p. 19).
   As for migrant workers, the governments of both Malaysia and Thailand

took quick action to repatriate them. Over 11,000 were deported from Malaysia from January to May 1998. Beginning January 1998, the Thai government took steps to deport the country's estimated 600,000 foreign workers, mostly Burmese (*Asian Labour Update,* 1998a, p. 3) Likewise, the South Korean government repatriated over 270,000 migrant workers in the first few months of the crisis (Lee, 1998, p. 19). Often these expulsions were carried out brutally and in ways designed to scapegoat these workers as a major cause of declining wages and rising unemployment rates.

3. The following sources offer brief discussions of the rise and contemporary politics of NGO movements: For South Korea see Hart-Landsberg (1998b, Chapter 7); for Thailand, see Ungpakorn (1999, Chapters 3 and 8), and Bello, Cunningham, and Li (1998, Chapter 12); for Indonesia, see *Links* (1997-98).

4. Some activists are reluctant to embrace Marxism and the political strategy of building an anti-capitalist movement with socialism as its goal because of their justifiably critical appraisal of the experience of countries that have declared themselves socialist, such as the former Soviet Union or the People's Republic of China. We do not think that the practices of these countries represented socialism, even though their respective revolutions were made in the name of socialism and many of their citizens hoped for and worked hard to create socialism. That is why in the Introduction we defined our goal as the creation of socialism from below. However, we doubt that even this emphasis on democratic control is sufficient to diminish popular reluctance to embrace a socialist project. The more general problem is that most people, even those critical of capitalism, have come to believe that there are no viable alternatives to capitalism.

5. For background to and analysis of these events, see *Links* (1997-98; 1999a; 1999b), Miah (1998a; 1998b), and Simanjuntak (1997).

6. In highlighting these challenges we do not mean to claim any originality in their formulation. Our understanding of the South Korean situation has been strongly influenced by the writings and activities of many South Korean activists. Not surprisingly, activists continue to reevaluate possibilities and are engaged in intense debates over strategy. Our intent is to generate further thought, discussion, and debate among those forces (within as well as outside South Korea) that share our general political perspective.

References

Abdullah, Syed R. S. and Tom Keenoy. 1995. "Japanese Managerial Practices in the Malaysian Electronics Industry: Two Case Studies," *Journal of Management Studies*, Vol. 32, No. 6, November, pp. 747–766.

Ahn Mi-Young. 1999, "Economy—South Korea: The Crisis Has Two Faces," *Interpress Service*, On-Line Edition, March 24.

Akamatsu, Kaname. 1961. "A Theory of Unbalanced Growth in the World Economy," *Weltwirtschaftliches Archiv*, Vol. 86, No. 1, pp. 196–217.

———. 1962. "A Historical Pattern of Economic Growth in Developing Countries," *Developing Economies*, Vol. 1, No. 1, March–August, pp. 3–25.

Allen, G. C. 1958. *Japan's Economic Recovery*. London: Oxford University Press.

AMPO. 1998. "The End of the Japanese Miracle? An Interview with Okumura Hiroshi," *AMPO Japan-Asia Quarterly Review*, Vol. 28, No 3, July, pp. 36–38.

Amsden, Alice H. 1989. *Asia's Next Giant: South Korea and Late Industrialization*. New York: Oxford University Press.

———. 1991. "Diffusion of Development: The Late-Industrializing Model and Greater East Asia," *American Economic Review*, Vol. 81, No. 2, May, pp. 282–286.

———. 1994. "Why Isn't the Whole World Experimenting with the East Asian Model to Develop?," *World Development*, Vol. 22, No. 4, April, pp. 627–633.

———. 1996. "Late Industrialization: Can More Countries Make It?," in Charles V. Whalen, ed., *Political Economy for the 21st Century*. Armonk, NY: M.E. Sharpe, pp. 245–261.

——— and Yoon-Dae Euh, 1997. "Behind Korea's Plunge," *New York Times*, November 27, p. A23.

Anderson, Perry. 1974. *Lineages of the Absolutist State*. London: New Left Books.

Aoki, Keisuke. 1991. "Flexible Work Organization and Management Control in Japanese-style Management," *International Journal of Political Economy*, Vol. 21, No. 3, Fall, pp. 49–69.

Asian Labour Update. 1998a. "The Asian Miracle/Mess," No. 27, February–May, pp. 1, 3-4.

———. 1998b. "Thailand: Dispute Ends," No. 27, February–May, pp. 28-29.

Associated Press. 1994. "Japanese Socialist Party Abandons Pacifist Policies," *Tribune-Star,* Terre Haute, September 4.

———. 1996. "Sexy Game Lets Japanese Men Raise 'Daughters'," *Tribune-Star,* Terre Haute, April 6, p. A4.

———. 1997. "China's New Threat: Army of Unemployment Creating Wave of Protests Across Nation," *New York Times,* December 26, p. B4.

———. 1998. "Retirees Block Trains in a Protest in China," *New York Times,* April 19, Section 1, p. 10.

———. 1999a. "Japanese Bankruptcies Second Highest Since WWII," *Tribune-Star,* Terre Haute, January 20, p. A5.

———. 1999b. "Shop till You Drop, and It's On the House: Japan Gives Away Vouchers to Shoppers," *Tribune-Star,* Terre Haute, January 31, p. A4.

———. 1999c. "Record Joblessness in Japan," *New York Times,* July 31, p. B2.

Athukorala, Prema-chandra and Jayant Menon. 1997. "AFTA and the Investment-Trade Nexus in ASEAN," *World Economy,* Vol. 20, No. 2, March, pp. 159-174.

Baker, Russ W. 1994. "The Deforesting of Irian Jaya," *The Nation,* February 7, pp. 162-164.

Balassa, Bela and John Williamson. 1987. *Adjusting to Success: Balance of Payments Policy in the East Asian NICs.* Washington, DC: Institute for International Economics.

Baran, Paul A. 1957. *The Political Economy of Growth.* New York: Monthly Review Press.

——— and Paul M. Sweezy. 1966. *Monopoly Capital: An Essay on the American Economic and Social Order.* New York: Monthly Review Press.

Bauer, John and Andrew Mason. 1992. "The Distribution of Income and Wealth in Japan," *Review of Income and Wealth,* Vol. 38, No. 4, December, pp. 403-428.

Beach, Sophie. 1999. "China's Unseen Unemployed," *The Nation,* February 15, pp. 20-23.

Beasley, W. G. 1987. *Japanese Imperialism, 1894-1945.* Oxford, UK: Clarendon Press.

———. 1995. *The Rise of Modern Japan: Political, Economic and Social Change Since 1850,* Second Edition. New York: St. Martin's Press.

Bello, Walden. 1992. *People and Power in the Pacific.* London: Pluto Press.

——— (with Shea Cunningham and Bill Rau). 1994. *Dark Victory: The United States, Structural Adjustment, and Global Poverty.* London: Pluto Press.

———. 1996a. "Neither Market Nor State: The Development Debate in South-East Asia," *The Ecologist,* Vol. 26, No. 4, July/August, pp. 167-175.

———. 1996b. "Japan's Strategy of Attrition in APEC," *Documentation for Action Groups in Asia,* Distributed Worldwide on APC Networks, September 4.

———. 1996c. "ASEAN and APEC: The Making of a Geo-Economic Rivalry," *Documentation for Action Groups in Asia,* Distributed Worldwide on APC Networks, November 4.

———. 1996d. "The Balance-of-Power Doomsday Machine: Resurgent U.S. Unilateralism, Regional Realpolitik, and the U.S.-Japan Security Treaty," *AMPO Japan-Asia Quarterly Review,* Vol. 27, No. 2, pp. 12-29.

———. 1997. "Addicted to Capital: The Ten Year High and Present Day Withdrawal Trauma of Southeast Asia's Economies," *Focus-On-Trade* (a publication of Focus on the Global South, Bangkok, Thailand), No. 20, December.

———. 1998. "Statement to the Subcommittee on General Oversight and Investigations," Committee on Banking and Financial Services, U.S. House of Representatives, *Focus-on-Trade,* On-Line Edition, No. 25, May.

——— and Stephanie Rosenfeld. 1990. *Dragons in Distress: Asia's Miracle Economies In Crisis.* San Francisco: Institute for Food and Development Policy.

Bello, Walden, Shea Cunningham, and Li Kheng Poh. 1998. *A Siamese Tragedy: Development and Disintegration in Modern Thailand.* New York: Zed Books.

Bennett, John W. and Solomon B. Levine. 1976. "Industrialization and Social Deprivation: Welfare, Environment, and the Postindustrial Society in Japan," in Hugh Patrick, ed., *Japanese Industrialization and Its Social Consequences.* Berkeley: University of California Press, pp. 439-492.

Benson, John. 1996. "A Typology of Japanese Enterprise Unions," *British Journal of Industrial Relations,* Vol. 34, No. 3, September, pp. 371-386.

Bernard, Mitchell. 1999. "East Asia's Tumbling Dominoes: Financial Crises and the Myth of the Regional Model," in Leo Panitch and Colin Leys, eds., *Socialist Register 1999: Global Capitalism Versus Democracy.* New York: Monthly Review Press, pp. 178-208.

——— and John Ravenhill. 1995. "Beyond Product Cycles and Flying Geese: Regionalization, Hierarchy, and the Industrialization of Asia," *World Politics,* Vol. 47, No. 2, January, pp. 171-209.

Bisson, T. A. 1947. "Reparations and Reform in Japan," *Far Eastern Survey,* Vol. 16, No. 21, December 17, pp. 241-247.

Blomqvist, Hans C. 1995. "Intraregional Foreign Investment in East Asia," *ASEAN Economic Bulletin.* Vol. 11, No. 3, March, pp. 280-297.

Bloomberg News. 1998a. "Japan Jobless Rate Remains at Record High," *New York Times,* July 1, p. C4.

———. 1998b. "Japanese Unemployment Stays at Rate of 4.3%," *New York Times,* October 28, p. C4.

Bowles, Paul. 1997. "ASEAN, AFTA and the 'New Regionalism'," *Pacific Affairs,* Vol. 70, No. 2, Summer, pp. 219-233.

——— and Brian MacLean. 1996. "Regional Trading Blocs: Will East Asia Be Next?," *Cambridge Journal of Economics,* Vol. 20, No. 4, July, pp. 393-412.

Drecher, Jeremy and Tim Costello. 1994. *Global Village or Global Pillage: Economic Reconstruction from the Bottom Up.* Boston: South End Press.

Bremner, Brian. 1998a. "The Jolt Japan Needs?," *Business Week,* April 13, pp. 28-29.

———. 1998b. "Japan's Real Crisis," *Business Week,* May 18, pp. 136-142.

——— and Moon Ihlwan. 1998. "Can Kim Cut It?," *Business Week,* June 8, pp. 52-53.

Brenner, Robert. 1998. "Uneven Development and the Long Downturn: The Advanced Capitalist Economies from Boom to Stagnation, 1950-1998." *New Left Review,* No. 229, May/June, pp. 1-265.

Broad, Robin, 1995. "The Political Economy of Natural Resources: Case Studies of the Indonesian and Philippine Forest Sectors," *Journal of Developing Areas,* Vol. 29, No. 3, April, pp. 317-340.

Broadbent, Jeffrey. 1998. *Environmental Politics in Japan: Networks of Power and Protest.* Cambridge, UK: Cambridge University Press.

Brohman, John. 1996. "Postwar Development in the Asian NICs: Does the Neoliberal Model Fit Reality?," *Economic Geography,* Vol. 72, No. 2, April, pp. 107-130.

Budiardjo, Carmel. 1993. "Indonesian Tyranny: A Price Worth Paying," *Lies of Our Times,* November, pp. 8-10.

Budiman, Arief. 1994. "Indonesia: Authoritarianism Backed by G7," in *The People vs. Global Capital: The G7, TNCs, SAPs, and Human Rights,* Report of the International People's Tribunal to Judge the G7; Tokyo, July 1993. Tokyo: Pacific Asia Resource Center, pp. 83-95.

Burkett, Paul. 1997. "Democracy and Economic Transitions," *Studies in Political Economy,* No. 52, Spring, pp. 111-136.

————. 1999. *Marx and Nature: A Red and Green Perspective.* New York: St. Martin's Press.

————. 1998. "East Asia and the Crisis of Development Theory," *Journal of Contemporary Asia,* Vol. 28, No. 4, pp. 435-456.

————. 2000. "Alternative Perspectives on Late Industrialization in East Asia: A Critical Survey," *Review of Radical Political Economics,* Vol. 32, No. 2, June.

———— and Martin Hart-Landsberg. 1996. "The Use and Abuse of Japan as a Progressive Model," in Leo Panitch, ed., *Socialist Register 1996: Are There Alternatives?.* London: Merlin, pp. 62-92.

Burton, John, 1999. "S. Korea Faces Bumpy Road to Recovery," *Financial Times,* May 7, p. 6.

Business Korea. 1996. "Outgoing to Meet New Flooding Challenges," March, pp. 17-21.

————. 1999. "Korea's Export Potential Erodes," April, p. 22.

Bussey, John. 1995. "Japan's Bungling Ministry of Finance," *Wall Street Journal,* November 10, p. A16.

Cary, James. 1962. *Japan Today: Reluctant Ally.* New York: Praeger.

Cassen, Robert and Sanjaya Lall. 1996. "Lessons of East Asian Development," *Journal of the Japanese and International Economies,* Vol. 10, No. 3, September, pp. 326-334.

Castley, R. J. Q. 1996. "The Role of Japan in Korea's Acquisition of Technology," *Asia Pacific Business Review,* Vol. 3, No. 1, Autumn, pp. 29-53.

Chandran, Premesh. 1998. "Malaysia in Crisis," *Asian Labour Update,* No. 29, September-December, pp. 23-24.

Chang, Ha-joon. 1997. "Perspective on Korea: A Crisis from Underregulation," *Los Angeles Times,* On-Line Edition, December 31.

Cheng, Eva. 1999. "China: Is Capitalist Restoration Inevitable?," *Links*, No. 11, January-April, pp. 44-66.

Chernow, Ron. 1997. "Grim Reckoning in Japan—and Beyond," *New York Times*, November 17, p. A19.

Cho, Soon. 1994. *The Dynamics of Korean Economic Development*. Washington, DC: Institute for International Economics.

Cho Yang-Ho. 1998. "Reforming the Chaebol: the Citizen's Fair Trade Commission," *Civic Society*, No. 4, July-August, p.5

Cho, Young-Hoon. 1996 "The Growth of Enterprise Welfare in Japan," *Economic and Industrial Democracy*, Vol. 17, No. 2, May, pp. 281-300.

Choi Jeong-Pyo. 1998. "Korean Chaebol Need Reform," *Civic Society*, No. 4, July-August, p 4.

Chossudovsky, Michel. 1999. "Global Falsehoods: How the World Bank and the UNDP Distort the Figures on Poverty," *Links*, No. 12, May-August, pp. 31-36

Chriszt, Michael J. 1993. "Are International Comparisons of Inflation and Employment Valid?," *Economic Review*, Federal Reserve Bank of Dallas, Vol. 78, No. 6, November-December, pp. 23-36.

Civic Society. 1998. "Publishers' Message," No. 4, July-August, p. 2.

Clark, Robert L. and Naohiro Ogawa. 1997. "Transitions from Career Jobs to Retirement in Japan," *Industrial Relations*, Vol. 36, No. 2, April, pp. 255-270.

Clarke, Simon. 1988. "Overaccumulation, Class Struggle and the Regulation Approach," *Capital & Class*, No 36, Winter, pp. 59-92.

———. 1990-91 "The Marxist Theory of Overaccumulation and Crisis," *Science & Society*, Vol. 54, No. 4, Winter, pp. 442-467.

Cleeve, Emmanuel. 1994. "Transnational Corporations and Internalisation: A Critical Review," *British Review of Economic Issues*, Vol. 16, No. 40, October, pp. 1-23.

Clifford, Mark (with Jennifer Veale). 1998. "Showdown in Seoul," *Business Week*, December 14, pp. 56-57.

Clinton, Bill and Al Gore. 1992. *Putting People First: How We Can All Change America*. New York: Times Books.

Cohen, Jerome B. 1949. *Japan's Economy in War and Reconstruction*. Minneapolis: University of Minnesota Press.

———. 1958. *Japan's Postwar Economy*. Bloomington: Indiana University Press.

Coleman, Joseph. 1999. "Japan Suicide Rates Surge," *Tribune-Star*, Terre Haute, July 3, p. A5.

Connors, Michael Kelly. 1999. "Political Reform and the State in Thailand," *Journal of Contemporary Asia*, Vol. 29, No. 2, pp. 202-226.

Corben, Ron. 1995. "Thailand-Environment: Economic Growth, But at What Price?," *InterPress Service*, Distributed Worldwide on APC Networks, November 28.

Cumings, Bruce. 1981. *The Origins of the Korean War, Volume I*. Princeton, NJ: Princeton University Press.

———. 1990. *The Origins of the Korean War, Volume II*. Princeton, NJ: Princeton University Press.

————. 1997a. "Korea's Labor War," *The Nation,* January 27, pp. 6-7.

————. 1997b. "Japan and Northeast Asia into the Twenty-first Century," in Peter Katzenstein and Takashi Shiraishi, eds., *Network Power: Japan and Asia.* Ithaca, NY: Cornell University Press, pp. 136-168.

Dahlby, Tracy. 1980. "The Japanese Supertraders," *Far Eastern Economic Review,* February 1, pp. 39-40.

Dassbach, Carl H.A. 1993. "The Japanese World of Work and North American Factories," *Critical Sociology,* Vol. 20, No. 1, pp. 3-30.

Dauvergne, Peter. 1997. *Shadows in the Forest: Japan and the Politics of Timber in East Asia.* Cambridge, MA: MIT Press.

DeMartino, George. 1996. "Industrial Policies Versus Competitiveness Strategies: In Pursuit of Prosperity in the Global Economy," *International Papers in Political Economy,* Vol. 3, No. 2.

Doner, Richard F. 1993. "Japanese Foreign Investment and the Creation of a Pacific Asian Region," in Jeffrey A. Frankel and Miles Kahler, eds., *Regionalism and Rivalry: Japan and the United States in Pacific Asia.* Chicago: University of Chicago Press, pp. 159-214.

Dos Santos, Theotonio. 1970. "The Structure of Dependence," *American Economic Review,* Vol. 60, No. 2, May, pp. 231-236.

Eckholm, Erik. 1997. "Chinese Democracy Campaigners Push for Free Labor Unions," *New York Times,* December 24, p. A3.

————. 1998. "Joblessness: A Perilous Curve On China's Capitalist Road," *New York Times,* January 20, pp. A1, A8.

Economist. 1995. "Japan: One in Ten?" July 1, pp. 26-27.

————. 1996. "Into China," March 16, pp. 63-64.

————. 1997a. "The Asian Miracle: Is It Over?," March 1, pp. 23-25.

————. 1997b. "When China and India Go Down Together," November 22, pp. 41-42.

————. 1998a. "Frozen Miracle: A Survey of East Asian Economies," March 7, pp. 1-18.

————. 1998b. "East Asia's New Faultlines," March 14, pp. 16-17.

————. 1998c. "Japan on the Brink," April 11, pp. 15-17.

————. 1998d. "Japan's Economic Plight," June 20, pp. 21-23.

————. 1998e. "Corporate Japan Goes to Waste," August 29, pp. 55-56.

————. 1998f. "Japanese Banks: Still Mired in the Mud," November 28, pp. 79-80.

————. 1998g. "Japan's Other Debt Crisis," December 12, pp. 71-72.

————. 1999a. "Japan's Constitution: The Call to Arms," February 27, pp. 23-25.

————. 1999b. "Old, Down and Out in Japan," March 13, p. 53.

————. 1999c. "Japan: The Darker Side of Cuteness," May 8, p. 32.

————. 1999d. "Japan's Unruly Classrooms," June 26, p. 48.

————. 1999e. "Japanese Finance: Born-Again Lender," July 10, p. 72.

————. 1999f. "Pushing the Euro, Pulling the Yen," July 17, pp. 65-66.

————. 1999g. "Economic Indicators," August 14, p. 80.

Editors. 1998. "A Letter From the Editors: the Spirit of Revolution," *Against the Current*, No. 75, July-August.

Elder, Sam and Constance Sorrentino. 1993. "Japan's Low Unemployment: An Update and Revision," *Monthly Labor Review,* Vol. 116, No. 10, pp. 56-63.

Engardio, Peter. 1996. "Is the East Asian Juggernaut Sputtering?," *Business Week,* August 26, p. 44.

————, Jonathan Moore, and Christine Hill. 1996. "Time for a Reality Check in Asia," *Business Week,* December 2, pp. 59-66.

Faison, Seth. 1997. "China's Economic Boss Resists Pressure to Devalue Currency," *New York Times,* December 1, p. A5.

Fallows, James. 1994. *Looking at the Sun: The Rise of the New East Asian Economic and Political System.* New York: Pantheon.

Fingleton, Eamonn. 1995. "Japan's Invisible Leviathan," *Foreign Affairs,* Vol. 74, No. 2, March/April, pp. 69-85.

Focus on the Global South. 1999. "Conference Calls for Radical Reform of International Finance," *Focus-on-Trade,* No. 34, April.

Folbre, Nancy. 1994. "Capitalists All," *In These Times,* Vol. 18, No. 19, August 8, pp. 26-27.

Forrest, Richard A. 1991. "Japanese Aid and the Environment," *The Ecologist,* Vol. 21, No. 1, January/February, pp. 24-32.

Freeman, Alan. 1996. "The Poverty of Nations: Relative Surplus Value, Technical Change and Accumulation in the Modern Global Market," *Links,* No. 7, July-October, pp. 35-57.

Friedman, Thomas. 1999. "Thailand's Situation Stable After Crisis Forced Needed Changes," *New York Times,* On Line Edition, March 23.

Fumio, Kaneko. 1993. "Funds for the World," *AMPO Japan-Asia Quarterly Review,* Vol. 24, No. 4, pp. 28-31.

Gargan, Edward A. 1997. "Currency Assault Unnerves Asians," *New York Times,* July 29, pp. C1, C15.

Gerson, Joseph. 1996. "Asian/Pacific Realpolitiks: The New World Order Is Everywhere," *Z Magazine,* Vol. 9, No. 7/8, July/August, pp. 40-48.

Gill, Stephen. 1999. "The Geopolitics of the Asian Crisis," *Monthly Review,* Vol. 50, No. 10, March, pp. 1-9.

Gill, Teena. 1995. "South-East Asia: Bigger Economic Pie, Thinner Slice for the Poor," *InterPress Service,* Distributed Worldwide on APC Networks, December 27.

Goad, G. Pierre (with Prangtip Daorueng). 1999. "Look Homeward Asia," *Far Eastern Economic Review,* June 10, pp. 10-13.

Goldsmith, Raymond W. 1983. *The Financial Development of Japan, 1868-1977.* New Haven, CT: Yale University Press.

Goldstein, Don. 1997. "Financial Structure and Corporate Behavior in Japan and the U.S.: Insulation Versus Integration With Speculative Pressures," *International Review of Applied Economics,* Vol. 11, No. 1, January, pp. 27-48.

Gonzalez, Michael. 1995. "Prices of Stocks and Bonds Sink in the U.S.," *Wall Street Journal*, October 24, p. C1.

Goodman, Peter S. 1993. "Plain and Simple: Reebok, Nike, and Levi Strauss on the Prowl for Cheap Labor in Indonesia," *The Progressive*, June, pp. 26-28.

Goodno, James B. 1996. "Capitalism's Latest Success: Social Progress and Social Problems in Southeast Asia," Discussion Paper, Freedom from Debt Coalition, Manila, Philippines.

———— and John Miller. 1994. "Which Way to Grow? Notes on Poverty and Prosperity in Southeast Asia," *Dollars and Sense*, July/August, pp. 26-29.

Gordon, David M. 1993a. "Clintonomics: The Upsides and the Downsides," *The Nation*, Vol. 256, No. 10, March 15, pp. 325, 329, 344.

————. 1993b. "Generating Affluence: Productivity Gains Require Worker Support," *Dollars and Sense*, November/December, pp. 20-22.

Graham, George. 1999. "Richest 6m in World Keep Getting Richer," *Financial Times*, May 17, p. 4.

Greenfield, Gerard. 1998a. "Transnational Capital and the State in China: Partners in Exploitation," *Against the Current*, Vol. 13, No. 1, March/April, pp. 34-38.

————. 1998b. "TNCs, Flexibility, and Workers in Asia," Paper Presented at the ASEM Conference on "The Asian Crisis: People's Realities, People's Responses," London, March 31 - April 1.

———— and Apo Leong. 1997. "China's Communist Capitalism: The Real World of Market Socialism," in Leo Panitch, ed., *Socialist Register 1997: Ruthless Criticism of All That Exists*. London: Merlin, pp. 96-122.

Ha Seung-Chang. 1998a. "Political Overview," *Civic Society*, No. 3, May-June, pp. 1-2.

————. 1998b. "Political Overview," *Civic Society*, No. 4, July-August, pp. 1-3.

Halliday, Jon. 1978. *A Political History of Japanese Capitalism*. New York: Monthly Review Press.

———— and Gavan McCormack. 1973. *Japanese Imperialism Today*. New York: Monthly Review Press.

Hamashita, Takeshi. 1997. "The Intra-regional System in East Asia in Modern Times," in Peter Katzenstein and Takashi Shiraishi, eds., *Network Power: Japan and Asia*. Ithaca, NY: Cornell University Press, pp. 113-135.

Hamilton, David P. 1996a. "Dependence on Memory Chip Could Hurt Japan's Firms," *Wall Street Journal*, February 27, p. B4.

————. 1996b. "Japanese Can Expect Little Help from Trade," *Wall Street Journal*, June 24, p. A1.

————. 1998. "Japan's Economy Is In Trouble, But Don't Tell That to Tokyo," *Wall Street Journal*, June 17, pp. A1, A9.

———— and G. Pierre Goad. 1994. "Japan's Chip Makers Pick Partners in Asia," *Wall Street Journal*, November 7, p. A11.

Hamilton, David P., Steve Glain, and Norihiko Shirouzu. 1996. "Japan's Economic Growth Shows Signs of Exhaustion," *Wall Street Journal*, June 20, p. A15.

Hart-Landsberg, Martin. 1993. *The Rush to Development: Economic Change and Political Struggle in South Korea.* New York: Monthly Review Press.

———. 1994. "Post-NAFTA Politics: Learning From Asia," *Monthly Review* Vol. 46, No. 2, June, pp. 12-21.

———. 1998a. "Inside the Asian Crisis: Causes and Consequences," *Against the Current,* Vol. 13, No. 1, March/April, pp. 26-29.

———. 1998b. *Korea: Division, Reunification, and U.S. Foreign Policy.* New York: Monthly Review Press.

——— and Paul Burkett. 1998. "Contradictions of Capitalist Industrialization in East Asia: A Critique of 'Flying Geese' Theories of Development," *Economic Geography,* Vol. 74, No. 2, April, pp. 87-110.

———. 1999. "East Asia in Crisis: Beyond TINA, Toward Socialism," *Monthly Review,* Vol. 51, No. 2, June, pp. 53-61.

Hatch, Walter and Kozo Yamamura. 1996. *Asia in Japan's Embrace: Building a Regional Production Alliance.* Cambridge, UK: Cambridge University Press.

Henwood, Doug. 1998. "The Bull's Sour 16," *The Nation,* September 7, p. 5.

Hewes, Laurence I. 1955. *Japan—Land and Men: An Account of the Japanese Land Reform Program—1945-51.* Ames, IA: Iowa State College Press.

Hideo, Totsuka, Nomura Masami, Kumazawa Makoto, Okamara Tatsuo, and Ota Mallku. 1994. "Myths of the Managed Society," *AMPO Japan-Asia Quarterly Review,* Vol. 25, No. 1, pp. 10-39.

Hill, Hal and Premachandra Athukorala. 1998. "Foreign Investment in East Asia: A Survey," *Asian-Pacific Economic Literature,* Vol. 12, No. 2, November, pp. 23-50.

Hill, M. Anne. 1996. "Women in the Japanese Economy," in Susan Horton, ed., *Women and Industrialization in Asia.* London: Routledge, pp. 134-164.

Hiroshi, Kanda, Fuke Yosuke, Nagase Riei, and Murai Yoshinori. 1993. "Snaring the World in Debt," *AMPO Japan-Asia Quarterly Review,* Vol. 24, No. 4, pp. 32-38.

Hitoshi, Hirakawa. 1993. "Investing in Asia," *AMPO Japan-Asia Quarterly Review,* Vol. 24, No. 4, pp. 22-27.

Hone, A. 1974. "Multinational Corporations and Multinational Buying Groups: Their Impact on the Growth of Asia's Exports of Manufactures," *World Development,* Vol. 2, February, pp. 145-149.

Hoogvelt, Ankie. 1995. "Japan and the World," *Review of International Political Economy,* Vol. 2, No. 4, Autumn, pp. 719-727.

Horioka, Charles Yuji. 1990. "Why Is Japan's Household Saving Rate So High? A Literature Survey," *Journal of the Japanese and International Economies,* Vol. 4, No. 1, March, pp. 49-92.

———, Norihiro Kasuga, Katsuyo Yamazaki, and Wako Watanabe. 1996. "Do the Aged Dissave in Japan? Evidence from Micro Data," *Journal of the Japanese and International Economies,* Vol. 10, No. 3, September, pp. 295-311.

Houseman, Susan and Machiko Osawa. 1995. "Part-time and Temporary Employment in Japan," *Monthly Labor Review,* Vol. 118, No. 10, October, pp. 10-18.

Howard, Michael C. 1993. "Introduction," in Michael C. Howard, ed., *Asia's Environmental Crisis*. Boulder, CO: Westview Press, pp. 1-35.

Hsing, Y. 1996. "Blood, Thicker Than Water: Interpersonal Relations and Taiwanese Investment in Southern China," *Environment and Planning*, Series A, Vol. 28, No. 12, December, pp. 2241-2261.

Huff, W. G. 1995. "What is the Singapore Model of Economic Development?," *Cambridge Journal of Economics*, Vol. 19, No. 6, December, pp. 735-759.

Hughes, Helen, ed. 1988. *Achieving Industrialization in East Asia*. Cambridge, UK: Cambridge University Press.

Hung, Rudy. 1996. "The Great U-Turn in Taiwan: Economic Restructuring and a Surge in Inequality," *Journal of Contemporary Asia*, Vol. 26, No. 2, pp. 151-163.

Hymer, Stephen. 1970. "The Efficiency (Contradictions) of Multinational Corporations," *American Economic Review*, Vol. 60, No. 2, May, pp. 441-448.

———. 1979. "The Multinational Corporation and the International Division of Labor," in *The Multinational Corporation: A Radical Approach*. New York: Cambridge University Press, pp. 140-164.

Ietto-Gillies, Grazia. 1988. "Internationalisation of Production: An Analysis Based on Labour," *British Review of Economic Issues*, Vol. 23, Autumn, pp. 19-47.

International Monetary Fund (IMF). 1996. *World Economic Outlook, May 1996*. Washington, DC: International Monetary Fund.

———. 1997a. *World Economic Outlook, May 1997*. Washington, DC: International Monetary Fund.

———. 1997b. *World Economic Outlook, Interim Assessment: Crisis in Asia*. Washington, DC: International Monetary Fund, December.

Ishizaki, Tadao. 1985-86. "Is Japan's Income Distribution Equal? An International Comparison," *Japanese Economic Studies*, Vol. 14, No. 2, Winter, pp. 30-55.

Ito, Takatoshi. 1996. "Japan and the Asian Economies: A 'Miracle' In Transition," *Brookings Papers on Economic Activity*, 1996, No. 2, pp. 205-272.

Itoh, Makoto. 1994. "Is the Japanese Economy in Crisis?," *Review of International Political Economy*, Vol. 1, No. 1, Spring, pp. 29-51.

Itsunori, Ikeda. 1994. "Giving the SDF New Fangs," *AMPO Japan-Asia Quarterly Review*, Vol. 25, No. 2, pp. 7-9.

James, Paul. 1997. "Postdependency?" *Alternatives*, Vol. 22, No. 2, pp. 205-26.

Jenkins, Holman W., Jr. 1995. "Japan's Quiet Bank Bailout," *Wall Street Journal*, October 17, p. A19.

Jeong, Seongjin and Jo-Young Shin. 1998. "Debates on the Current Economic Crisis within the Korean Left," Paper Presented at the Summer Conference of the Union for Radical Political Economics, Bantam, CT, August 22-25.

Johnson, Chalmers. 1982. *MITI and the Japanese Miracle: The Growth of Industrial Policy, 1925-75*. Stanford, CA: Stanford University Press.

Jomo K. S. 1998. "Introduction: Financial Governance, Liberalization and Crises in East Asia," in Jomo K. S., ed., *Tigers in Trouble: Financial Governance, Liberalization and Crises in East Asia*. London: Zed Books, pp. 1-32.

Jones, Sidney. 1998. "Social Cost of Asian Crisis: The Region's Economic Upheaval May Lead to a Human Rights Disaster," *Financial Times*, On-Line Edition, January 26.

Jordan, Mary. 1998. "S. Korea's Wage Earners Pay the Price for Nation's Bailout," *Washington Post*, On-Line Edition, May 5.

Jussaume, R.A. 1998. "Globalization, Agriculture, and Rural Social Change in Japan," *Environment and Planning*, Series A, Vol. 30, No. 3, March, pp. 401-413.

Kahn, Joseph. 1998. "IMF Concedes Its Conditions for Thailand Were Too Austere," *New York Times*, February 11, p. C8.

Kanabayashi, Masayoshi. 1996a. "Japan's Shipping Concerns Tread Water: High Costs at Home Send Many Operators Abroad," *Wall Street Journal*, March 19, p. A10.

———. 1996b. "Work in Japan," *Wall Street Journal*, August 20, p. A1.

Kang Soo-dol. 1998. "The International Monetary Fund's Structural Adjustment Program in Korea," *Youndae* (Solidarity), No. 1, September, pp. 22-29.

Karmin, Craig. 1999. "Rallies in Japan, Brazil Offset Duds in Europe," *Wall Street Journal*, April 1, p. C12.

Kates, Carol, Ben Watanabe, John Price, Jane Slaughter, and Frank Hammer. 1992. "Special Report on Japan: Are These Our Enemies . . . Or Our Friends?," *Labor Notes*, No. 159, June, pp. J1-J8.

Katz, Richard. 1998. "A Crisis? Don't Tell the Japanese," *New York Times*, July 8, p. A21.

Kazuoki, Ohno. 1997. "Japanese Agriculture Today: The Roots of Decay," in Joe Moore, ed., *The Other Japan: Conflict, Compromise, and Resistance Since 1945*, New Edition, Armonk, NY: M.E. Sharpe, pp. 176-198.

Kim Chong-Tae. 1997. "Falling Farther and Farther Behind," *Business Korea*, July, pp. 14-16.

———. 1999. "U.S., Korea on Collision Course," *Business Korea*, March, p. 13.

Kim June Dong. 1994. "Incidence of Protection: The Case of Korea," *Economic Development and Cultural Change*, Vol. 42, No. 3, April, pp 617-629.

Kolko, Gabriel. 1968. *The Politics of War: The World and United States Foreign Policy, 1943-1945*. New York: Random House.

Kolko, Joyce and Gabriel Kolko. 1972. *The Limits of Power: The World and United States Foreign Policy, 1945-1954*. New York: Harper and Row.

Komin, Suntaree. 1993. "A Social Analysis of the Environmental Problems in Thailand," in Michael C. Howard, ed., *Asia's Environmental Crisis*. Boulder, CO: Westview Press, pp. 257-274.

Korea Herald. 1998. "80 Percent of Families Suffer Pay Cuts Since IMF Bailout," On-Line Edition, May 14.

Korhonen, Pekka. 1994. "The Theory of the Flying Geese Pattern of Development and Its Interpretations," *Journal of Peace Research*, Vol. 31, No. 1, February, pp. 93-108.

Krause, Lawrence B. and Sueo Sekiguchi. 1976. "Japan and the World Economy," in Hugh Patrick and Henry Rosovsky, eds., *Asia's New Giant: How the Japanese Economy Works*. Washington, DC: Brookings Institution, pp. 383-458.

Kristof, Nicholas D. 1997a. "Real Capitalism Breaks Japan's Old Rules," *New York Times,* July 15, pp. A1, A6.

————. 1997b. "Battered Economies in Asia Raise Fears of Unrest," *New York Times,* November 30, pp. A1, A6.

————. 1997c. "Asian Democracy Has Two Masters," *New York Times,* December 21, Section 4, p. 4.

————. 1998. "Shrugging Off Doom: A Special Report; Shops Closing, Japan Still Asks, 'What Crisis?'," *New York Times,* April 21, pp. A1, A6.

————. 1999a. "Tokyo Lawmakers Pass Bill to Improve Military Ties With U.S.," *New York Times,* April 28, p. A5.

————. 1999b. "Japan: Making Patriotism Official," *New York Times,* June 12, p. A5.

———— and Sheryl WuDunn. 1998. "A Lot of Talk About Russia, But the Numbers Shout Japan," *New York Times,* August 29, pp. A1, B2.

Kunio, Yoshihara. 1988. *The Rise of Ersatz Capitalism in Southeast Asia.* New York: Oxford University Press.

Kwak Young-sup. 1999. "Korea's Overseas Direct Investment Plunging: Nosedive Feared to Cut into Mid- and Long-Term Global Competitiveness of Local Corporations," *Korea Herald,* On-Line Edition, May 5.

Kwang-yong, Kim. 1999. "The Greater China Economic Area and East Asia," *East Asian Review,* Vol. 11, No. 1, Spring, pp. 95-109.

Lande, Laurie. 1999. "Asian Funds are Getting Bullish on Japan," *Wall Street Journal,* March 18, p. C23.

Lazonick, William. 1998. "The Japanese Financial Crisis, Corporate Governance, and Sustainable Prosperity," Working Paper No.227, The Jerome Levy Economics Institute, February.

Lee Jai Yun. 1998. "Thoughts on the Causes of the Korean Economic Crisis and Its Impact on Workers," *Asian Labour Update,* No. 27, February-May, pp. 17-19.

Lee, Jaymin. 1997. "The Maturation and Growth of Infant Industries: The Case of Korea," *World Development,* Vol. 25, No. 8, August, pp. 1271-1281.

Lee, Jongsoo. 1997. "The 'Crisis' of Non-Perfoming Loans: A Crisis for the Japanese Financial System?," *Pacific Review,* Vol. 10, No. 1, pp. 57-83.

Lee, Kiong-Hock and A. Sivananthiran. 1996. "Contract Labour in Malaysia: Perspectives of Principal Employers, Contractors and Workers," *International Labour Review,* Vol. 135, No. 6, pp. 75-91.

Leventhal, Paul L. 1994. "The New Nuclear Threat," *Wall Street Journal,* June 8.

Lever-Tracy, Constance, David Ip, and Noel Tracy. 1996. *The Chinese Diaspora and Mainland China: An Emerging Economic Synergy.* London: Macmillan.

Levine, David I. and Laura D'Andrea Tyson. 1989. "No Voice for Workers: U.S. Economy Penalizes Worker Participation," *Dollars and Sense,* December 1989, pp. 20-22.

Lim, Linda Y. C. 1978. "Women Workers in Multinational Corporations: The Case of the Electronics Industry in Malaysia and Singapore," *Occasional Papers in Women's Studies,* University of Michigan, No. 9, Fall.

———. 1995. "Southeast Asia: Success Through International Openness," in Barbara Stallings, ed., *Global Change, Regional Response: The New International Context of Development.* Cambridge, UK: Cambridge University Press, pp. 238-271.

Lim Young-Il. 1998. "The Economic Crisis and Labor Movement in Korea," unpublished manuscript, Kyungnam University, November 11.

Limqueco, Peter, Bruce McFarlane, and Jan Odhnoff. 1989. *Labor and Industry in ASEAN.* Manila, Philippines: Journal of Contemporary Asia Publishers.

Links. 1997-98. "Indonesia: Organizing the Mass Struggle for Real Democracy," No. 9, November-February, pp. 5-26.

———. 1999a. "Indonesia: The Unfinished Struggle," No. 11, January-April, pp. 79-94.

———. 1999b. "Interview with the Editor of 'Pembebasan'," No. 11, January-April, pp. 91-94.

Lippit, Victor D. 1993. "But What About China?," *Rethinking Marxism,* Vol. 6, No. 1, Spring, pp. 128-138.

Lummis, Douglas. 1999. "Article 9: And Now It's Gone?," *AMPO Japan-Asia Quarterly Review,* Vol. 29, No. 1, pp. 12-15.

Luxemburg, Rosa. 1970. "Reform or Revolution," in Mary-Alice Walters, ed., *Rosa Luxemburg Speaks.* New York: Pathfinder Press, pp. 33-90.

Macedo Cintra, Marcos Antonio. 1994. "Financial Repression and the Latin American Finance Pattern," *CEPAL Review,* No. 53, August, pp. 31-47.

Magdoff, Harry. 1992. "Globalization—To What End?, Part I," *Monthly Review,* Vol. 43, No. 9, February, pp. 1-18.

———. 1993. "What is the Meaning of Imperialism?," *Monthly Review,* Vol. 45, No. 4, September, pp. 1-7.

Mandel, Michael J. (with Pete Engardio, Emily Thornton, and Chris Farrell). 1997. "The Threat of Deflation," *Business Week,* November 10, pp. 55, 58-59.

Martin, Philip. 1996. "Migrants on the Move in Asia," *Asia Pacific Issues,* No. 29, December, pp. 1-7.

———, Andrew Mason, and Ching-lung Tsay, eds. 1995. "Special Focus: Labour Migration in Asia," *ASEAN Economic Bulletin,* Special Issue, Vol. 12, No. 2, November.

Marx, Karl. 1967. *Capital,* Vol. I. New York: International Publishers.

——— and Frederick Engels. 1975. *Selected Correspondence.* Moscow: Progress Publishers.

Mason, Mark. 1992. "The Origins and Evolution of Japanese Direct Investment in Europe," *Business History Review,* Vol. 66, No. 3, Summer, pp. 435-474.

McCormack, Gavan. 1978. "Japan and South Korea, 1965-75: Ten Years of 'Normalisation'," in Gavan McCormack and Mark Selden, eds., *Korea North and South: The Deepening Crisis.* New York: Monthly Review Press, pp. 171-187.

———. 1991. "The Price of Affluence: The Political Economy of Japanese Leisure," *New Left Review,* No. 188, July/August, pp. 121-134.

———. 1996. *The Emptiness of Japanese Affluence.* Armonk, NY: M.E. Sharpe.

254 References

McDermott, John and Chris Tilly. 1994. "Japan in Recession: A Conversation with Ronald Dore," *Dollars and Sense,* March/April, pp. 20-21, 37-38.

McNally, David. 1998. "Globalization on Trial: Crisis and Class Struggle in East Asia," *Monthly Review,* Vol. 50, No. 4, September, pp. 1-14.

Medley, Joseph. 1997. "(Post-)Modern Imperialism: Class Relations in the North Pacific Political Economy," Paper Presented at the Annual Meetings of the Union for Radical Political Economics, New Orleans, LA, January 4-6.

Meisner, Maurice. 1997. "The Other China," *Current History,* Vol. 96, September, pp. 264-269.

Miah, Malik. 1998a. "Indonesia: Repression and Revival," *Against the Current,* No. 72, January-February, pp. 13-18.

———. 1998b. "Indonesia's Unfolding Democratic Revolution," *Against the Current,* No. 75, July-August, pp. 6-8.

Michell, Tony. 1988. *From a Developing to a Newly Industrialized Country: The Republic of Korea, 1961-82.* Geneva, Switzerland: International Labor Organization.

Miller, John A. 1997. "Does Capitalist Growth Alleviate Poverty? Lessons from Southeast Asia about Rapid Growth, the Capitalist State, and Social Movements," Paper Presented at the Annual Meetings of the Union for Radical Political Economics, New Orleans, LA, January 4-6.

Millman, Joel. 1999. "Is the Mexican Model Worth the Pain?," *Wall Street Journal,* March 8, p. A1.

Minami, Ryoshin. 1998. "Economic Development and Income Distribution in Japan: An Assessment of the Kuznets Hypothesis," *Cambridge Journal of Economics,* Vol. 22, No. 1, January, pp. 39-58.

Montagnon, Peter. 1999. "False Dawn in Asia," *Financial Times,* April 19, p. 17.

Moon Ihl-wan. 1997. "Seoul is Still Teetering on the Edge," *Business Week,* December 29, pp. 56-57.

Moon, Seong-ki. 1995. "O'seas Invst. By Electronics Cos. Raises Concerns About Lack of Localization," *Korea Economic Daily,* September 25, pp. 1, 24.

Moore, Joe. 1983. *Japanese Workers and the Struggle for Power, 1945-1947.* Madison, WI: University of Wisconsin Press.

———. 1997. "Production Control: Workers' Control in Early Postwar Japan," in Joe Moore, ed., *The Other Japan: Conflict, Compromise, and Resistance Since 1945,* New Edition. Armonk, NY: M.E. Sharpe, pp. 4-48.

Morioka, Koji. 1991. "Structural Changes in Japanese Capitalism," *International Journal of Political Economy,* Vol. 21, No. 3, Fall, pp. 8-31.

Morris-Suzuki, Tessa. 1996. "Japan: Beyond the 'Lessons of Growth'," *Social Justice,* Vol. 23, No. 1-2, Spring-Summer, pp. 275-292.

Moseley, Fred. 1999. "The United State Economy at the Turn of the Century: Entering a New Era of Prosperity?," *Capital and Class,* No. 67, Spring, pp. 25-45.

Mydans, Seth. 1997. "Thailand Economic Crash Crushes Working People," *New York Times,* On-Line Edition, December 15.

Nadler, Eric. 1994. "North Korea's Nuclear Neighbors," *The Nation,* July 4, pp. 17-19.

Nakajo, Seiichi. 1980. "Japanese Direct Investment in Asian Newly Industrializing Countries and Intra-Firm Division of Labor," *Developing Economies,* Vol. 18, No. 4, December, pp. 463-483.

Nakarmi, Laxmi. 1995. "Seoul Yanks the *Chaebol's* Leash: A Sudden Policy Shift Could Slow Investment Abroad," *Business Week,* October 30, p. 58.

Naruse, Tatsuo. 1991. "Taylorism and Fordism in Japan," *International Journal of Political Economy,* Vol. 21, No. 3, Fall, pp. 32-48.

Naughton, Keith and Amy Borrus. 1996. "America's No.1 Car Exporter is . . . Japan?," *Business Week,* February 26, p. 113.

Neff, Robert. 1998. "Why Japan Won't Act to Save Itself," *Business Week,* May 18, p. 144.

Netto, Anil Noel. 1996. "Malaysia: Rural and Migrant Workers Pinched by Housing Squeeze," *InterPress Service,* Distributed Worldwide on APC Networks, August 9.

O'Connor, James. 1998. *Natural Causes: Essays in Ecological Marxism.* New York: Guilford.

Ofreneo, Rene F. 1993. "Japan and the Environmental Degradation of the Philippines," in Michael C. Howard, ed., *Asia's Environmental Crisis.* Boulder, CO: Westview Press, pp. 201-219.

Ogawa, Naohiro and Robert L. Clark. 1995. "Earnings Patterns of Japanese Women: 1976-1988," *Economic Development and Cultural Change,* Vol. 43, No. 2, January, pp. 293-313.

Ohkawa, Kazushi and Henry Rosovsky. 1973. *Japanese Economic Growth: Trend Acceleration in the Twentieth Century.* Stanford, CA: Stanford University Press.

Oizumi, E. 1994. "Property Finance in Japan: Expansion and Collapse of the Bubble Economy," *Environment and Planning,* Series A, Vol. 26, No. 2, February, pp. 199-213.

Ott, David J. 1961. "The Financial Development of Japan, 1878-1958," *Journal of Political Economy,* Vol. 69, No. 2, April, pp. 122-141.

Ozawa, Masako. 1985-86. "Myths of Affluence and Equality," *Japanese Economic Studies,* Vol. 14, No. 2, Winter, pp. 56-99.

Ozawa, Terutomo. 1993. "Foreign Direct Investment and Structural Transformation: Japan as a Recycler of Market and Industry," *Business & the Contemporary World,* Vol. 5, No. 2, Spring, pp. 129-150.

———. 1996. "The New Economic Nationalism and the 'Japanese Disease': The Conundrum of Managed Growth," *Journal of Economic Issues,* Vol. 30, No. 2, June, pp. 483-491.

———. 1999. "The Rise and Fall of Bank Loan Capitalism: Institutionally Driven Growth and Crisis in Japan," *Journal of Economic Issues,* Vol. 33, No. 2, June, pp. 351-358.

Pacelle, Mitchell. 1995. "Japan's Banks Sell More Real Estate in U.S. at Big Losses," *Wall Street Journal,* December 5, p. A5.

Park Byung-Ok. 1998. "CCEJ Efforts to Alleviate Mass Unemployment," *Civic Society,* No. 3, May-June, pp. 5-6.

Park, Won-suk. 1999. "A Little War for Democracy: Citizen's Action on Regaining Rights," *Youndae* (Solidarity), No. 2, March, pp. 12–13.

Parker, Mike. 1994. "Trouble in Paradise: Election of Dissident Reveals Discontent at Model 'Team Concept' Plant," *Labor Notes*, No. 184, July, p. 2.

Participatory Economic Committee. 1999. "Minority Shareholders Campaign," *Youndae* (Solidarity), No. 2, March, pp. 8–11.

Passell, Peter. 1997. "South Korea Is Facing Some Difficult Economic Choices," *New York Times*, December 18, p. C2.

Paterniti, Michael. 1998. "Indonesia," *Rolling Stone*, On-Line Edition, April 30.

Patnaik, Prabhat. 1990. "Whatever Happened to Imperialism?" *Monthly Review*, Vol. 42, No. 6, November, pp. 1–6.

Pempel, T. J. 1996/97. "Gulliver in Lilliput: Japan and Asian Economic Regionalism," *World Policy Journal*, Vol. 13, No. 4, Winter, pp. 13–26.

Petras, James. 1998a. "The Asian Crisis," *Z Magazine*, Vol. 11, No. 1, January, pp. 10–11.

———. 1998b. "The Americanization of Asia: The Rise and Fall of a Civilization," *Journal of Contemporary Asia*, Vol. 28, No. 2, pp. 149–158.

——— and Tienchai Wongchaisuwan. 1993. "Thailand: Free Markets, AIDs, and Child Prostitution," *Z Magazine*, Vol. 6, No. 9, September, pp. 35–38.

Pitelis, Christos N. and Roger Sugden. 1991. "On the Theory of the Transnational Firm," in Christos N. Pitelis and Roger Sugden, eds., *The Nature of the Transnational Firm*. London: Routledge, pp. 9–15.

Pollack, Andrew. 1997. "Sony Posts Huge Increases in Net for Quarter and Year: Company Benefits from Weaker Currency," *New York Times*, May 9, p. C2.

Pollin, Robert. 1993. "Public Credit Allocation through the Federal Reserve," in Gary A. Dymski, Gerald Epstein, and Robert Pollin, eds., *Transforming the U.S. Financial System*. Armonk, NY: M.E. Sharpe, pp. 321–354.

Press, Eyal. 1996. "Jim Bob's Indonesian Misadventure: A U.S. Mining Company Clashes With Indigenous Peoples," *The Progressive*, June, pp. 32–35.

Prosterman, Roy L. and Jeffrey M. Riedinger. 1987. *Land Reform and Economic Development*. Baltimore: Johns Hopkins University Press.

Raines, J. Patrick and Charles G. Leathers. 1995. "Veblen's Theory of Institutional Change: An Explanation of the Deregulation of Japanese Financial Markets," *American Journal of Economics and Sociology*, Vol. 54, No. 3, July, pp. 357–367.

Rasiah, Rajah. 1988. "The Semiconductor Industry in Penang: Implications for the New International Division of Labor Theories," *Journal of Contemporary Asia*, Vol. 18, No. 1, pp. 24–46.

Ravenhill, John. 1995. "Economic Cooperation in Southeast Asia: Changing Incentives," *Asian Survey*, Vol. 35, No. 9, September, pp. 850–866.

Rebick, Marcus E. 1995. "Rewards in the Afterlife: Late Career Job Placements as Incentives in the Japanese Firm," *Journal of the Japanese and International Economies*, Vol. 9, No. 1, March, pp. 1–28.

Reitman, Valerie. 1996a. "Sales of Import Cars Jump in Japan As its Makers Ship From Overseas," *Wall Street Journal,* February 7, p. A10.

———. 1996b. "Japan's New Growth Industry: Schoolgirl Prostitution," *Wall Street Journal,* October 2, p. A8.

Robinson, Lillian S. 1993. "Touring Thailand's Sex Industry," *The Nation,* November 1, pp. 492–497.

Rodrik, Dani. 1994. "Getting Interventions Right: How South Korea and Taiwan Grew Rich," Working Paper No. 4964, National Bureau of Economic Research, December.

Rowley, Chris and Mark Lewis 1996. "Greater China at the Crossroads?," *Asia Pacific Business Review,* Vol. 2, No. 3, Spring, pp. 1–22.

Rytting, James. 1989. "Class Struggles in Japan," *Against the Current,* Vol. 4, No. 1, March–April, pp. 26–29.

Sachs, Jeffrey D. 1997. "The Wrong Medicine for Asia," *New York Times,* On-Line Edition, November 3.

Sah, Dong-seok. 1995. "Deficit with Advanced World Surging: Enjoining Surplus with Developing Nations," *Korea Times,* June 24, p. 6.

Sakurai, Joji. 1999. "Defense Report Reflects Japan's Anxiety Over Asian Security," *Tribune-Star,* Terre Haute, July 28, p A7.

Sanger, David E. 1997. "The Overfed Tiger Economies," *New York Times,* August 3, Section 4, p. 3.

———. 1998, "Japan's Bad Debt Is Now Estimated Near $1 Trillion," *New York Times,* July 30, pp. A1, A8.

Sapsford, Jathon. 1995a. "Yen's Climb Causes Jobless Rate to Rise to 3.2% in Japan," *Wall Street Journal,* May 31, p. B9.

———. 1995b. "Japanese Banks Get New, Lower Ratings," *Wall Street Journal,* August 22, pp. A2, A6.

———. 1995c. "Japan to Propose New Bank Safeguards," *Wall Street Journal,* September 25, p. A10.

———. 1995d. "Japan Posts Rise in Bank Loans Unlikely to Be Repaid; Facts May Be Even Worse," *Wall Street Journal,* November 15, p. A16.

———. 1995e. "Tokai Bank to Aid in Japanese Rescue of Credit Union," *Wall Street Journal,* December 8, p. A8.

———. 1995f. "Japan Approves Unpopular Bailout Plan," *Wall Street Journal,* December 20, p. A10.

———. 1997. "Japanese Banks 'Dumping' Loans in Asia," *Wall Street Journal,* May 9, p. A14.

Schive, Chi. 1993. "Cross Investment in the Asia-Pacific: The Case of Taiwan's Inward and Outward Investment," *Business & the Contemporary World,* Vol. 5, No. 2, Spring, pp. 89–104.

Schuman, Michael, 1996. "Korea Inc. Speeds its Global Expansion As Life Grows Tougher in Home Market," *Wall Street Journal,* May 14, p. A13.

————. 1999. "Korea's Fast Recovery Suggests That Reform Isn't the Only Answer," *Wall Street Journal,* May 14, pp. A1, A6.

————, Namju Cho, and Michael Williams. 1996. "Convictions in Korea Highlight Anxieties Over Economy, Politics," *Wall Street Journal,* August 27, pp. A1, A9.

Seguino, Stephanie. 1997a. "Economic Liberalization, Export-Led Growth, and Gender Wage Differentials in South Korea and Taiwan," Paper Presented at a Joint Session of the Association for Social Economics and the International Association for Femininist Economics, at the 1997 Meetings of the Allied Social Science Associations, New Orleans, LA, January 3-6.

————. 1997b. "Gender Wage Inequality and Export-Led Growth in South Korea," *Journal of Development Studies,* Vol. 34, No. 2, December, pp. 102-132.

Seki, Mitsuhiro. 1995. "The Destruction of the Full-Set Industrial Structure—East Asia's Tripolar Structure," *Japanese Economic Studies,* Vol. 23, No. 1, January-February, pp. 3-28.

Selden, Mark. 1997. "China, Japan, and the Regional Political Economy of East Asia, 1945-1995, " in Peter Katzenstein and Takashi Shiraishi, eds., *Network Power: Japan and Asia.* Ithaca, NY: Cornell University Press, pp. 306-340.

Sender, Henry. 1995. "Offshore Attractions," *Far Eastern Economic Review,* June 15, pp. 48-52.

Sesit, Michael R. and Bill Spindle. 1999. "Japan Intervenes to Weaken Yen," *Wall Street Journal,* January 13, pp. A2, A12.

Shari, Michael. 1999. "Mystery Woman: What is Megawati's Economic Program Likely to Be?," *Business Week,* June 21, pp. 52-53.

Sheridan, K. 1995. "Japan's Direct Investment, Its Development Pattern and Future Direction," *Journal of Contemporary Asia,* Vol. 25, No. 4, pp. 473-491.

Shimbun, Asahi. 1998. "No Jobs In Japan for Those Over 50," Worldwide Internet Release, Institute for Global Communications, July 24.

Shin, Yoon Hwan and You-Il Lee. 1995. "Korean Direct Investment in Southeast Asia," *Journal of Contemporary Asia,* Vol. 25, No. 2, pp. 179-196.

Shu-Ki, Tsang. 1996. "The Political Economy of Greater China," *Asia Pacific Business Review,* Vol. 2, No. 3, Spring, pp. 23-43.

Simanjuntak, Togi. 1997. "Indonesia's New Workers' Movement," *Against the Current,* No. 69, July-August, pp. 15-20.

Sivaraman, Satya. 1997. "Thailand-Economy: A Tiger Losing Its Stripes," *InterPress Service,* Distributed Worldwide on APC Networks, August 12.

Smith, Neil. 1984. *Uneven Development: Nature, Capital and the Production of Space.* Oxford, UK: Basil Blackwell.

Smith, Richard. 1997. "Creative Destruction: Capitalist Development and China's Environment," *New Left Review,* No. 222, March/April, pp. 3-41.

Solomon, Jay and Kate Linebaugh. 1998. "Medicine Grows Dangerously Scarce in Indonesia As Currency Plunge Makes It Prohibitively Dear," *Wall Street Journal,* February 4, pp. A17, A18.

Song, Byong-Nak. 1990. *The Rise of the Korean Economy.* New York: Oxford University Press.

Spindle, Bill. 1999. "Japan's Economy Shrank 0.8% in Quarter," *Wall Street Journal,* March 15, p. A15.

Stanfield, J. R. 1994. "Learning from Japan About the Nurturance Gap in America," *Review of Social Economy,* Vol. 52, No. 1, Spring, pp. 2-19.

Steiner, Robert. 1995. "Daiwa Scandal, Loan Woes Boost Rate Japanese Banks Pay to Borrow Money," *Wall Street Journal,* October 25, p. A17.

Steven, Rob. 1983. *Classes in Contemporary Japan.* Cambridge, UK: Cambridge University Press.

————. 1988a. "The Japanese Working Class," in E. Patricia Tsurumi, ed., *The Other Japan: Postwar Realities.* Armonk, NY. M.E. Sharpe, pp. 91-111.

————. 1988b. "The High Yen Crisis in Japan," *Capital & Class,* No. 34, Spring, pp. 76-118.

————. 1990. *Japan's New Imperialism.* Armonk, NY: M.E. Sharp.

————. 1996. *Japan and the New World Order, Global Investments, Trade and Finance.* New York: St. Martin's Press.

————. 1997. "Japanese Investment in Thailand, Indonesia, and Malaysia: A Decade of JASEAN," in Joe Moore, ed., *The Other Japan: Conflict, Compromise, and Resistance Since 1945,* New Edition. Armonk, NY: M.E. Sharpe, pp. 199-245.

Stiglitz, Joseph. 1997. "How to Fix the Asian Economies," *New York Times,* October 31, p. A19.

Strauss, Neil. 1998. "A Japanese TV Show That Pairs Beauty and Pain," *New York Times,* July 14, p. B2.

Strom, Stephanie. 1997. "While Markets Toss and Turn, Japan Enjoys Relative Calm," *New York Times,* October 25, pp. B1, B2.

————. 1998a. "Disappointing Raises Set for Japan's Workers," *New York Times,* March 21, p. B2.

————. 1998b. "A Surprising Jump in Japanese Joblessness," *New York Times,* April 29, p. C3.

————. 1998c. "As the Yen Falls, Markets Fear Japanese Savers Will Look Elsewhere," *New York Times,* August 12, p. C5.

————. 1998d. "Japan Business Executives Are Even Gloomier Than Expected," *New York Times,* October 2, p. C4.

————. 1998e. "Yen's Rise Against Dollar Is Threatening Japanese Exports," *New York Times,* October 10, pp. B1, B2.

————. 1999a. "Japan's Legislators Tighten The Ban on Under-Age Sex," *New York Times,* May 19, p. A6.

————. 1999b. "Japan Announces a Plan to Create 700,000 Jobs," *New York Times,* July 12, p. B2.

Sung, Yun-Wing. 1993. "China's Impact on the Asian Pacific Regional Economy," *Business & the Contemporary World,* Vol. 5, No. 2, Spring, pp. 105-128.

Sweezy, Paul M. 1980. "Japan in Perspective," *Monthly Review*, Vol. 31, No. 9, February, pp. 1-14.

———— and Harry Magdoff. 1988. *The Irreversible Crisis.* New York: Monthly Review Press.

Tabb, William K. 1992. "Vampire Capitalism," *Socialist Review*, Vol. 22, No. 1, January-March, pp. 81-93.

————. 1994. "Japanese Capitalism and the Asian Geese," *Monthly Review*, Vol. 45, No. 10, March, pp. 29-40.

————. 1996. "The East and the World Today," *Social Justice*, Vol. 23, No. 1-2, Spring-Summer, pp. 250-261.

————. 1999. "Japan's Recession: The 800-Pound Crisis," *Dollars and Sense*, March/April, pp. 10-13, 40.

Takahashi, Yukichi. 1997. "The Labor Market and Lifetime Employment in Japan," *Economic and Industrial Democracy*, Vol. 18, No. 1, February, pp. 55-66.

Teranishi, Juro. 1996. "Shared Growth and the East Asian Miracle," *Journal of the Japanese and International Economies*, Vol. 10, No. 3, September, pp. 312-317.

Terry, Edith. 1996. "An East Asian Paradigm?," *Atlantic Economic Journal*, Vol. 24, No. 3, September, pp. 183-198.

————. 1998. "Crisis? What Crisis?," Working Paper No. 50, Japan Policy Research Institute, October.

Thompson, Herb and James Duggie. 1996. "Political Economy of the Forestry Industry in Indonesia," *Journal of Contemporary Asia*, Vol. 26, No. 3, pp. 352-365.

Tsuru, Shigeto. 1993. *Japan's Capitalism: Creative Defeat and Beyond.* Cambridge, UK: Cambridge University Press.

Tsuru, Tsuyoshi. 1994. "The Social Structure of Accumulation Approach and the Regulation Approach: A US-Japan Comparison of the Reserve Army Effect," in David M. Kotz, Terrence McDonough, and Michael Reich, eds., *Social Structures of Accumulation: The Political Economy of Growth and Crisis.* New York: Cambridge University Press, pp. 274-291.

———— and James B. Rebitzer. 1995. "The Limits of Enterprise Unionism: Prospects for Continuing Union Decline in Japan," *British Journal of Industrial Relations*, Vol. 33, No. 3, September, pp. 459-492.

Tsuruoka, Doug. 1992. "Hey, Big Spenders: Malaysia's Consumers Worry Economic Planners," *Far Eastern Economic Review*, July 9, p. 58.

Ungpakorn, Ji Giles. 1999. *Thailand: Class Struggle in an Era of Economic Crisis.* Hong Kong: Asia Monitor Resource Center.

United Nations Conference on Trade and Development (UNCTAD). 1993. *Trade and Development Report 1993.* New York: United Nations.

————. 1995. *World Investment Report 1995.* New York: United Nations.

————. 1996a. *Trade and Development Report 1996.* New York: United Nations.

————. 1996b. *World Investment Report 1996.* New York: United Nations.

Updike, Edith and Laxmi Nakarmi. 1995. "A Movable Feast for Mitsubishi," *Business Week*, August 28, pp. 50-51.

Van Der Meulen Rodgers,Yana. 1996. "Indonesia's Macroeconomic and Trade Performance," *Journal of Developing Areas,* Vol. 30, No. 2, January, pp. 149-166.

———. 1998. "A Reversal of Fortune for Korean Women: Explaining the 1983 Upward Turn in Relative Earnings," *Economic Development and Cultural Change,* Vol. 46, No. 4, July, pp. 727-748.

Veale, Jennifer. 1999. "Is This Recovery For Real?," *Business Week,* January 25, pp. 54-55.

Vickers, Marcia. 1997. "In Japan's Rebound, Exporters May Be the Stars," *New York Times,* June 29, Section 3, p. 4.

Wade, Robert. 1990. *Governing the Market: Economic Theory and the Role of the Government in East Asian Industrialization.* Princeton, NJ: Princeton University Press.

———. 1992. "East Asia's Economic Success: Conflicting Perspectives, Partial Insights, Shaky Evidence," *World Politics,* Vol. 44, No. 2, January, pp. 270-320.

———. 1993. "The Visible Hand: The State and East Asia's Economic Growth," *Current History,* Vol. 92, December, pp. 431-440.

———. 1996. "Japan, the World Bank, and the Art of Paradigm Maintenance: The East Asian Miracle in Political Perspective," *New Left Review,* No. 217, May/June, pp. 3-37.

——— and Frank Veneroso, 1998. "The Asian Crisis: The High Debt Model Versus the Wall Street-Treasury-IMF Complex," *New Left Review,* No. 228, March/April, pp. 2-23.

Watanabe, Ben. 1993. "'Promise of 'Lifetime Employment' is Disappearing in Japan," *Labor Notes,* No. 170, May, pp. 1, 13.

Weinberg, Neil. 1998. "What Devaluation Hath Wrought," *Forbes,* October 5, p. 53.

White, Gordon and Robert Wade. 1988. "Developmental States and Markets in East Asia: An Introduction," in Gordon White, ed., *Developmental States in East Asia.* New York: St. Martin's Press, pp. 1-29.

Williams, Michael. 1994. "Japan's Shoppers Bring a New Era to Economy," *Wall Street Journal,* June 20, p A1.

——— —. 1995. "Japan Will Improve Supervision of Branch Banks, Add Inspectors," *Wall Street Journal,* November 13, p. A11.

——— and Jathon Sapsford. 1995. "Japan's Slow Response to Bank Crisis Shows Its Big, Basic Problems," *Wall Street Journal,* June 14, pp. A1, A8.

——— and Robert Steiner. 1995. "Japan Finally Begins Its Huge Bank Bailout, Seizing Two Lenders," *Wall Street Journal,* August 31, pp. A1, A5.

Wolferen, Karel van. 1993. "Interview: Japan in the Age of Uncertainty," *New Left Review,* No. 200, July/August, pp. 15-40.

Woo-Cumings, Meredith. 1997. "How Industrial Policy Caused South Korea's Collapse," *Wall Street Journal,* Interactive Edition, December 8.

World Bank, 1993. *The East Asian Miracle: Economic Growth and Public Policy.* New York: Oxford University Press.

WuDunn, Sheryl. 1997a. "Television Is a Window To the Silly Side of Japan," *New York Times,* March 8, p. A4.

————. 1997b. "Japanese Economy Follows Zigzag: Exporters Thrive as Other Sectors Shrink," *New York Times,* August 16, pp. C1, C5.

————. 1998a. "Japan's Economy Appears Bleaker," *New York Times,* June 13, pp. A1, B2.

————. 1998b. "As Japan Goes, So Goes the Neighborhood," *New York Times,* June 16, p. C8.

————. 1998c. "Asia's Tigers Lick Wounds and Worry," *New York Times,* September 16, pp. C1, C6.

————. 1998d. "Japan's Plan: A Big Shrug," *New York Times,* November 17, p. A5.

———— and Nicholas D. Kristof. 1998. "Crisis in Banking Is Japanese, But Implications Are Global," *New York Times,* June 27, pp. A1, B2.

Wysocki, Jr., Bernard. 1999. "Should Japan Cheer About a Strong Yen?" *Wall Street Journal,* January 11, p. A1.

Yam, Tan Kong. 1995. "China and ASEAN: Rivals for Foreign Direct Investment," *Asia Pacific Business Review,* Vol. 2, No. 1, Autumn, pp. 50-67.

Yamamura, Kozo. 1967. *Economic Policy in Postwar Japan: Growth Versus Economic Democracy.* Berkeley: University of California Press.

————. 1972. "Japan 1868-1930: A Revised View," in Rondo Cameron, ed., *Banking and Economic Development: Some Lessons of History.* New York: Oxford University Press, pp. 168-198.

————. 1976. "General Trading Companies in Japan: Their Origins and Growth," in Hugh Patrick, ed., *Japanese Industrialization and Its Social Consequences.* Berkeley: University of California Press, pp. 161-199.

Yamazawa, Ippei and Hirohisa Kohama. 1985. "Trading Companies and the Expansion of Foreign Trade: Japan, Korea, and Thailand," in Kazushi Ohkawa and Gustav Ranis (with Larry Meissner), eds., *Japan and the Developing Countries: A Comparative Analysis.* Oxford, UK: Oxford University Press, pp. 426-446.

Yamin, Mohammad. 1991. "A Reassessment of Hymer's Contribution," in Christos N. Pitelis and Roger Sugden, eds., *The Nature of the Transnational Firm.* London: Routledge, pp. 64-80.

Yasuba, Yasukichi. 1976. "The Evolution of Dualistic Wage Structure," in Hugh Patrick, ed., *Japanese Industrialization and Its Social Consequences.* Berkeley: University of California Press, pp. 249-298.

Yeung, Henry Wai-chung. 1997. "Business Networks and Transnational Corporations: A Study of Hong Kong Firms in the ASEAN Region," *Economic Geography,* Vol. 73, No. 1, January, pp. 1-25.

Yoshino, Toshihiko. 1977. "The Creation of the Bank of Japan—Its Western Origins and Adaptation," *Developing Economies,* Vol. 15, No. 3, September, pp. 381-401.

Young, Alexander K. 1979. *The Sogo Shosha.* Boulder, CO: Westview Press.

Yue, Chia Siow. 1993. "Foreign Direct Investment in ASEAN Economies," *Asian Development Review,* Vol. 11, No. 1, pp. 60-102.

Zhao, Suisheng. 1997. *Power Competition in East Asia: From the Old Chinese World Order to Post–Cold War Regional Multipolarity.* New York: St. Martin's Press.

Ziemba, William T. 1991. "The Chicken or the Egg: Land and Stock Prices in Japan," in William T. Ziemba, Warren Bailey, and Yasushi Hamao, eds., *Japanese Financial Market Research.* Amsterdam: North-Holland, pp. 45-68.

Index